Journey Through the New Testament

Author
Teresa LeCompte

Theological Consultant
Rev. Robert J. Hater, Ph.D.

Harcourt Religion Publishers
www.harcourtreligion.com

Nihil Obstat
Reverend Steven Olds, S.T.D.

Imprimatur
✠ Most Reverend Thomas G. Wenski, Bishop of Orlando
February 1, 2005

The Ad Hoc Committee to Oversee the Use of the Catechism, United States Conference of Catholic Bishops, has found this catechetical text, copyright 2006, to be in conformity with the *Catechism of the Catholic Church.*

For permission to reprint copyrighted material, grateful acknowledgment is made to the following sources:

Costello Publishing Company, Inc., Northport, NY: From *Vatican Council II: The Basic Sixteen Documents,* edited by Rev. Austin Flannery, O. P. Text copyright © 1996 by Reverend Austin Flannery, O. P.

International Commission on English in the Liturgy: From the English translation of "Renewal of Baptismal Promises" in the *Rite of Christian Initiation of Adults.* Translation © 1985 by International Committee on English in the Liturgy, Inc. From the English translation of the *Rite of Confirmation,* 2nd Edition. Translation © 1975 by International Committee on English in the Liturgy, Inc.

International Consultation on English Texts: English translation of the Apostles' Creed, The Lord's Prayer, The Hail Mary, Lamb of God, the Magnificat, and the Nicene Creed by the International Consultation on English Texts.

National Council of the Churches of Christ in the U.S.A.: Scripture quotations from the *New Revised Standard Version Bible: Catholic Edition.* Text copyright © 1993 and 1989 by the Division of Christian Education of the National Council of the Churches of Christ in the U.S.A.

United States Conference of Catholic Bishops, Washington, D. C.: From *Economic Justice for All* by United States Catholic Bishops. Text copyright © 1986 by United States Conference of Catholic Bishops. From the English translation of the *Catechism of the Catholic Church: Modifications from the Editio Typica for the United States of America.* Text copyright © 1997 by the United States Catholic Conference, Inc.—Libreria Editrice Vaticana.

Librairie Arthème Fayard: A Poem by Dom Helder Camara from *The Violence of a Peacemaker* by José de Broucker. English translation © 1970 by Orbis Books.

Additional acknowledgments and credit can be found on page 262.

Printed in the United States of America

ISBN 0-15-901666-5

4 5 6 7 8 9 10 059 10 09 08 07

Contents

Introduction

Called to Journey vi

Chapter 1

Called Into Relationship 2

"In this you rejoice, even if now for a little while you
have had to suffer various trials."

1 Peter 1:6

The People of God
Explore the Land: The Land of Canaan
Special Feature: A Shared Land

Judaism at the Time of Jesus
Explore the Land: Map of Palestine
Special Feature: Dead Sea Scrolls

Politics and Society of the Time

Development of Scripture
Special Feature: How the Canon Came to Be

Witness of Faith: Dorothy Day

Prayer and Review

Personal Journey

Chapter 2

Called to Follow Jesus 32

"For once you were darkness, but now in
the Lord you are light. Live as children of
the Light."

Ephesians 5:8

What Does It Mean to Follow Jesus?
Special Feature: John the Baptist

Beginnings of the Church
Special Feature: Confirmation
Special Feature: Continuing the Mission of the Apostles

The Life of Early Christians
Special Feature: An Accepted Religion

**Development of the Gospels
and the New Testament**
Special Feature: The Gospels
Explore the Land: Early Growth of the Church

Witness of Faith: Sister Thea Bowman, FSPA

Prayer and Review

Personal Journey

Chapter 3

Called to Be Like Jesus 62

"For where your treasure is, there your heart will be also."
Matthew 6:21

The Gospel According to Matthew
Explore the Land: Antioch
Special Feature: A New Rabbi

Jesus' Birth and Beginning Ministry
Special Feature: The History of the Crèche

The Christian Life
Special Feature: The Parables

The Community and Just Actions
Special Feature: Peter, the Rock

Witness of Faith: Sister Dorothy Stang

Prayer and Review

Personal Journey

Chapter 4

Called to Believe 92

"If any want to become [Jesus'] followers, let them deny themselves and take up their cross and follow [him]."
Mark 8:34

The Gospel According to Mark
Explore the Land: The City of Rome

The Beginning of Jesus' Ministry
Special Feature: Traveling in the Time of Jesus

The Misunderstood Messiah
Special Feature: The Suffering Servant

The Paschal Mystery

Witness of Faith: Saint Pio of Pietrelcina

Prayer and Review

Personal Journey

Chapter 5

Called to Justice. 122

"[L]ove the Lord your God with all your heart, . . . soul, . . . strength, . . . and mind; and your neighbor as yourself."
Luke 10:27

The Gospel According to Luke
Explore the Land: Greece
Special Feature: Shema

The Response of Love
Special Feature: Honoring Mary

Who Is My Neighbor?

Table Fellowship

Witness of Faith: Blessed Kateri Tekakwitha

Prayer and Review

Personal Journey

Chapter 6

Called to Love 150

"I am the light of the world. . ."
John 8:12

The Gospel According to John
Explore the Land: The Seven Churches of Revelation

The Ministry and Signs of Jesus

Jesus' Teachings and Example
Special Feature: Symbols of the Holy Spirit
Special Feature: Week of Prayer for Christian Unity

The Glory of the Cross of Jesus
Special Feature: Vocations

Witness of Faith: Dom Helder Camara

Prayer and Review

Personal Journey

Chapter 7

Called to Share the Good News . . 178

" . . . you will be my witnesses in Jerusalem . . . and to the ends of the earth."

Acts of the Apostles 1:8

The Acts of the Apostles
Explore the Land: Early Journeys

Outreach to Gentiles
Special Feature: The Christian Symbol of the Fish

Paul's Missionary Journeys
Special Feature: Living Out the Good News

The Martyrdom of the Disciples
Special Feature: The Sacraments of the Catholic Church

Witness of Faith: Doctors of the Church: Saint Catherine of Siena, Saint Teresa of Ávila, Saint John of the Cross

Prayer and Review

Personal Journey

Chapter 8

Called to Be Church 210

"Bear with one another and, if anyone has a complaint against another, forgive each other. . . ."

Colossians 3:12

Overview of the Letters
Explore the Land: Expansion of the Early Church

The Pauline Letters
Special Feature: The Marks of the Church

Messages for Everyone
Special Feature: Stations of the Cross

Messages of Hope in the World
Special Feature: Symbolism in Revelation

Witness of Faith: Pope John Paul II

Prayer and Review

Personal Journey

Catholic Source Book 242

Scripture & Liturgy
The Seven Sacraments
The Mass
The Liturgical Year
Vocations

Scripture & Morality
The Ten Commandments
The Great Commandment
The New Commandment
The Beatitudes
Works of Mercy
Virtues
Precepts of the Church
Catholic Social Teaching

Catholic Prayers and Practices
The Lord's Prayer
Hail Mary
Magnificat
The Rosary
The Stations of the Cross

Glossary 258
Index 261

Called to Journey

"Follow me." *Mark 2:14*

Throughout the Gospels, we read of Jesus' calling people to follow him. He calls you to follow him, too. In your study of the New Testament, Jesus speaks to you and invites you to live as his disciple. As his disciple, you can grow into the person God made you to be. You can make a difference in the world around you.

Responding to the Invitation

When Jesus called his first disciples to follow him, he cared about their willingness to follow. He wasn't stopped by their past but he wanted them to change how they currently lived. He would not accept their uncertainty—he just called them even more intently.

You are no different. Jesus loves you for who you are right now. He does not base his love for you on what you have or have not done, but calls you to begin now to make a difference in the world and in yourself. Can you make the leap of faith that the first disciples and countless others have made throughout history? Can you follow Jesus and trust in him, knowing that he has a plan for your life?

Most of us cannot easily answer these questions. However, they require a faith-filled and committed response. Following Jesus is both an exciting and a challenging endeavor.

You began your journey at Baptism, and your family, parish community, and the Church around the world have accompanied you on this journey of faith thus far. Your journey involves—is actually dependent upon—personal experience. An *experience* is something that you personally encounter, undergo, or live through. You live out your faith through personal and communal experiences. You learn about yourself, God, and the world through interactions with other people, especially with your family and the Church community. Examining your experiences, coming to understand yourself, and being open to God and others are ongoing steps in your journey with Jesus.

Where Are You Now?

Reflect on the following statements. Be honest with yourself, but don't be hard on yourself. Remember Jesus loves you as you are. It is important to love and respect yourself in the same way.

My greatest accomplishment in the past year was . . .

My greatest challenge in the past year was . . .

The person or persons in my life that mean the most to me are . . .

The thing that gives me the greatest joy is . . .

My greatest fear is . . .

What motivates me the most is . . .

I define my family as . . .

I define my friends as . . .

For me, God is . . .

What I know about Jesus is . . .

My concept of the Bible is . . .

What to Bring

You have entered an exciting time in your life—new challenges, relationships, and experiences await you. This is also a time filled with pitfalls and danger. Peer pressure to do things you know are wrong is an ever-present challenge.

In many ways you resemble the early Christians who looked forward to the future, but also had concerns about their personal needs and wants. Following Jesus gave them hope, but it frequently did not give them what they wanted. Christ challenged them to look beyond their personal needs to the needs of others—to consider the good of the whole community and of the Church.

Jesus told his Apostles, "As you go, proclaim the good news, 'The kingdom of heaven has come near.' Cure the sick, raise the dead, cleanse the lepers, cast out demons. You received without payment; give without payment. Take no gold, or silver, or copper in your belts, no bag for your journey, or two tunics, or sandals, or a staff . . ." (*Matthew 10:7–10*).

As the Apostles traveled with Jesus, he told them, "Whoever welcomes you welcomes me, and whoever welcomes me welcomes the one who sent me" (*Matthew 10:40*). He gave them confidence and courage. They were able to face the hardships and setbacks that came their way. Even through the darkest days of persecution, the early Christians sustained their trust in God. And as God promised, they were rewarded. The early Christians grew in numbers. They grew also in their passion for God. They came to realize that God truly was with them through every trial.

God is also with you through the dark times—through what might seem like endless difficulty. Taking the next step on this journey requires the same confidence, courage, and trust that the early Christians had. Armed with the word of God, strengthened by faith in Jesus, and empowered by the Holy Spirit, you, too, can overcome all challenges.

What could you bring to aide you on a journey through the New Testament? You have some of the same things that the early Christians did—knowledge of God, Scripture, and the saving works of Jesus. In addition, these followers had the gift of the Holy Spirit guiding them and leading the Apostles to establish the Church community. Early Christians received God's grace in the celebration of the sacraments. The Holy Spirit is also with you, and the Church celebrates the sacraments to give you grace. As you explore the New Testament and the world at the time of Jesus, think about how God calls you to participate in the life of the Church community.

Faith is a gift of God. It is an authentically human act, by which we trust in God and believe in his revelation to us. It is also an act of the Church in that the Church's faith supports and nourishes our faith. We learn about faith from the faith and example of the Church and other people of faith. Our faith development begins in our family life. With our family members and among our friends and acquaintances, our faith grows. Our faith grows as our relationship with God and with the Church community grows.

A Journey of Knowledge

Many people talk about the difference between "knowing" Jesus and "knowing about" Jesus. Distinguish between the two for yourself, and then share your thoughts with a partner.

Getting Ready to Go

Where do you want to go? All journeys begin with a destination. In life, as in a journey, knowing where you are going is important. A map provides direction—a plan for your travels. Like a compass, it helps you choose your course.

Having a map, or a plan of action, will help you face challenges in life with confidence. The Bible and the Church provide a kind of map for living. Through Scripture and Tradition we receive God's directions and guidance on how to live as his children. Learning about God the Father, the Son, and the Holy Spirit will help you prepare for and confront the joys and sorrows, the victories and defeats that are a part of every life.

The theme of "journey" is common in both the Old and New Testaments. Often, those who were on the path to God did not know where it would lead them or how they would get there. They had to trust God and remember that they were not alone on their journey. God was always there to guide them, just as he is present to guide us.

What Is Your Destination?

My present dreams include . . .

My hopes for the future are . . .

My goals for the coming year are . . .

My faith influences my life and goals by . . .

Some "roadblocks" that may keep me from reaching my destination are . . .

Following Jesus can help me reach my goals by . . .

I will journey with . . .

I can help others on their journey by . . .

Beginning the Journey

The journey is more than traveling from place to place. It is an inner journey as well—one that leads from the mind to the heart to the soul. During this journey, the Word of God is a light for our path. We must incorporate it into our lives and use it as a guide for our choices and actions. This will help us develop our conscience.

In studying the Scriptures, you will learn about not only the saving actions of Jesus while he lived, but also how Jesus continues to save us today. Jesus is present among us when we gather to pray as a Church, to celebrate the sacraments, and in all the Church's liturgy and worship. Through the liturgy of the Church, we come to appreciate one another as part of the Body of Christ. As Jesus told his disciples, "For where two or three are gathered in my name, I am there among them" (*Matthew 18:20*).

What Does Scripture Say about Scripture?

"All scripture is inspired by God and is useful for teaching, for reproof, for correction, and for training in righteousness, so that everyone who belongs to God may be proficient, equipped for every good work."

2 Timothy 3:16–17

"You have been born anew, not of perishable but of imperishable seed, through the living and enduring word of God. For 'All flesh is like grass and all its glory like the flower of grass. The grass withers, and the flower falls, but the word of the Lord endures forever.' The word is the good news that was announced to you."

1 Peter 1:23–25

"Indeed, the word of God is living and active, sharper than a two-edged sword, piercing until it divides soul from spirit, joints from marrow; it is able to judge the thoughts and intentions of the heart."

Hebrews 4:12

"So faith comes from what is heard, and what is heard comes through the word of Christ."

Romans 10:17

"The time is fulfilled, and the kingdom of God has come near; repent, and believe in the good news."

Mark 1:15

"Take the helmet of salvation, and the sword of the Spirit, which is the word of God."

Ephesians 6:17

"The tempter came and said to him, 'If you are the Son of God, command these stones to become loaves of bread.' But he answered, 'It is written, "One does not live by bread alone, but by every word that comes from the mouth of God."'"

Matthew 4:3–4

c. **2000** B.C.
Birth of
Abraham

c. **1900** B.C.
Migration of Abraham
to Canaan

c. **1290** B.C.
Exodus of Israelites
from Egypt

c. **1370** B.C.
Birth of Moses

c. **1030** B.C.
David's slaying of Goliath

2000 B.C.

1330 B.C.

CHAPTER 1

Called Into Relationship

"In this you rejoice, even if now for a little while you have had to suffer various trials."

1 Peter 1:6

Chapter Goals

In this chapter, you will:

- learn about God's covenant with his people and the new covenant established by Jesus his Son.
- explore the Judaism of Jesus' time.
- understand the political and social environment at the time of Jesus.
- examine Scripture and Tradition as the divine revelation of God.
- learn about Dorothy Day.

961–922 B.C.
Reign of Solomon, king of Israel, builder of first Temple in Jerusalem

336–323 B.C.
Conquest and rule by Alexander the Great

105 B.C.
First signs of Dead Sea community at Qumran

27 B.C.
Rule of Augustus over the Roman Empire begins

660 B.C.

A.D. 10

994–962 B.C.
King David's reign over Israel

c. 587–586 B.C.
Temple destroyed by invading Babylonians

46–44 B.C.
Julius Caesar's rule over most of Mediterranean

37–4 B.C.
Herod the Great's rule of Palestine; rebuilding of Temple in Jerusalem

4 B.C.
Births of Jesus and John the Baptist

The People of God

The study of the New Testament centers on the life and mission of Jesus. To gain insight into the meaning and value of the New Testament for us today, we have to look at who Jesus was and what he said and did.

The study of the New Testament also requires acceptance that the religious message of the New Testament emerges from a historical context. God reveals himself in and through history, and so it is that the early Church—inspired by the Holy Spirit—recorded the events of Jesus Christ.

Jesus was a Jew who preached the nearness of the kingdom of God to his fellow Jews. He was influenced by the Jewish culture. The Jewish people's relationship to Jesus drew them deeper into divine revelation with God. Jesus fulfilled the Law of Moses by giving a new law of love and by teaching that God's covenant of love extends beyond the Chosen People to people everywhere. Jesus fulfilled the promise of the Old Testament prophets. As God's Son, his words and actions showed that God the Father was present in the world—actively healing, saving, and redeeming the people who had sinned and turned away.

And so, it is essential to understand and appreciate the important connection between the Old and the New Testaments. *Old* does not imply that these Scriptures are out of date. Rather, they are the record of **salvation history**, the saving action of God through human history. Together with the New Testament, these sacred writings are integral to our understanding of Jesus and Christianity. The New Testament has to be read in the light of the Old Testament. The Old Testament has to be read in the light of Jesus' death and Resurrection. The unity of the Old and the New Testaments comes from the unity of God's plan and his truth that is recorded in the Bible—both the Old and the New Testaments.

▲ Stained glass window featuring Jesus Christ at Abbey Church, Dorchester-on-Thames, England.

God's Covenant in the Old Testament

Within the diverse religious panorama of the Greco-Roman world, Judaism was a strong, visible presence. It was also unique in professing only one God. God had entered into a special relationship with the Jewish people and had acknowledged his continued presence in their history.

Here are some of the core beliefs shared and remembered by Jews at the time of Jesus and by Jews today:

Core Beliefs

There is one God.

God created everything, including humans, whom he made in his image—male and female.

He chose a people with whom to share his revelation and to carry his blessing through history. These people were originally called the Israelites. After the fall of the Temple in Jerusalem, they became known as the Jews. They are also known as the Hebrews.

God made a **covenant** with the Israelites (Jews). The covenant, a sacred agreement between God and the Jewish people, began approximately 1,900 years before Jesus was born, when God selected Abraham to be the father of the *chosen* people.

▲ The March of Abraham by Jozsef Molnar, late 19th century.

The concept of **monotheism**, belief in one God, was almost unknown at this time. An equally unfamiliar idea was that a god would initiate a relationship with humans and take an active role in their lives. People who lived during this time usually made sacrifices to their gods in the hope that the gods would not interfere in their lives. Jewish beliefs and practices were very different.

Abraham in Canaan
→ Abraham's route to Egypt and return to Canaan
--→ Abraham's route of battle with enemy kings

Mediterranean Sea

EGYPT

Way to Shur

On (Heliopolis)

Noph (Memphis)

Gulf of Suez

Wilderness of Shur

Wilderness of Paran

Kadesh-barnea (En-mishpat)

AMALEKITES

Gaza
Gerar

Beersheba

Negeb

AMORITES

Valley of Siddim

Arabah

Zered River

Petra

Gulf of Aqabah (Eilat)

Dan

Sea of Galilee

Acco

Dor

Beth-shan

Samaria

Shechem

Bethel • Ai

Mamre • Hebron (Kiriath-arba)

Dead Sea

ZUZIM REPHAIM

EMIM

HORITES

Syro-Arabian Desert

0   25   50 mi
0   25   50 km

Explore the Land

The Land of Canaan This map shows how the Middle East looked during the time of Abraham. You can see how far Abraham and his family journeyed.
What do you think Abraham and his wife faced during the long journey? How do you think this region has changed since the time of Abraham?

The Chosen People

The God of Abram established a relationship with Abram and promised him descendants and land. Genesis recounts Abram's first meeting with God:

scripture

"Now the LORD said to Abram, 'Go from your country and your kindred and your father's house to the land that I will show you. I will make of you a great nation, and I will bless you, and make your name great, so that you will be a blessing. I will bless those who bless you, and the one who curses you I will curse; and in you all the families of the earth shall be blessed'" (*Genesis 12:1–3*).

Abram did as the Lord instructed, left his hometown of Ur, and began a journey into the unknown. Abram took his wife Sarai and everything they owned. After facing and overcoming many obstacles, they reached the land of Canaan.

"The LORD came to Abram in a vision, 'Do not be afraid, Abram, I am your shield; your reward shall be very great.' But Abram said, 'O Lord GOD, what will you give me, for I continue childless, and the heir of my house is Eliezer of Damascus?' And Abram said, 'You have given me no offspring, and so a slave born in my house is to be my heir.' But the word of the LORD came to him, 'This man shall not be your heir; no one but your very own issue shall be your heir.' He brought him outside and said, 'Look toward heaven and count the stars, if you are able to count them.' Then he said to him, 'So shall your descendents be'" (*Genesis 15:1–5*). On that day the Lord made a covenant with Abram and gave him land.

Later in the journey, "The LORD appeared to Abram and said to him, 'I am God Almighty; walk before me, and be blameless. And I will make my covenant between me and you, and will make you exceedingly numerous.' Then Abram fell on his face; and God said to him, 'As for me, this is my covenant with you: You shall be the ancestor of a multitude of nations. No longer shall your name be Abram, but your name shall be Abraham; for I have made you the ancestor of a multitude of nations. I will make you exceedingly fruitful; and I will make nations of you, and kings shall come from you. I will establish my covenant between me and you, and your offspring after you throughout their generations, for an everlasting covenant, to be God to you and to your offspring after you. And I will give to you, and to your offspring after you, the land where you are now an alien, all the land of Canaan, for a perpetual holding; and I will be their God'" (*Genesis 17:1–8*).

Faith Activity

Family Tree Draw your family tree. On the reverse side of it, write the name of a person in your family who most models obedience, faith, and trust in God. Describe this person and your relationship with him or her. How can this living example of obedience, faith, and trust in God help you have a stronger faith conviction?

God and his People Abram was not the first person to whom God spoke. God made himself known to our first parents, and to us through creation. After the fall, God spoke to Adam and Eve. He promised them salvation, and in this way he remained active in the lives of his people.

We see this in God's relationship with Noah, with whom he made an everlasting covenant.

Find the verses in Genesis that detail these covenant relationships. Discuss in small groups how they affect your lives today.

▲ The Sacrifice of Isaac by Michelangelo Merisi da Caravaggio, c. 1603–1604.

A Name Change The change in names given to Abraham and his wife, Sarah, held special meaning. It signified the important vocation and mission given them by God. Of Sarah, God said, "I will bless her, and moreover I will give you a son by her. I will bless her, and she shall give rise to nations; kings of peoples shall come from her" (*Genesis 17:16*). The promise was fulfilled in the birth of their son Isaac. Through them, God began a covenant that would ultimately reach its fulfillment in Jesus. The blessing of this covenant was passed down through the lineage of the patriarchs.

Abraham was more than the father of a family. He was the father of faith. His obedience to God as he walked in faith models for us perfect obedience and trust in God. As we journey with God, we are also called to obey, to have faith, and to trust God.

The Law of the Covenant

Covenant is a key concept in our understanding of the Old and the New Testaments. A *covenant* is an agreement between two or more persons that is binding on both parties. When used in the Old Testament, it describes a faithful relationship between God and the Hebrew people, and the challenges presented as that relationship evolves.

When Isaac's son Jacob renewed the covenant with God, his name was changed to Israel. From his lineage evolved the twelve tribes of Israel. The descendants of Abraham—Isaac, Israel, and Joseph—are considered the patriarchs of the tribes of Israel.

The patriarchal period began from approximately 1900 B.C. and continued for about two hundred years. After the patriarchs, God, through the Exodus, formed Israel. The Hebrew Exodus from Egypt was the defining event in Israelite history. In this event, God entered

Faith Activity

The Ten Commandments Read the Ten Commandments (See *Exodus 20:1–17*.) and then interpret them in today's language. Present your interpretation to your class.

into a new relationship with the Israelites. Through Moses, God freed the chosen people from slavery and made a covenant with them on Mount Sinai.

In the Mount Sinai event, Israel was given its identity as a nation. God told Moses, "Now therefore, if you obey my voice and keep my covenant, you shall be my treasured possession out of all the peoples. Indeed, the whole earth is mine, but you shall be for me a priestly kingdom and a holy nation" (*Exodus 19:5–6*).

The Ten Commandments The Law is God's caring instruction that sets forth ways that lead to happiness forever with him. From the beginning God has created people with an awareness of his law, which can be known by reason. God explicitly named this law in the **Ten Commandments** which God gave Moses and his people at Mount Sinai. Following the Ten Commandments was the Israelites' way to be faithful to the covenant. The Ten Commandments summarize the law and state grave obligations that apply to all people.

Keeping the Covenant Years later, King David brought the Ten Commandments, and the Ark of the Covenant that housed them, to Jerusalem. God established an eternal covenant between King David and his future generations. This covenant obliged David and his descendants to follow the law of God or be punished. But David and his ancestors often broke their covenant with God.

Prophets arose to be the *conscience* of the Jewish people and to attempt to bring them back to God. The prophets Jeremiah and Ezekiel revealed a *new* covenant on the horizon—one that would be written on the hearts of people rather than on stone. (See *Jeremiah 31:31–34* and *Ezekiel 36:23–28*.) The prophets called for a new kingdom in which a Messiah, sent from God, would lead the people back to him. This hope for a Messiah, known as messianic hopes, became a significant theme in the preaching of the prophets, particularly Isaiah.

Hence the Old Testament is important in understanding the old and the new covenant, because these are the Scriptures that Jesus prayed with, studied, and used to direct his mission. Studying the Old Testament helps in understanding Jesus, his life, and his mission.

The Covenant Is Fulfilled in Jesus

For the Jewish people, the Book of Exodus contains many of the defining moments in their journey with God. First is the story of the Passover, or *Pesach*. In this event, God's angel of death struck down the first-born of the Egyptians, but passed over the homes of the Israelites. The Israelites were protected because, at God's command, they had placed the blood of a lamb on the doorposts of their homes and eaten a meal of the lamb's flesh.

Following the Passover story is the story of the Exodus. With the guidance of Moses, the Israelites passed through the waters of the Red Sea to freedom in the promised land. The Passover, the Exodus from Egypt, and the covenant at Mount Sinai are central events in the history of Israel. For

Jesus and his fellow Jews, these events were reminders of the tenderness of God's love for the people and their need to be faithful to the covenant. We read in the Old Testament how the Israelites struggled to remain faithful to the covenant, and how God continued to remain merciful and faithful to the Israelites.

Jesus, through his death and Resurrection, fulfilled the old covenant. The Church is the People of God in Christ, redeemed from sin by Jesus' death. The Israelites were called to be the People of God; now all people are called to be part of the New People of God and Body of Christ. Through his sacrifice and death on the cross, Jesus became the Passover Lamb and the Exodus—the way out—for all humankind to be released from the bonds of sin and death. Through his Resurrection, all are welcomed to the promised land of God's kingdom. Jesus gave himself as the ultimate gift of mercy, forgiveness, and love in his new covenant.

Jesus as Fulfillment of the Covenant		
The Passover/Sinai Experience Connected to the Present		
	Old Covenant	**New Covenant**
The People	Israelites	Followers of Jesus
Slaves to	Egypt	Sin
Saved by the	Blood of the lamb	Jesus, Lamb of God
Crossed the waters of	Red Sea	Baptism
Celebrated through the	Ritual of Passover meal	Eucharist
Law	Letter of the law (Ten Commandments)	Law of love (Beatitudes)

Break open the Word

Messianic Themes Read Ezekiel 36:22–32, and then using a concordance, look up two other messianic-themed passages in the Old Testament. What similarities and differences do you see between the two readings? What passages in the New Testament coincide with the passages that you looked up? Which of these passages relate most to your life?

← Important

A SHARED LAND

God's covenant with Abraham also included land: "To your descendants I give this land, from the river of Egypt to the great river, the river Euphrates . . ." (*Genesis 15:18*) Land was important because it was a symbol of power and a visible source of identity.

Generations of Abraham's children were blessed with land. In Israel, also called the Holy Land, the Temple was built, the one true God was worshiped, and many of the events recorded in the Old Testament took place. In fact, all three major religions that have emerged from Abraham's family tree claim the capital of Israel—Jerusalem—as their sacred city.

For the Jews, Jerusalem was the home of their most sacred site—the Temple. Built by King Solomon in 950 B.C. and destroyed by the Babylonians in c. 587–586, the Temple was the center of Jewish identity and religion. All that remains of the Temple is the Western Wall, sometimes formerly known as the *Wailing Wall*. Jews from all over the world go there to pray.

For Christians, Jerusalem is the place of Jesus' Passion, death, and Resurrection. Christians from all over the world go there on pilgrimages and to pray.

For Muslims, the third holiest place for pilgrimages, after the cities of Mecca and Medina, is the Dome of the Rock in Jerusalem. This mosque enshrines the black rock on which Muslims believe Abraham nearly sacrificed his son Ishmael. This story is similar to the Old Testament story of Abraham and his son Isaac. Muslims also believe that Muhammad, the founder of their faith, ascended to heaven from this site.

This land has not been shared without conflict. For centuries among the descendants of Abraham, the ownership of the land has been a source of hatred, violence, and murder.

Faith Activity

Conflict in Jerusalem Form a discussion group that can be broken into two smaller groups. In the smaller groups, look online or in a newspaper for articles about the city of Jerusalem and the surrounding lands. Come together into the larger group to discuss various aspects of the conflict over the city of Jerusalem and the area surrounding it.

Judaism at the Time of Jesus

important

The *Promised Land*. The *Holy Land*. The *Land of Israel*. The *Land of Canaan*. More than the names of a geographical site on a map, these words describe the ancestral and spiritual connection held within the hearts of Jews. The land of Palestine was the sign of God's everlasting covenant with them.

Explore the Land

Map of Palestine This is the land that Jesus knew. Identify which villages and cities Jesus visited.

Why are these locations important to our understanding of the life and ministry of Jesus?

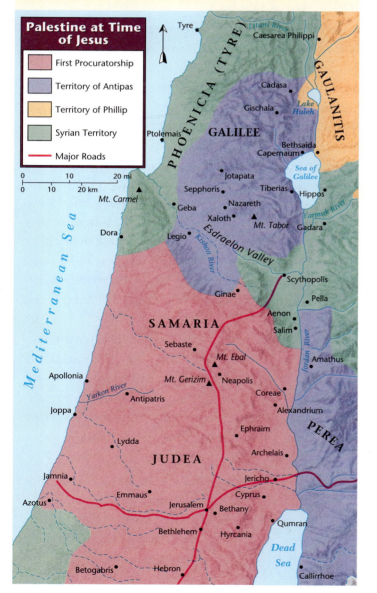

Palestine at Time of Jesus

- First Procuratorship
- Territory of Antipas
- Territory of Phillip
- Syrian Territory
- — Major Roads

Jesus, as the Son of the covenant, rooted his mission and spiritual message in this holy land. It was and still is a land swelling with life, diversity, beauty, and tension. It is a land formed by hills and plains, mountains and valleys, bodies of water and desert. As Jesus walked this land, he must have been drawn to the sights, the sounds, and the fragrances that surrounded him. The influence of this land on Jesus is captured in the many references to nature noted in Scripture.

The land is divided into several regions. Geographically, the major provinces noted in Scripture are Judea, Samaria, and Galilee. These divisions, however, were more than geographic. Each region had its own cultural, social, and religious identity.

Judea Those living in Judea considered their region to be most sacred. Within the boundaries of Judea lay Jerusalem, the City of David. Jerusalem was both the political and spiritual capital of the country. Jews living here tended to be orthodox and nationalistic. This sacred city was connected to many important events in biblical history. With the dawning of a *new Jerusalem,* the city would become the site where ancient biblical prophecies would be fulfilled through Jesus.

By the time Jesus was born, Jerusalem had formed the heart of Jewish existence for ten centuries. Jesus appeared to love this city. The Temple was located here. Jews viewed the Temple as the center of the universe—the connecting point where God and humans met. The Temple was central to the ritual worship of God that had been practiced for centuries.

Samaria The region of Samaria had at one time been the northern capital of Israel. In 721 B.C. Assyria conquered Samaria, whose inhabitants then went into exile. Only a small number of Israelites remained. Many of those who remained intermarried with the foreign occupants of the land. Consequently, most Jews in the southern regions of Israel despised the Samaritans and considered them outcasts.

Galilee Farther north was the region of Galilee. *Galilee* means "circle of Gentiles." True to its name, Galilee was encircled by Gentiles (non-Jews). Many of the Jewish people living in Galilee adopted some of the customs of their Gentile neighbors. For this reason, the Jews of Judea often looked down on the Galileans.

According to the Gospels, Jesus spent most of his life and ministry in Galilee. His hometown of Nazareth was part of the province of Galilee. It was here and in Judea that the message of Christianity was first preached.

The Importance of Family in Jewish Life

Every culture has norms that guide human behavior and social interactions. Today, when we think about *family life* and *marriage*, the meanings we associate with these words are directly connected to our own cultural experience. The institutions of family and marriage at the time of Jesus also highlight religious cultural attitudes and perspectives.

Family life formed the heart of the Jewish culture. Family members provided for their basic needs within the household: they prepared food, weaved clothing, made furniture, and fashioned tools. Also, property stayed within the family from one generation to the next.

The home—the center of Jewish social life—focused on the family. Rules based in the Torah, or Law, governed family relationships. Children were expected to honor their parents, and parents cared diligently for their children. Religious and societal norms called for all family members to behave in ways that would not bring dishonor to the other family members. When parents became older, responsibilities shifted, and children assumed the care of their parents.

Religion played the most important part in Jewish family life. Jewish worship most commonly took place in the home. The religious and social center rested on and around the dinner table. Festive meals in celebration of holy days and the Sabbath were among the most important family occasions. Members of the family had special roles in these religious celebrations. These celebrations were a time of prayer, joy, and fellowship with family and other Jews of the community.

Jewish Marriages Marriages were arranged as a legal and social contract between two families. The families hoped the marriage would enhance their status, produce male heirs, and preserve and transfer family property to the next generation. Marriage arrangements focused on finding an honorable family. The bride's family usually looked for someone who could provide for their daughter, was a respected citizen, and would be a good father.

Marriage and family remain central to Jewish faith, and from the very beginning of the Church, the significance of family and home has been stressed. As with Jews in Jesus' time, the Christian home is where children first earn and experience their faith. Families have a responsibility to create a community of prayer, virtue, and love. Parents live out their marriage covenant in many ways, but especially through the welcoming and forming in faith any children they may have. Parents and guardians are called to meet the physical, emotional, and spiritual needs of their children, guiding them to follow Jesus. Children, in turn, live out their faith by showing their parents and guardians respect, obedience, and appreciation for all that they do.

Faith Activity

Family Meals Today
How do you think that family meals today differ from family meals in the time of Jesus? How are they similar?

Groups Within Judaism

Historians speculate that five groups of Jews lived within Israel during the time of Jesus and early Christianity: Pharisees, Sadducees, Essenes, Zealots, and the largest segment of the population, those who were poor. Each group seems to have had distinct cultural characteristics as well as varying, and often conflicting, political and religious ideologies.

Pharisees The **Pharisees** were the most influential religious sect during the lifetime of Jesus and the religious group mentioned most often in the New Testament. As well-educated religious leaders, they focused on keeping the Jews faithful to the Law. Their interpretation of the Law focused on a strict observance of the Sabbath and on obeying purity laws, dietary rules, and ritual cleansings. Pharisees also acknowledged the oral traditions of the elders.

The New Testament portrays the Pharisees as people who were models of obedience to the Law. Jesus sometimes criticized them for worrying too much about superficial matters and not caring enough for the spirit of the Law. We read in the Gospels that they excluded the *unclean* from table fellowship. The *unclean* included those who were physically or emotionally ill and tax collectors. Some of the Pharisees in the Gospels appear as hostile questioners of Jesus. Others apparently liked him and were curious about his teachings. Of them Jesus said, "The scribes and the Pharisees sit on Moses' seat; therefore, do whatever they teach you and follow it; but do not do as they do, for they do not practice what they teach" (*Matthew 23:2–3*). Some Pharisees were sincere in their practice of the religious traditions. One of Jesus' Apostles, Matthew, was a Pharisee, as was Saint Paul. Jesus shared certain beliefs with the Pharisees: the resurrection of the righteous, the existence of angels and spirits, and a final judgment.

Interpret the Art

The Sabbath Pharisees Instructing a Man Not to Transport a Bed on the Sabbath by Cristoforo de Predis, 1476. The Pharisees followed the Law explicitly, several times chiding Jesus and his followers. Read John 5:1–18. *What does Jesus instruct the man to do? Why do you think he instructed the man as he did?*

Break open the Word

Jesus and the Law

In pairs or small groups, discuss three of the following Gospel references. What is happening in the stories you have chosen? In each, how would you describe the relationship between the Pharisees or Sadducees and Jesus?

Matthew 9:9–17

Matthew 12:1–4

Matthew 16:1–12

Matthew 22:15–46

Mark 7:1–13

Mark 10:2–9

Mark 12:18–27

Luke 5:17–26

Luke 11:37–54

John 9:13–41

Sadducees The **Sadducees** did not believe in anything that wasn't mentioned in the Torah. For example, they did not believe in life after death. As part of the wealthy, conservative, aristocratic ruling class, many Sadducees actively worked with the Romans. This relationship helped them maintain their economic power. They were also powerful in the religious community because, by heredity, they were the chief priests and elders of the people.

Although the Sadducees are seldom mentioned in the New Testament, they were a small but significant group within the landscape of Judaism. Because the Temple was the most important religious symbol to the Jews, the Sadducees occupied an important position. Sadducees were responsible for preserving the sanctity of the Temple and for managing it. They also composed the majority of the seventy-one-member Sanhedrin, the highest court of Israel. They emphasized temple sacrifice, which is one reason the group declined after the Temple was destroyed in A.D. 70.

Scribes The **scribes**, who interpreted and taught the Law, were most closely affiliated with the Pharisees, but they were also associated with the Sadducees. Scribes were not a religious party; rather, they were the Jewish scholars who assisted in writing and telling Jews about their religious traditions. At that time, many people in the Mediterranean world were unable to read or write. Scribes were responsible for writing and keeping records for the people. In addition, they may have served at synagogue services by reading and explaining the Jewish Scriptures.

Essenes Unlike the Sadducees, the **Essenes** are believed to have withdrawn completely from the world and from political activity to prepare for the imminent coming of God. They typically avoided all contact with foreign cultures and followed the Law of Moses to the last detail. Believing that Temple worship was impure and that the Jews had become lax in living the Law, the Essenes withdrew to desert communities to live a pure, monastic lifestyle. This sect probably influenced John the Baptist. Although not mentioned in the Bible, sources indicate their existence as part of the Qumran movement—a group of Essenes that settled in the desert area around the Qumran riverbed.

Zealots Another group, the **Zealots**, formed a rebellious movement of militant Jews who yearned and battled for the recovery of Jewish independence. They considered the acceptance of foreign government and the subsequent payment of taxes to Rome as blasphemy against God.

Other groups within Judaism held this minority sect in contempt. The Zealots were primarily responsible for the outbreak of violence against Rome from A.D. 66 to 70. Eventually, this uprising resulted in the destruction of the Temple and the Jewish community in Jerusalem. Only the Pharisees survived this disaster. After the fall of Jerusalem, the Zealots, the Sadducees, and the Essenes either disappeared or were drastically reduced in number.

The Great Majority In contrast to the groups just discussed, the majority of the Jewish population was poor. The mission of Jesus was most clearly linked to these people. At the beginning of his public ministry, Jesus stated:

scripture

"The Spirit of the Lord is upon me,
> because he has anointed me
> > to bring good news to the poor.
He has sent me to proclaim release
> to the captives
> and recovery of sight to the blind,
> to let the oppressed go free,
to proclaim the year of the Lord's
> favor."

Luke 4:18–19

In this passage Jesus described the following important parts of his mission:

- to preach the good news to the poor
- to help people be free to really live
- to perform acts of mercy
- to work toward social justice
- to celebrate and proclaim the arrival of deliverance

DEAD SEA SCROLLS

Although not mentioned in the Bible, sources indicate that an Essene community possibly existed in the Qumran riverbed near the northwest shore of the Dead Sea.

In the spring of 1947, a shepherd by the name of Jum'a from the nomadic Bedouin Ta'amireh tribe was looking for a lost sheep. In his search, he accidentally discovered a cave where the Wadi Qumran descends into the Dead Sea. In the cave, jars containing parchment scrolls were discovered. These manuscripts, known as the Dead Sea Scrolls, date back to between the first century B.C. to the first century A.D.

The scrolls are believed to have been hidden in the cave between A.D. 66 and 70 to protect them from the invading Roman army.

Fragments from nearly every book of the Old Testament have been found. These scrolls also contain information about the beliefs and the lifestyle of the Jewish people and of the Essenes, part of the religious group responsible for writing and preserving the scrolls. Members of this sect were Jews, considering themselves the people of the new covenant. Most of them were spread out in Judean towns and villages. They strictly observed the law. Membership in the community is estimated to have been as high as 4,000.

Connect to the Past

An Amazing Discovery Written nearly 2,000 years ago—the Dead Sea Scrolls were discovered in several caves in the Qumran region near the Dead Sea nearly half a century ago. The Qumran region was abandoned in about A.D. 70.
What historical events may have led to the hiding of the Dead Sea Scrolls and the abandonment of the Qumran?

Politics and Society of the Time

To become aware of the values of the ancient world, it helps to consider the religious, political, social, and cultural environment at the time of Jesus. Looking back can help us better appreciate our relationship to the first followers of Christ.

At the beginning of the Christian era, the Greco-Roman world was politically united under Roman rule and culturally unified through the **Hellenistic**, or Greek, influence. Many different religions and cults, however, characterized the religious sphere because of the Roman policy not to disturb the religious practices of the territories they conquered. Although these beliefs existed alongside each other, they sometimes rivaled one another for dominance.

The Political Scene

One way that Rome ensured stability throughout its empire was its policy of appointing a leader from within the conquered people. When Jesus was born, Herod the Great was the handpicked Roman choice to govern Palestine. But Herod was not a pure Jew; in other words, his bloodline and social background were not completely Jewish. His mother was an Arabian princess. Also, Herod was an Idumaean Jew. Idumaeans were forced to accept Judaism when they were conquered by the Hasmonaean ruler John Hyrcanus. Consequently, Herod was distrusted and hated by most Jews in the region.

Herod's own personality traits reinforced this distrust. Even though Herod was a genius at political and military maneuvers, he was also ambitious, ruthless, violent, and cruel. The Jews further despised him because he was a puppet of Rome and the visible symbol of the foreign rule and tyranny they were under.

Herod's violent and suspicious nature also affected his family. He is believed to have ordered the execution of a wife, three of his sons, a brother-in-law, and several other relatives. The Gospel according to Matthew records Herod's attempt to kill the infant Jesus by massacring all the male infants in Bethlehem. He apparently feared competition for being king of the Jews.

▼ Jews pray at the Western Wall during Passover.

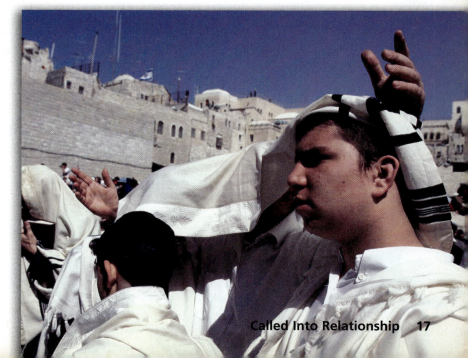

On the other hand, Herod prompted cultural and religious progress. One of Herod's accomplishments was in architecture. He reconstructed areas of Jerusalem, Jericho, and Caesarea. He built theaters, amphitheaters, and the hippodromes for Grecian games to honor Augustus. Most favorable in the eyes of the Jews were his efforts to reconstruct the Temple of Jerusalem. Yet these buildings were paid for at the expense of the people, who were taxed almost out of existence.

When Herod died in 4 B.C., three of his sons divided the territory. Herod Antipas (4 B.C.–A.D. 39) gained Galilee and Perea. He is the Herod mentioned most frequently in Scripture and was responsible for the execution of John the Baptist by beheading and for returning Jesus to Pilate.

The Roman Empire In addition to the territories governed by Herod's sons, the Roman Empire stretched from Syria to the British Isles, encompassing most of Western Europe except for part of Germany and Scandinavia. By the end of the first century A.D., the empire is estimated to have included 100 million people of different customs, cultures, and faiths.

The Peace of Rome, or *Pax Romana*, was in effect. Unity, relative peace, and law enforcement allowed for improved trade and increased business within the Roman Empire. Roads were built and maintained throughout the regions. Sea trade also flourished, allowing Rome to connect and trade with such faraway lands as China and India.

Although Rome had developed the web of roads and sea transportation for business and military purposes, early Christianity also profited from their construction. This network provided a means for the messengers of the *word* to spread the Good News of Jesus throughout the Empire.

Just as the transportation system provided for the spread of the Gospel, the Greek culture and language aided in spreading the word of God. Alexander the Great, who lived hundreds of years before Jesus, was responsible for making *koine,* or common Greek, the common language of the Mediterranean world. The New Testament was written in Greek, and in most areas of the empire, the Gospel was preached in Greek. The spread of Christianity in the first centuries happened almost entirely in regions under Greek influence.

Hellenism was primarily a reflection of the culture and beliefs of the city of Athens and other Greek cities. Classical literature, art and architecture, and extensive trade among regions characterized the culture. The Greek pagan religion was based on myths and legends surrounding the dramas of the god Zeus and a host of other gods. The spread of this culture into surrounding regions greatly influenced the Mediterranean culture.

Social Classes

Cultural anthropologists have determined eight social classes, which moved in a downward ranking, within the Mediterranean world.

These eight social classes were divided into two economic classes: those who were rich and those who were poor. The wealthy owned businesses or land. They made and enforced the rules. A small number of people owned the majority of the land and its resources. The poor class included the peasants who worked the land, artisans, unskilled laborers, and those who were destitute. Most of the population was made up of simple, ordinary people. They lived in debt as a result of the taxes imposed on them by the government and by their religious leaders. Some were even forced to sell themselves and their families into slavery.

Approximately 90 percent of the population lived in poverty. Those who were poor were generally illiterate, with limited opportunities for education. They passed down their histories orally and frequently used songs as teaching tools. Most of the population knew Greek and possibly also spoke a language native to their area of the country. It was not unusual for poor people to die by age thirty from disease, lack of hygiene, or an inadequate diet.

In general Jesus' public ministry took place among the majority population—those who were poor. He empathized with them. The teaching and example of Jesus often focused on alleviating the plight of the poor population. He welcomed those who were poor and included everyone in his invitation to follow him. In fact, many members of the early Church

Work with the Chart

Discussion Group Discuss in a small group the social classes you perceive in our culture.
1. *What factors determine a person's class?*
2. *What was Jesus' attitude toward the social divisions of his time?*
3. *How do you think he would react to the divisions in our society?*

Social Classes		
Classification	**Who are they?**	**Example**
Ruler	People of great power and influence in a large region, often obtaining power through war or inheritance	Julius Caesar
Governor	Often appointed by the ruler to control a smaller area, a province, or a city	Herod
Merchant	People who traded goods from different regions, as well as the military and the bureaucracy	Zacchaeus
Peasant	Farmers who worked the land and occasionally owned it, but frequently lost their land due to taxation. They often became tenant farmers and worked their own land for someone else. Fisherman also fell into this classification.	Simon Peter
Artisan	Bartered the goods they created	Joseph
Unclean	Generally peasants or artisans who failed and then attempted to make their living as beggars or bandits. Included in this group were the poorest people, often afflicted with medical conditions.	The Lepers

were among the ordinary people, who labored long hours to provide for their families.

Other early Christians lived in cities with affluent families. The head of the household was wealthy and influential. Unlike today, where many homes contain only one family, Hellenistic households might have had several generations of extended family living together. In addition, slaves and employees were counted as members of the household. This type of living arrangement benefited the expansion of Christianity: when the head of the household became a believer and was baptized, usually all members of the household followed.

Cult Practices

Christianity was born into a culture that was predominantly **polytheistic**, meaning that many gods were worshiped. (Judaism, by contrast, was monotheistic and exclusive.) In fact, it was normal for non-Jews to participate in the practice of more than one religion. People could choose from many religions and philosophies. A small sampling of the religious beliefs and rituals that existed at the dawn of Christianity are listed in the following paragraphs. Many followers of the mystery cults came to accept Christianity.

For the most part, we know little of the origins of the mystery cults. Only those who had been fully initiated into the worship knew the secret ceremonies and rituals. As the Eastern cults filtered into the Greco-Roman Empire, traditional beliefs declined. The demise of ancient Roman religion followed a similar path.

The Eastern mystery cults had a considerable impact on Greco-Roman civilization. These cults offered answers to questions about one's life in the next world and gave people a sense of hope. The Greeks in Asia Minor quickly accepted these religious ideas and blended them into existing religious traditions.

One of the mystery cults was the cult of Isis. This cult emphasized chastity and morality, and promised followers immortality. The cult of

◀ A statue of the Roman god Vulcan.

Demeter promised its followers deliverance and a better fate in the world beyond. Some of the cults, such as the cult of Dionysus, had secret rites. This cult revolved around the death and resurrection of Dionysius. The cult of Mithras also had its own secret rites. It was an offshoot of the ancient Persian religion of Zoroastrianism and was at one time a strong rival to Christianity.

The cult of the emperor was not a mystery religion—public acknowledgment of the emperor was promoted as a sign of political submission. Those who refused to acknowledge the cult were persecuted and martyred. Many of those who chose to follow Christ instead of the emperor were also persecuted, and some were even martyred.

Philosophical Movements

In addition to these cults, several schools of philosophy were popular. These philosophies aided people in considering how they should live their lives. They helped some people feel more secure in their unstable world. People attracted to these philosophical ideas were typically well educated.

Philosophies

The Epicureans promoted several ideas: the pleasure of the mind is to contemplate the pleasure of the body; the safest social pleasure was friendship; and if gods did exist, they did not become involved in human affairs.

Unlike Epicureans, Cynics believed that all pleasures of life were evil and should be scorned. They advocated returning to a simple, natural lifestyle.

While Stoicism evolved from Cynicism, Stoics believed that all life is part of a single system called *nature* and that life is good when one is in harmony with nature.

Magic and More Magical practices and the conjuring of spirits were also common at this time. Many people believed in and feared demons. Professional magicians used magic to ward off the power of the demons. The magician and his followers believed that both the power of the stars and all the good and evil forces in the universe could influence most aspects of life.

Millions of people looked to the stars as deities and believed they were as powerful as the gods Jupiter, Isis, and Osiris. They thought the movements of the heavenly bodies controlled their lives. Emperor and subject alike held profound belief in astrology.

While these beliefs and ceremonies clearly contradict the practices and teachings of the Church, the persistence of the Jews and the Christians in worshiping the one true God appeared atheistic to the people of this period. The only beliefs or religions that have survived from this time are all monotheistic: Christianity, Judaism, Islam, and Zoroastrianism. Eventually all pagan cults and religions other than Christianity were prohibited in the late fourth century in an edict issued by Emperor Theodosius I.

▲ Priests attend the Zoroastrian initiation ceremony known as *Navjote*.

BREAK OPEN the *Word*

Live in Christ Early followers of Jesus experienced firsthand the struggles and temptations of living in their society. Read Ephesians 4:17–24 to learn about Saint Paul's advice to an early Christian community, then answer the following questions:

1. Write a two-paragraph response to the advice given in this passage.
2. How do the values in this passage contradict those of the mystery cults and philosophical schools of the first-century world?
3. Why is the advice in this passage still good to follow today?

Development of Scripture

The Temple, the sacred Scriptures and the law, the Covenant, and the messianic hopes of the Jewish people formed the central structures of Judaism at the time of Jesus and set the foundation for the writing of the New Testament. Also integral in understanding the connection between Judaism and the New Testament writers is the presence of Jesus in the cities of Rome, Athens, Corinth, Alexandria, and Antioch of Syria. In these cities around the Roman Empire but outside of Israel, Christian communities first developed. The early Church there was influenced by the Jewish synagogue, worship, and practice.

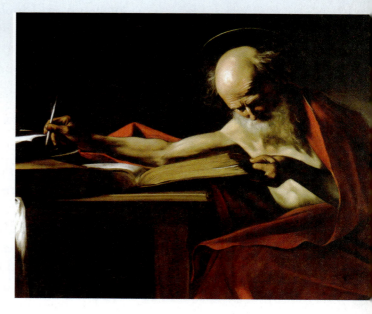

▲ Saint Jerome Writing by Michelangelo Merisi da Caravaggio, c. 1606.

The Jews in these areas were also deeply influenced by the surrounding Hellenism. Most of the Jews in these communities had little or no ability to understand the Scriptures written in Hebrew and their Aramaic translations. Consequently, Greek translations of the Scriptures of the Jewish people developed. The New Testament writers most often cited the Greek translations of these Scriptures, which are now part of the Old Testament.

The Old Testament sets the stage for the arrival of the Messiah. The New Testament chronicles the remarkable life of Jesus and the birth of the early Church. These Scriptures are the major source of our knowledge and understanding of Jesus. How this Scripture originated is a vital part of any study of Jesus' life and the **Tradition** of the Catholic Church. *Tradition* is the living and authentic transmission of the teachings of Jesus in the Church. Tradition is revealed in the creeds, liturgy, and prayers of the Church and in the authentic teachings of the popes and the bishops.

Both the Old and the New Testaments form the Bible—God's word recorded by humans. They also both depict peoples' lived experience and response to the presence of God in their lives. Attention must be given to the content and unity of the whole Scripture, the living tradition of the Church, and the coherence of the truths of faith among themselves and within the whole plan of God's revelation. To understand how the Old and the New Testaments were developed, we must look at biblical inspiration and revelation, the canon of sacred Scripture, and the interpretation of Scripture.

Divine Inspiration and Revelation

Our Bible was written gradually over a span of about 1,000 years. These writings are God's words written in human words. God inspired human authors to reveal his truths. He acted through them, and they used their own abilities to communicate God's word. **Biblical inspiration** is the process by which God the Holy Spirit assisted a human author in writing a book of the Bible. Because of this, God is the author of the Bible, and the truth that he willed us to know was conveyed without error. The inspired words of the Bible:

- are ". . . pure and unfailing fount of spiritual life" (*Dei Verbum, 21*).

- can lead us toward a deeper love and understanding of Jesus.

- teach us about the power of the Trinity to spread the Word.

Biblical inspiration is rooted in God's dealings with the Hebrew people where we find witness of God inspiring the entire Old Testament. The books of the Old Testament gave witness to how God and human authors worked together to produce a writing that can rightfully be called the word of God. Paul writes, "We also constantly give thanks to God for this, that when you received the word of God that you heard from us, you accepted it not as a human word but as what it really is, God's word, which is also at work in you believers" (*1 Thessalonians 2:13*). Even in the oral communication of God's word, those who heard early preachers understood that they heard not just the word of humans, but also the word of God.

God's Word **Divine revelation** is God's communicating of himself and his plan of goodness throughout history. Scripture and Tradition make up the one source of his revelation. God reveals his ultimate plan of love and salvation in the New Testament through his Son, Jesus. Jesus is the full revelation of God the Father. The inspired accounts about Jesus—his life, his work, his saving death and Resurrection—are lasting testimonies of his divine plan. These testimonies have been communicated through the centuries of the Church's history to the followers of Jesus (like ourselves) who no longer see, hear, or touch Jesus as the original disciples did.

The "Dogmatic Constitution on Divine Revelation" (Dei Verbum) part of the documents of the Second Vatican Council, says:

"Those things revealed by God which are contained and presented in the text of sacred scripture have been written under the inspiration of the holy Spirit. For holy mother church, relying on the faith of the apostolic age, accepts as sacred and canonical the books of the Old and New Testaments . . . written under the inspiration of the holy Spirit[1], they have God as their author, and have been handed on as such to the church itself.[2] . . . [A]ll that the inspired authors, or sacred writers, affirm should be regarded as affirmed by the holy Spirit, we must acknowledge that the books of scripture, firmly, faithfully, without error, teach the truth . . .[3] Thus 'all scripture is inspired by God, and is useful for teaching, for reproof, for correction and for training in righteousness, so that everyone who belongs to God may be proficient, equipped for every good work'[4]" (*Dei Verbum, 11*).

Dei Verbum emphasizes that the Bible is the work of God. The human authors who wrote the texts were inspired and empowered by the Holy Spirit as he directed them. Biblical inspiration applies to the whole Bible. We cannot divide the Bible into the texts that are the word of God and others that are not.

Dei Verbum also deals with the question of error in the Bible. If God is the author of the books of Scripture, then we must acknowledge that Scripture is without error and that he confided it for the sake of our salvation. By linking the inerrancy of the Bible to the truth of salvation that is present in every statement of Scripture, the Second Vatican Council shows that inerrancy applies to the whole Bible. In fact, to the extent that a passage expresses a saving truth, to that same extent the passage is without error.

Not everything in the Bible is literally true, but the fundamental beliefs and teachings of the Bible are without error. This freedom from error is called **biblical inerrancy**. The books of Scripture faithfully and without error teach the truth that God, for the sake of our salvation, wishes to have communicated through the Sacred Scriptures.

Faith Activity

A Prayer for Guidance
Choose a psalm that reflects a positive attribute, such as courage, strength, faith, or dignity. Quietly reflect on the psalm. Then write a prayer asking God to grant you the ability to read, understand, and integrate the Bible into your life.

Interpreting the Scriptures

Biblical exegesis is the explanation or critical interpretation of a passage of sacred Scripture. The Second Vatican Council, especially in Dei Verbum, addressed the interpretation of Scripture. It says:

> "Seeing that, in sacred scripture, God speaks through human beings in human fashion,[5] it follows that the interpreters of sacred scripture, if they are to ascertain what God has wished to communicate to us, should carefully search out the meaning which the sacred writers really had in mind, that meaning which God had thought well to manifest through the medium of their words.
>
> In determining the intention of the sacred writers, attention must be paid, among other things, to *literary genres*.
>
> The fact is that truth is differently presented and expressed in the various types of historical writing, in prophetical and poetical texts, and in other forms of literary expression . . . Rightly to understand what the sacred authors wanted to affirm in their work, due attention must be paid both to the customary and characteristic patterns of perception, speech, and narrative which prevailed in their time, and to the conventions which people then observed in their dealings with one another.[6]"
> (*Dei Verbum, 12*)

We concentrate on the intention of the human author when we interpret the Scriptures. In searching for the meaning of a biblical text, discovering the author's intention becomes the central task. However, we need the guidance of the Holy Spirit, who first inspired the authors, to help us understand the truth God wishes to convey.

Literary Forms Choose the form that you relate to most. Then choose a story—one not already listed as an example—from the New Testament that fits the form you have chosen. Present the following to the class:
How did the literary form used in the story help you integrate its teachings into your life?

Literary Forms in the Bible

- Forms are the names given to the different styles of writing found in the Bible.
- Descriptions tell the characteristics of the writing style.
- Examples are books or stories in the Bible that demonstrate the literary form.

Forms	Descriptions	Example(s)
Historical accounts	Accounts written to reveal God's activity in the world	The Books of Chronicles, Kings, and Acts
Parables	Short stories told to answer a question or illustrate a deeper point	The prodigal son, the sower
Letters	Messages addressed to early Christians by the Apostles and their followers	The Letters of Paul
Apocalyptic literature	Writing that describes the destruction of evil and the coming of God's reign	The Book of Revelation
Psalms and canticles	Poems and prayers once sung	The Book of Psalms

Of further importance is considering the literary form used. The way a biblical text expresses the truth must first be understood in order to understand the truth it expresses. If the literary form is misunderstood, the message of the text may be misunderstood or even lost.

Trying to understand the author's intention involves several steps:

- understanding the historical setting in which the author wrote
- knowing the meaning of key concepts (such as sin or redemption) as the author uses them and not as defined in modern terms
- appreciating the literary forms chosen by the author

How the Canon Came to Be

Important

The Catholic Bible contains the faith story of the people of Israel—the Old Testament of forty-six books—and of Christians—the New Testament of twenty-seven books. These books are referred to as the canon of the Bible, that is, the official collection of inspired books of sacred Scripture that contain the witness and instruction for our faith.

Canon is rooted in the Greek word *kanon*, which means "reed or measuring stick." The sacred canon of Catholic Scripture is the measure of authenticity that books are regarded to have as being revealed and inspired by God. The Old Testament and the New Testament are the collection of books recognized by the teaching authority of the Church as the true measure of our faith.

The Old Testament was written in Aramaic or Hebrew. However, as a result of the Babylonian exile, many Jews were dispersed and living in a world influenced by Greek culture and language. Therefore, the books were translated into Greek probably in the second century B.C. This translation is referred to as the *Septuagint*, meaning "seventy." This word was used because some believe that seventy scholars translated in seventy days what we call the Old Testament.

Some Jews used the Septuagint to compose their own canon and selected books not considered part of the traditional Jewish canon. These books are the Wisdom of Solomon, Baruch, Judith, 1 and 2 Maccabees, Sirach/Ecclesiasticus, and Tobit. They were probably chosen because of their Greek overtone. At times these books are referred to as the Apocrypha (hidden books) or Deuterocanonicals (second canon). The Deuterocanonicals are included in the Catholic Bible.

The first Christians and the Church used the Greek version for the first fourteen centuries. However, Protestants rejected these books at the beginning of the Protestant Reformation when Martin Luther rejected all the books not identical to the traditional Jewish canon. However, Catholics maintain the Deuterocanonicals.

Today, Christians agree on the canon of the New Testament. These books hold the true message of Jesus as discerned through the apostolic Tradition of the Church. The canonical books reflected the faith of the early Christians, a faith that preceded the writing of the New Testament. Therefore, the canon of Scripture reflects the faith of the Church.

The canon was developed with divine guidance. We must read and interpret the Scriptures with God's guidance and with the help of the Church in our own day. When reading the Bible, we enter into a tradition and a relationship with the earliest Christian communities responsible for writing and preserving the texts. Reading it demands a respect for the faith of the Church and for the inspiration of the Holy Spirit.

Faith Activity

Which Book Is Which? What are the first and the last books of the Old Testament? What are the first and the last books of the New Testament? How many chapters do each of the four books contain? Interview a family member and find out what her or his favorite book of the Old Testament is. Choose a story from it and write a half-page analysis of it.

Dorothy Day (1897–1980)

Dorothy Day was a woman of profound faith who was deeply committed to living the values of the Gospel even when it went against the cultural practices of her time. However, this was not the way her life had been. In fact, for most of her childhood and early adult life, Dorothy would have labeled herself an atheist. In her early years she lived a life very distant from the vision of Jesus.

As a child, Dorothy was raised in a home where religion was not practiced. Yet, as Dorothy matured, she developed strong ideas about an ideal society and empathy for those living on the fringe. She channeled her energy for these causes by working as a journalist. She also campaigned for radical causes, such as the right of women to vote.

During these early years, Dorothy was part of a rather radical lifestyle of the Greenwich Village Community in New York City. Her personal life was in tumult. She became pregnant and had an abortion. Then she entered into a common-law marriage with Foster Batterham. Joy and happiness filled Dorothy's spirit when she realized she was pregnant. She was grateful that God had given her another chance to bring life into the world. This was the beginning of a lifelong conversion experience for Dorothy.

Drawn to prayer and to the Eucharist and to meditating on the Scriptures, Dorothy came to understand that love for God moves one to love of neighbor. These were more than pious thoughts for Dorothy. Living this belief became her life. In fact, Dorothy chose a life of voluntary poverty, saying, "The mystery of poverty is that by sharing in it, making ourselves poor in giving to others, we increase our knowledge and belief in love."

One night in 1932, after reporting on a hunger march in Washington, D.C., for *Commonweal* magazine, Dorothy went to pray at the National Shrine of the Immaculate Conception. There she pleaded with God that she "might find something to do in the social order besides reporting conditions." Her prayer was answered by the arrival of Peter Maurin, a former Christian brother from France. Like Dorothy, Peter was burning with a passionate desire to reform the injustices found in society. Together, in 1933, they founded the Catholic Worker Movement and the *Catholic Worker,* a newspaper that challenged people to live the teachings of Jesus. While Dorothy described Peter as the "spirit and founder of the movement," she became the energy and heart of it. Her hope was that the Catholic Worker Movement would create a permanent revolution in the life of the Church as it called upon its members to make personal responses that would make a difference in the world. Dorothy's commitment to nonviolent social change led to her involvement in protests against injustices and war. She was arrested many times for her convictions. Dorothy is an example of a loved sinner who became a loving servant.

Prayer

Begin by praying the Sign of the Cross.

Leader: As we begin our journey, we ask that you help us better understand the old covenant with Abraham and the new covenant with Jesus.

All: Lord, guide us on our journey.

Leader: May we reflect on the trust that the ancient Israelites placed in you and find that same trust in ourselves.

All: Lord, guide us on our journey.

Leader: May we show compassion for all peoples, regardless of color or class, just as Jesus did.

All: Lord, guide us on our journey.

Leader: May we live the Ten Commandments and the Beatitudes in our lives, and through our actions spread God's word.

All: Lord, guide us on our journey.

Leader: May we ask for God's help when we don't know what to do, and listen to his response.

All: Lord, guide us on our journey.

Leader: May we read the Bible with your help and the help of the Church, and better understand it and make it part of our lives.

All: Lord, guide us on our journey.

Leader: Take a moment and reflect on your life and how the Bible can help us live more Christ-like lives . . .

All: Lord, guide us on our journey.

Leader: We ask this in your name, almighty Lord . . .

All: Amen.

End by praying the Sign of the Cross.

Review

1. What did God promise Abram? How has this promise come true?

2. Why is the Passover event so important to the Jewish people?

3. How did Jesus fulfill the new covenant? How are the old and the new covenant connected?

4. Describe the regions and the peoples of Judea, Samaria, and Galilee.

5. Describe the roles and responsibilities of family members at the time of Jesus. What role did religion play in Jewish family life?

6. Compare the differences among the five main groups within Judaism.

7. Describe Herod the Great's personality. What is he responsible for in the life of Jesus?

8. Describe the differences in social classes in Jesus' time. With which class of people did Jesus spend most of his time? Why?

9. What are the four monotheistic religions that survived Jesus' time? How do they differ?

10. What is biblical inspiration? What is divine revelation? Describe biblical inerrancy.

11. What is biblical exegesis? What must be considered when interpreting the Scriptures?

12. Briefly summarize the literary forms found in the Bible.

Key Words

biblical exegesis (p. 25)—This is the explanation or critical interpretation of a passage of sacred Scripture.

biblical inerrancy (p. 25)—Freedom from error is called this. The books of Scripture faithfully and without error teach the truth that God, for the sake of our salvation, wishes to have communicated through the sacred Scriptures.

biblical inspiration (p. 24)—This is the process by which God the Holy Spirit assisted a human author in writing a book of the Bible. Because of this, God is the author of the Bible, and the truth that he willed us to know was conveyed without error.

covenant (p. 5)—A solemn promise, or agreement, made between two parties; the word means testament.

divine revelation (p. 24)—This is God's communicating of himself and his plan of goodness throughout history.

Essenes (p. 15)—They withdrew completely from the world and political activity to prepare for the imminent coming of God. They typically avoided all contact with foreign cultures and followed the Law of Moses to the last detail.

Hellenistic (p. 17)—This is another word for Greek influence.

monotheism (p. 5)—This is the belief in one God.

Pharisees (p. 13)—They were the most influential religious sect during the lifetime of Jesus. As well-educated religious leaders, they focused on keeping the Jews faithful to the law. They also acknowledged the oral traditions of the elders.

polytheistic (p. 20)—This means that many gods were worshiped.

Sadducees (p. 14)—They did not believe in anything that wasn't mentioned in the Torah. As part of the wealthy, conservative, aristocratic ruling class, many Sadducees actively worked with the Romans.

salvation history (p. 4)—This is the saving action of God through human history.

scribes (p. 14)—They were the interpreters and the teachers of the law most closely affiliated with the Pharisees, but also associated with the Sadducees. Scribes were not a religious party; rather, they were the Jewish scholars who assisted in writing and telling Jews about their religious traditions.

Ten Commandments (p. 8)—These ten laws—often called the Decalogue and given by God to Moses—prescribed the moral obligations for the Israelites. The commandments later evolved into the 613 laws which comprise the Torah, the written law of the Hebrew people.

Tradition (p. 23)—This is the living and authentic transmission of the teachings of Jesus in the Church.

Zealots (p. 15)—They formed a rebellious movement of militant Jews who yearned and battled for the recovery of Jewish independence. They considered the acceptance of foreign government and the subsequent payment of taxes to Rome as blasphemy against God.

Personal Journey

Teen to Teen

Who supports you on your journey with Christ? How do you support others in return?

Every day, you encounter choices—some big, some seemingly insignificant. But every choice leads you down one path and not another. Choices ultimately determine your direction—where you are headed and where you'll end up. It is not always easy to see where the road leads. When you surround yourself with positive people, pray, and involve yourself in the life of the Church, you are given a road map to help you choose the right direction.

"My mom supports me. She's always thinking about other people. If I'm mad at someone at school, she'll say, 'How do you think you made that person feel?' I don't always like her advice, but she usually ends up being right."
Terrence M.

"My best friend isn't afraid to speak her mind. When we're with a group that wants us to do something we're not supposed to, she won't go along with it. I admire her courage—she gives me the courage to walk away too."
Maria Elena C.

"I try to be a good example for my younger brother. Even though we argue a lot, I know he looks up to me. I feel responsible for keeping him out of trouble."
Alexander W.

Personal Challenge

Be supportive of your friends and family. It's so easy to follow the crowd these days—to call people names or insult them. Make a conscious effort to be more mindful of people's feelings and opinions. Support people who need help, physically or spiritually. Find a day that you can volunteer your time to help a neighbor, serve at a soup kitchen, or collect food and clothing for a homeless shelter.

Break open the Word

Showing Your Love

Read Matthew 22:34–40. Jesus reveals God as love itself—unselfish, unconditional love. As followers of Jesus, we are above all commanded to love. Jesus taught us that by following the commandments with our actions and also with our hearts, we grow closer to God the Father.

1. How can you show your love for your family and friends?
2. How does your church show love to the community? To the rest of the world?

A.D. **14–37**
Tiberius ruler
over Roman Empire

A.D. **28–29**
John the Baptist's
active ministry

A.D. **33**
Crucifixion, death, and
Resurrection of Jesus

A.D. 14-37

A.D. 47

A.D. **26–36** Pontius Pilate
the Roman procurator
over Judea and Samaria

A.D. **29**
Jesus' baptism; beginning
of his public ministry

Called to Follow Jesus

"For once you were darkness, but now in the Lord you are light. Live as children of the Light."

Ephesians 5:8

Chapter Goals

In this chapter, you will:

- examine what it means to follow Jesus.
- explore the beginnings of public ministry and the Church.
- experience the life of early Christians.
- examine the development of the Gospels and the New Testament.
- learn about Sister Thea Bowman.

A.D. 66–70
Dead Sea Scrolls hidden in Qumran region

A.D. 70
Second Temple destroyed

A.D. 69

A.D. 102

A.D. 64
Rome ravaged by fire

C. A.D. 65
Gospel according to Mark written

What Does It Mean to Follow Jesus?

On **Pentecost**, the fiftieth day following Easter, the Holy Spirit was made present, given, and communicated as a divine Person of the Trinity. From that time on, the Church has looked back, remembered, and passed on the stories of Jesus. Because of Pentecost, many have come to believe in and share the Good News. Two thousand years later, the story of Jesus continues to unfold. We are part of that story as we ask questions—questions that have been asked by his followers throughout the ages:

Who was Jesus?

Who were his followers?

How do the Gospels reveal the life and mission of Jesus?

How does God reveal himself as Father, Son, and Holy Spirit?

How does the Holy Spirit guide the Church?

What does it mean to be a member of the Church?

What are the responsibilities of the Church's leaders?

What does it mean to follow Jesus, and how does it affect our lives and the choices we make?

As with the Apostles, Jesus calls us to follow him into relationship with the Holy Spirit and God the Father. A study of the Scripture is a study of relationship. The Scriptures call us into a relationship with God—Father, Son, and

Holy Spirit—and challenge us to be aware of how that relationship affects the way we live and how we treat others.

What does it mean to follow Jesus? As Christians, we are called to walk in Christ's footsteps. To follow Jesus' example and to become more like him, we need to get to know him—to learn about his life and teachings.

Following Jesus, however, is more than studying a historical description of his life. We are called to take a faith journey with Jesus—to believe in him and to have a personal relationship with him. Believing in Jesus is about responding to the gift of his divine love. Responding to Jesus' love for us leads to a greater appreciation of our own worth. Believing in Jesus means understanding and believing in ourselves—and that, in turn, means acting like Jesus—letting ourselves become instruments of God the Father's love in the world. We are able to love others in new ways because of the life and love Jesus shares with us. We can become examples of faith, hope, and love, as Jesus is.

John the Baptist believed that the messianic hopes of the Jews would soon be fulfilled. He proclaimed to his followers, "I baptize you with water for repentance, but one who is more powerful than I is coming after me; I am not worthy to carry his sandals. He will baptize you with the Holy Spirit and fire" (*Matthew 3:11*). In spite of John's insistence that he was not the Messiah, people continued to flock to him to be baptized and to hear him preach.

Jesus came to John seeking a baptism of repentance, as did many other Jews. John knew from the moment he saw Jesus that Jesus was truly the Messiah. As Jesus approached the banks of the Jordan River, John proclaimed to the crowds, "Here is the Lamb of God who takes away the sin of the world!" (*John 1:29*). John also expressed a degree of unworthiness—because he recognized Jesus as God's Son—when he asked Jesus, "I need to be baptized by you, and do you come to me?" (*Matthew 3:14*). John knew that the baptisms he conferred using water in the Jordan amounted to very little compared to the Baptism the Messiah would grant through the Holy Spirit. Jesus, however, rebuked John and instructed him to proceed, saying that it must be done. After Jesus was baptized, "the heavens were opened to him and he saw the Spirit of God descending like a dove and alighting on him. And a voice from heaven said, 'This is my Son, the Beloved, with whom I am well pleased'" (*Matthew 3:16–17*).

The baptism given by John was a sign of a person's willingness to turn from sin and toward God. Even though Jesus was without sin, he sought baptism. This showed his connectedness with God's people.

Break Open the Word

John's Message The story of John the Baptist appears in each of the Gospels in varying detail. Read about John the Baptist in each of the Gospels. Compare and contrast the stories and what John proclaims in each Gospel. What differences do you see? What symbols of the Holy Spirit are present?

Faith Activity

Symbols of the Trinity

Many symbols of the Trinity are commonly used in the Church to represent the Father, Son, and Holy Spirit. Among them are the trefoil, the triquetra, the equilateral triangle, an interwoven circle, and a circle of fish. Two themes are common to each symbol: the incorporation of the number three and an image that shows balance between each of the three sides. What other images do you associate with the Trinity? Draw another symbol for the Trinity.

The Mystery of the Trinity

Through the baptism and the teachings of Jesus and through their own experiences, Jesus' followers were aware of a relationship between God, whom Jesus called Father, Jesus, and the Holy Spirit. God's revelation of the nature of the Trinity continued through Church Tradition and Scripture.

The New Testament provides us with the concept of the **Holy Trinity**— the belief that three Persons exist in one God. The Church proclaims the Trinity as three Persons: the Father, the Son, and the Holy Spirit, distinct from one another, yet united in one divine nature. He taught his disciples to form a close relationship with God the Father when he taught them the Lord's Prayer. (See *Luke 11:1–4.*)

Luke gives us a deeper insight into the relationship between Father and Son. In Luke Jesus states, "All things have been handed over to me by my Father; and no one knows who the Son is except the Father, or who the Father is except the Son and anyone to whom the Son chooses to reveal him" (*Luke 10:22*). The baptism of Jesus also presents the three distinct persons of the Trinity.

The mystery of the Trinity is the central mystery of Christian faith. God is made known to us by revealing himself as Father, Son, and Holy Spirit. The divine Persons are inseparable in what they are and in what they do. Yet each shows forth what is proper to him in the Trinity, especially the Son of God's Incarnation and the gift of the Holy Spirit. Christians sometimes associate aspects of God as Creator, Redeemer, and Sanctifier with different Persons of the Holy Trinity, although all three Persons do the work of creating, redeeming, and making holy.

Our Identity Although we cannot fully understand the mystery of the Trinity, it is integral to understanding that as Christians, we are called into relationship. Out of love God has revealed himself to us, creating us to live in relationship and happiness with him. Like the Trinity, we are to live our lives in relationship to God, to one another, and to the Church. In this way, we imitate God and reflect the image of the Trinity, and in a special way, the image of our God who became one of us: "Man is predestined to reproduce the image of God's Son made man, the 'image of the invisible God'[7], so that Christ shall be the first-born of a multitude of brothers and sisters[8]." (*Catechism of the Catholic Church, 381*).

Christian Baptism

The baptisms conferred by John the Baptist were symbolic. Unlike the **Baptism** we now share in the Church, recipients did not receive forgiveness of sin or the gift of the Holy Spirit; they did not come to share in the life of the Trinity. The baptism of John was not a **sacrament**—an effective sign that conveys grace established by Jesus and given to the Church. People went to John to show repentance and sorrow for their sins. Devout Jews of John's time knew and believed that only God could forgive sin.

Baptism is the first sacrament of forgiveness and the first of three Sacraments of Initiation—Confirmation and Eucharist are the others—in which God forgives both original sin and any personal sins committed before Baptism. Those who are baptized are united to Jesus and become members of the Body of Christ, the Church.

In the Sacrament of Baptism, the Church continues the mission Jesus gave his Apostles to "go therefore and make disciples of all nations, baptizing them in the name of the Father and of the Son and of the Holy Spirit, and teaching them to obey everything that I have commanded you" (*Matthew 28:19–20*).

Baptism in the New Testament Several of the New Testament letters, including the First Letter of Peter, express the importance of Baptism in the early Christian Church. While Scripture does not describe the entire ritual of Baptism, the letters of Paul give us some clues concerning what the rite

▼ Roberto Arno Ramirez is baptized—as his sponsor looks on—months after coming to the U.S. to have corrective surgery for his legs.

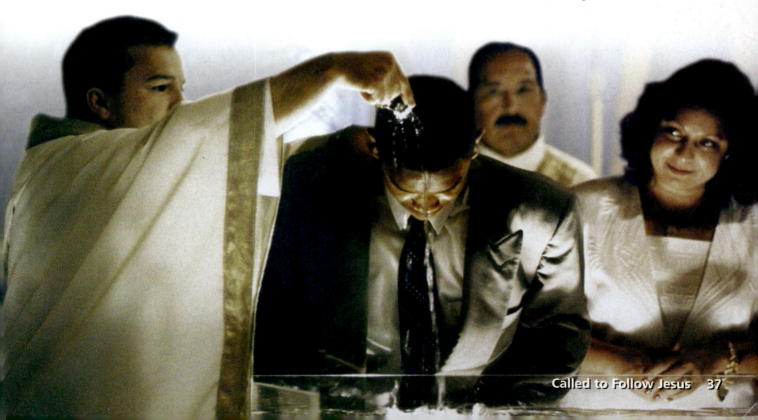

of Baptism involved. In Galatians 6:6 Paul describes the distinctive relationship between the person performing the ceremony and the initiate. In Galatians 3:27 the church recognizes a metaphor for the special garment worn by the newly baptized person that symbolizes new life in Christ. Paul also notes the ritual of anointing in Ephesians 1:13.

Faith Activity

Baptism Look in your parish bulletin or on its Web site to find out when your parish will next celebrate Baptisms. With a group of classmates, attend the Baptism, and participate in the ceremony. What symbolism do you see? How is this ceremony different from the early Church ceremony? How is the Trinity invoked?

Scripture

"Do you not know that all of us who have been baptized into Christ Jesus were baptized into his death? Therefore we have been buried with him by baptism into death, so that, just as Christ was raised from the dead by the glory of the Father, so we too might walk in the newness of life."

Romans 6:3–4

"For in the one Spirit we were all baptized into one body—Jews or Greeks, slaves or free—and we were all made to drink of one Spirit."

1 Corinthians 12:13

". . . for in Christ Jesus you are all children of God through faith. As many of you as were baptized into Christ have clothed yourselves with Christ."

Galatians 3:26–27

"There is one body and one Spirit, just as you were called to the one hope of your calling, one Lord, one faith, one baptism . . ."

Ephesians 4:4–5

These Scripture verses from Saint Paul's writings teach us that, through Baptism, we find salvation—freedom from everlasting sin and restored friendship with God. Baptism is necessary for this salvation and for membership into the People of God, the Church. All are welcome, and all those baptized are united to one another no matter their life situation, their geographical location, or their age.

The Ritual of Baptism In the early Church, those being baptized were immersed in water three times. The Trinitarian baptismal formula was recited over them during this immersion: "In the name of the Father, and of the Son, and of the Holy Spirit." After the third—and longest—immersion, those receiving the Baptism came up gasping for air.

In the Sacrament of Baptism, we die to everything that separates us from God—we die in our sins—and we rise to new life in Jesus Christ. Baptism frees us from sin and unites us with Jesus and all who are baptized. Some parishes continue the practice of immersion today. The other form for the celebration of the sacrament is the pouring of holy water three times over the head of the person being baptized. In both cases, the action of pouring or immersion is accompanied by the words: "In the name of the Father, and of the Son, and of the Holy Spirit."

Today some people refer to Baptism as christening, which means to join with Christ. This term reminds us that the Sacrament of Baptism joins us to

Christ and we become members of the Church. The word *Christ* means "anointed one." In the Old Testament, priests, prophets, and kings were anointed with oil to signify their special vocation. Christians are anointed with oil at Baptism to exemplify their calling to share in the role of Jesus as priest, prophet, and king. They are consecrated to participate in Christian worship. The oil used for anointing is called *chrism* and is blessed by a bishop on Holy Thursday for use throughout the next year.

Baptismal Fonts The baptismal font is located in the baptistery or occasionally, in the narthex of the church. The baptismal font should be clean, beautiful, and constructed of a material fitting for Baptisms—generally wood, metal, or stone. Many baptismal fonts are constructed in such a way that they may be used for either the Baptism of infants in a smaller basin or for the Baptism of adults in a larger pool.

In the time of the Apostles, people were baptized either in rivers or in pools of water; specially constructed fonts were not used. When the early churches began to appear, baptismal fonts were sometimes constructed. Many early fonts echoed the historical locations of Baptism in the Church; the fonts were dug into the earth and appeared as a small cross-shaped pool inside the church, fed by a nearby stream. Decorations and other ornamentation were common in the freestanding fonts that appeared in later churches. Most fonts were circular or octagonal in shape, as are many today, though some were cross-shaped.

▲ A priest blesses a child during a Baptismal mass in Victoria, Seychelles.

Faith **Activity**

Baptismal Fonts Go to your church and explore the baptistery. Explore the baptisteries of other Catholic churches in your area as well. Compare the fonts found in your church with the others. If no other churches are in your area, look on the Internet or in the library for photos of other baptismal fonts.

Beginnings of the Church

scripture

"When the day of Pentecost had come, they were all together in one place. And suddenly from heaven there came a sound like the rush of a violent wind, and it filled the entire house where they were sitting. Divided tongues, as of fire, appeared among them, and a tongue rested on each of them. All of them were filled with the Holy Spirit and began to speak in other languages, as the Spirit gave them ability."

Acts 2:1–4

▲ Pentecost by El Greco, c. 1604–1614.

Imagine being present at Pentecost. Who do you think was there? Certainly Mary, the mother of Jesus, was present, as well as the Apostles and other disciples, both men and women. What do you think their relationship had been with Jesus? We know from Scripture that they heard his teachings firsthand and witnessed the miracles he performed. They also shared in the joys, sorrows, and challenges of daily living. As close as many of these people were to Jesus, most of them denied and deserted him in his time of need. Yet these were the people Jesus chose to carry on his mission. At Pentecost the Holy Spirit filled them with the wisdom to accept Jesus' call and with the courage and love to proclaim his message.

The Holy Spirit in the Church

As promised, Jesus sent the Holy Spirit to his disciples. It's important to realize the same Spirit is acting throughout history. We find in the Old Testament many references to the Spirit of the Lord. The Hebrew people before Jesus' time believed in the one true God, but the Trinity had not been revealed to them yet. With the coming of the Son of God and later the Holy Spirit at Pentecost, the Holy Spirit was revealed as a divine Person of the Trinity.

The Hebrew people were aware of the Spirit of the Lord working in the world. In fact, the gifts of the Holy Spirit recognized at Confirmation have their root in the Hebrew Scriptures. Isaiah 11:1–2 states, "A shoot shall come out of the stump of Jesse, and a branch shall grow out of his roots. The spirit of the LORD shall rest on him, the spirit of wisdom and understanding, the spirit of counsel and might, the spirit of knowledge and the fear of the LORD."

The Gospel writers mention the Holy Spirit early in their accounts. We learn of the Holy Spirit in Matthew in reference to the conception of Jesus, and in the other Gospels at the baptism of Jesus. The Gospels according to Matthew and Mark usually mention him with reference to God the Father. The Gospels according to Luke and John, on the other hand, present Jesus as a vehicle through which the Holy Spirit is given to the Church.

The Life of Early Christians

The first followers of Jesus were excited by his message. Under the leadership of Peter and the other Apostles, the Church grew rapidly. The followers of Jesus soon included people who had not met Jesus, but who came to believe in him because of the Holy Spirit and the work of the Apostles and the disciples, Mary, and the other women who were eyewitnesses to Jesus' life, death, and Resurrection. The early Christians developed the oral tradition of telling and retelling the stories surrounding the life of Jesus.

After Pentecost the followers of Jesus followed Jesus' command from the Last Supper to gather and break bread in his memory. On Sunday, the day of the Lord's Resurrection, they gathered to celebrate the Eucharist. Everyone was invited—rich or poor—to these gatherings, usually held in a larger home. Within these house churches, Christians worshiped, received instruction, and cared for the needs of others.

House churches developed, in part, because local governors and other Roman officials did not consider the followers of Christ to be practicing a legal religion. Also, the Jewish community had begun to expel Christians from the synagogues. As a result, early Christians distanced themselves from Judaism, abandoning some of the Jewish fast days and adopting Sunday as their day of worship. To avoid the scrutiny of Roman and Jewish leaders, the early Christians began gathering and holding Mass in the homes of fellow believers.

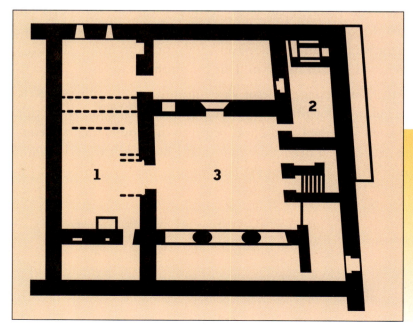

Faith Sharing

Encountering God

Spend some time considering how your relationship with God has been part of your life, and then complete the following activities:

1. Write about a time you experienced God's presence.
2. Write about a person through whom you found God.

Break Open the Word

Communal Life

Acts 2:42–47 describes the life of the early Church.

1. Summarize how the first Christians lived their daily lives.
2. What could you do to live this same way with your family? With your friends? With your classmates?

Connect to the Past

House Churches Plan of the house church at Dura Europos. The layout of early house churches depended on the layout of the house. Most of the houses were small—three to five rooms. Those who gathered in these house churches often used objects from their home to celebrate the Eucharist. Eventually, specially decorated items became more common.

1. Assembly room with dais at east end
2. Room for baptisms
3. Open courtyard

These Christian gatherings allowed the followers of Jesus to grow in openness to his message. The Church continued to grow through the Sacrament of Baptism. Church members prayed together and celebrated the Eucharist.

Jesus' celebration of the Eucharist and his saving actions on the cross established the sacramental life of the Church. During his life, Jesus welcomed, fed, healed, and forgave people. After his death he continued to share God's life with his followers through the Church's sacraments. In the sacraments, instituted by Jesus and given to the Church, the Trinity shares his life with us.

Mission

The Holy Spirit was sent upon the Church to launch her mission in the world. Jesus gave the Holy Spirit to the Church to preserve her in truth and to remind her of all Christ said and did. He makes present in the Church the mystery of salvation and draws members of the Church more deeply into union with the Trinity and with one another.

In fulfilling the prophesies of the Old Testament, Jesus united those present at Pentecost in a deeper union and communion of love with him as he released the gifts of the Holy Spirit upon them. These gifts and his unifying love were not meant for the use of the individual, but for the good of the Church.

The actions of the Holy Spirit are most visible in the Acts of the Apostles; the Spirit confers power, wisdom, faith, and prophecy to the Apostles. The Apostles, in doubt and fear following the Ascension of Jesus, are granted by the Holy Spirit the power to overcome their fears and preach to the masses.

For fifteen to twenty years, the disciples told and retold the stories of Jesus and how the gifts they received at Pentecost were shared with the early Church community. When Saint Paul began his missionary journeys (A.D. 46–47), he wrote letters to the newly formed Christian churches. Paul's letters recounted the gifts of the Holy Spirit. These letters with their words of encouragement were a source of hope and faith, prompting the early Christian churches to remain strong in their commitment to Jesus.

An Era Ending The message of Jesus was imprinted on the minds, hearts, and lives of his followers long before anything was recorded in a manuscript. As the original bearers of the Good News began to die (some, such as Peter and Paul, were martyred), a need arose to formally document the life, death, and Resurrection of Jesus, as well as the faith of the early Church.

Continuing the Mission
of the Apostles

Jesus chose twelve Apostles to carry on his work in the world in a special way. Of the Apostles, Jesus chose Peter to lead them. After his death and before his Ascension into heaven, Jesus appeared to the Apostles, saying, "'Peace be with you. As the father has sent me, so I send you.' When he had said this, he breathed on them and said to them, 'Receive the Holy Spirit . . .'" (*John 20:21–22*). In continuing Jesus' mission, the Apostles became the leaders of the early Church. They were commissioned by Jesus to teach, to sanctify, and to lead.

Peter and the other Apostles chose leaders to carry out Jesus' mission and gave them the title of *bishop*. These bishops chose other bishops to form a lineage that extends 2,000 years into the Church leadership today. The continuity of shepherding responsibility given by Christ to the Church leadership is realized in the line of authority passing from the Apostles to each of their legitimate successors. (See *John 20:23; Matthew 28:19.*) This uninterrupted succession of bishops is called **apostolic succession**. The pope, the bishop of Rome and thus the successor of Peter, is first among the world's bishops. He is the leader of the bishops and the pastor of the whole world.

Like the first Apostles, today's bishops have the task of teaching, governing, and making holy in Jesus' name. The responsibilities of all ordained ministers include the following:

- They teach the true faith. This happens when they give homilies at Mass and teach in various situations.
- They sanctify, or make holy, the Church by celebrating the sacraments with the people and praying the Liturgy of the Hours.

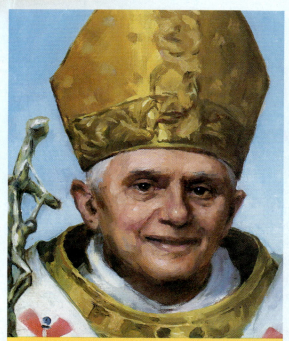

Connect to the Past

Crosiers Because of the roles of the bishops and Jesus' instruction to Peter to "tend my sheep" (*John 21:16*), the pope and the bishops are known as the shepherds of Christ's flock, the Church. This is why they have a *crosier,* or shepherd's crook. *How do the pope and bishops lead and care for Catholics today?*

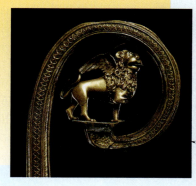

- They govern, or lead, the Church. Bishops and priests serve the people as true pastors. Most bishops head geographic areas in the Church known as dioceses.

An Accepted Religion

Imagine the year is A.D. 64. Rome has burned to the ground, and Nero has accused the followers of Christ of setting the blaze. Open persecution against Christians has sporadically taken place in parts of the Roman Empire. Imagine being in the small home of a fellow Christian, celebrating the Eucharist in dim candlelight. Filled with the Holy Spirit, you and other Christians gather to celebrate the Eucharist and remember the life and teachings of Jesus.

For nearly 250 years, Christians took the risk of practicing an illegal religion. Yet during these years, the Apostles and those who followed them set out into the Mediterranean region, spreading God's Word and baptizing in the name of the Father, Son, and Holy Spirit, as Jesus had commanded them. House churches served as meeting places for these early travelers when they returned to areas where communities of believers had already been established.

Persecution and violence against Christians continued in the Roman Empire. Then Constantine, a worshiper of the pagan sun god, became the emperor of Rome. In an amazing turn of events, Constantine turned his allegiance to the Christian God and religion: Constantine was preparing for a battle in which his troops were heavily outnumbered. According to legend, he had a vision of a flaming cross emblazoned across the sky and the Latin words: *In hoc Signo Vinces*, which means "by this sign thou shalt conquer." After winning the battle, Constantine converted to Christianity and in 313 instituted the Edict of Milan, which mandated toleration of Christians in the Roman empire. He established governmental neutrality toward all religions, though eventually Constantine recognized Christianity as the one true religion.

Connect to the Past

Conversion Illustration of the conversion of Roman Emperor Constantine I to Christianity, 1869. *Can you think of two conversion experiences that are recounted in the New Testament?*

The Shift from Oral to Written Tradition

Eventually, the early Christian communities began to write about the life and teachings of Jesus and about the ways they celebrated and followed him. These writings flowed from the living Tradition of early ecclesial communities to form the basis of the New Testament Scriptures.

We cannot separate the written Scripture from the living Tradition of the Church. The revelation of God's truth in Jesus Christ was handed on in Scripture as well as by the preaching of the Apostles and their example in the Christian community. The Apostles' mission was to continue Jesus' work after he was gone. Their beliefs and teachings are preserved both in Scripture and in Tradition. We can identify three stages of New Testament and early church development.

The Life and Teaching of Jesus,
4–6 B.C.—A.D. 30–33

The life of Jesus had an incredible impact in the world, despite the absence of rapid transportation or communication. Thousands of people witnessed the miracles he performed—signs that he was the Son of God. In addition, his message of the kingdom of God and salvation changed people in revolutionary ways. Jesus' followers witnessed his being truly raised from the dead by God the Father. Even though Jesus died, his Apostles and disciples saw him after his Resurrection. His appearances to them produced followers who knew beyond the shadow of a doubt that Christ had been raised from the dead. His life, death, and Resurrection sparked the beginnings of the early Church and changed history.

Jesus had many opponents who were upset with his teaching, miracles, and befriending of outcasts. The chief priests, scribes, and elders accused him of blasphemy, trying to abolish the Law, and trying to make himself God. Jesus was put to death. On the third day after his Passion and death, Jesus rose from the dead, and a new age dawned. Salvation was won for all people and a broken world was renewed. Jesus, the Son of God, came to reveal the truth about God, to save humankind from its sins, and to inaugurate the kingdom of God. His Church is the seed of the kingdom of God on earth.

▼ Antique paten with precious stones and glass from the court of Charles the Bald, c. 950.

The Parables

Jesus told a story like no other. People of different backgrounds and geographical locations flocked to hear his words. Jesus used **parables** to connect his message of the kingdom to the everyday life experiences of his listeners. The Synoptic Gospels include parables, and in the Gospel according to Matthew, they are a part of all five major discourses and narrative sections.

Centuries after Jesus lived, these parables continue to draw us into the timeless realities of God's presence in our ordinary lives. These stories lead us on a journey toward wholeness and truth. When these parables become a part of our lives, they summon a response from us to put them into action through acts of love. Jesus calls us to follow his lead—our lives are to be parables in action.

■ Parables provide us with a religious or moral lesson about the kingdom of God.

■ Parables were taken from the circumstances in the everyday lives of Jesus' audience.

■ Parables reveal truths to believers and conceal truths from nonbelievers.

■ Parables have surprise endings.

■ Parables present listeners with a challenge to respond to the word of God.

Levels of Meaning Jesus structured his parables with the beginning phrase "The kingdom of heaven is like" or "The reign of God is like." His parables are metaphors or similes drawn from common life experiences or nature to illustrate moral or spiritual truths. A parable elicited a search for the meaning of the story and prompted the listener to apply its message to life.

The parables convey a meaning on two levels: the literal level and the spiritual level. Although the literal level describes the story itself, the spiritual level teaches about God, truth, and the kingdom. We need to move from the literal level to the spiritual level to grasp the deeper spiritual meaning of the parables. When our minds and hearts are open to the spiritual truth, it becomes the lived truth in our dealings with others.

Open to the Message Jesus realized that not everyone would be open to accepting the challenges that the kingdom of God required.

The disciples asked Jesus why he spoke to them and to the crowds in parables. Jesus responded that ". . . seeing they do not perceive, and hearing they do not listen, nor do they understand" (*Matthew 13:13*). To believers, the truth is revealed; to nonbelievers, the truth is concealed. Some people are open to the message; others are closed.

The Parables

The House Built on Rock	The Sheep and the Goats
The Sower	The Two Debtors
The Seed Grows of Itself	The Good Samaritan
The Weeds Among the Wheat	The Importunate Friend
The Mustard Seed	The Rich Fool
The Yeast	The Servants Who Waited
The Found Treasure	The Barren Fig Tree
The Pearl of Great Value	The Last Seat
The Net	The Great Supper
The Unmerciful Servant	The Lost Sheep
The Laborers in the Vineyard	The Lost Coin
The Two Sons	The Prodigal Son
The Tenants	The Dishonest Steward
The Marriage Feast	The Rich Man and Lazarus
The Wedding Garment	The Persistent Widow
The Ten Virgins	The Pharisee and the Tax Collector
The Talents	The Gold Pieces

Faith Activity

Act it Out Break into small groups. First choose a parable and find it in one of the Gospels. Summarize its message, and then act it out in a modern setting. Have your classmates guess which parable you acted out.

Connect to the Past

The Church of the Holy Sepulchre The Church of the Holy Sepulchre is among the oldest churches remaining in the world. It is built upon what is believed to be the site of Jesus' crucifixion. Go to the library, and research when the oldest church in the world was constructed. Find out when the oldest church in your area was built and when the oldest church in the United States was built.

Faith Activity

Individual or Community

Contemporary society tends to emphasize individualism. Yet we are called to community in different aspects of our lives—in our family, our school, our church, our neighborhood, and the global community. Fold a sheet of paper in half. On one side, list the benefits and challenges of individualism. On the other side, list the benefits and challenges of being part of a community. What conclusions can you draw from your reflection?

Oral Proclamation, A.D. 30–65

After the Resurrection and Pentecost, Jesus' Apostles and disciples shared what they had seen with people throughout the Mediterranean region. The early Christians remained faithful to Jesus' teaching. They believed he was the Messiah sent by God. Other people who heard the message of Jesus from the Apostles or from other eyewitnesses also became believers. As these new believers helped spread the Gospel, the early Church began to grow. Under the leadership of Paul, the Good News spread throughout the Roman Empire.

Preaching the Gospel took on these important forms during this time:

■ First, preaching to those who had not witnessed the saving acts of Jesus involved passing on the message of Jesus' life—his deeds, Passion, death, Resurrection, and Ascension. This vitally important message of salvation was called the *kerygma,* the Greek word for "proclamation." To further illustrate Jesus' message of salvation, the kerygma included the miracles and parables of his ministry. These preachers often used the Old Testament Scriptures to show how Jesus fulfilled the messianic prophecies.

- Second, preaching helped those who had accepted Jesus. This instruction, known as the *didache,* the Greek word for "teaching," reinforced the living message within the kerygma. The kerygma inspired those preaching it to live a more Christ-centered life.

- Third, celebrating the Eucharist and retelling stories of the life of Jesus helped preserve the Scripture and Traditions of the Church. The *liturgia,* meaning "Christian worship," recalled key events such as the teachings and prayers of Jesus (including the Lord's Prayer), and his words and actions at the Last Supper. Remembering the life and teachings of Jesus through the liturgia was a vital part of early Church celebrations. This Christian worship enlivened and sustained the faith of these people in a time when Christians were being persecuted for their beliefs.

Written Proclamation, A.D. 50–110

The events of Jesus' remarkable life and death preserved a faith account of his Gospel message. The early Christians believed strongly that Jesus would return in their lifetimes to judge the living and the dead. At first they did not write down the testimony they had heard or had proclaimed. But then the eyewitnesses to Jesus' life began to die, be persecuted, or be put to death, as Peter had been. The early Christians shifted their belief that the second coming of Christ was imminent. Because they realized that Christ might not come soon, they began to preserve the stories and testimony of Jesus in writing.

Passing on Jesus' message, the kerygma, by word of mouth left that message open to different interpretations, distortions, and omissions. To preserve and pass on the authentic teachings of Jesus to succeeding generations, more formal written records were needed. These written records provided an accurate testimony to Jesus' teaching and the faith of the early Church.

Jesus' Miracles   All four Gospels record Jesus' **miracles**. His miracles confirmed his power over the power of evil. In his miracles Jesus overcame the mystery of evil with the power of goodness. The synoptic Gospels call miracles the "deeds of power," because they show Jesus' power over evil. The Gospel according to John calls them "signs" because the miracles reveal Jesus as divine and God's power over evil and sin. When performing these miracles out of love and compassion for those who were afflicted, Jesus was a sign of God's mercy and love. The authors recorded these miracles because they knew something extraordinary was happening through Jesus. Divine power was at work in Jesus, his Son. Jesus made God real to people in ways they had never before experienced. The Gospel writers included the numerous miracles in their Gospels to illustrate a basic truth: that Jesus is the Son of God and that something amazing happened in and through his life.

In the Gospel according to Luke, Jesus is a healer. He shows his love for others through his healing touch. Jesus extends his healing touch not only to people, but also to the natural world. Jesus touches the dead and they rise to

Faith Activity

Meditation   Think about what it means to you when you bless yourself with the Sign of the Cross. Begin making the Sign of the Cross. As you silently pray, touch your forehead and pray for those who live in the northern part of the world. Touch the middle of your chest, remembering and praying for those who live in the southern part of the world. Finally, touch both shoulders and call to mind and pray for those who live around you. What is one way you can be a sign of God's presence in the world today?

Faith Activity

Saints   In the Catholic Church, one miracle is required for someone to be beatified; two miracles through the candidate's intercession must be verified before that person can be canonized a saint. Choose a particular saint and check a Catholic almanac, the Vatican Web site, or Butler's Lives of the Saints to discover the miracles attributed to him or her.

Work with the Chart

Miracles Select three of the miracles in the Gospel of Luke. Read each passage, and then answer the following questions:
1. Who had the gift of faith in each passage?
2. Was it the person who was healed or was it someone else?
3. How does Jesus interact with the sick in each story?

Four Categories of Miracles	
Miracles of Healing: Jesus cured people of various illnesses, including leprosy, paralysis, blindness, fever, deafness, and dropsy.	
Jesus cleansing a leper	Matthew 8:1–4; Mark 1:40–45; Luke 5:12–16
Jesus healing many at Peter's house	Matthew 8:14–17; Mark 1:29–34; Luke 4:38–41
Jesus healing a crippled woman	Luke 13:11–13
Miracles of Exorcism: Jesus has power over demons and evil spirits.	
Jesus curing a boy with a demon	Matthew 17:14–21; Mark 9:14–29; Luke 9:37–43
Jesus healing those possessed with demons	Matthew 8:16–17; Mark 1:32–34; Luke 4:40–41
Jesus healing a Canaanite woman's daughter	Matthew 15:21–28; Mark 7:24–30
Miracles over Nature: Jesus controls the forces of nature by stilling a storm, feeding multitudes, turning water into wine.	
Jesus calming the storm	Matthew 8:23–27; Mark 4:35–41; Luke 8:22–25
Jesus walking on water	Matthew 14:22–33; Mark 6:45–52; John 6:16–21
Jesus and the wedding at Cana	John 2:1–11
Miracles over Death: Jesus restores the life of a person.	
Jesus and Jairus's daughter	Matthew 9:18–19 23–26; Mark 5: 21–24, 35–43; Luke 8:40–42, 49–56
Jesus and the widow's son at Nain	Luke 7:11–17
Jesus and Lazarus	John 11:1–44

new life; he touches the sick and they are made well; he touches those possessed by evil spirits and they are filled with goodness; he touches the elements of nature like bread, water, and wine and they are transformed.

The Necessity of Faith Someone who hoped to be healed by the supernatural power of Jesus usually had to have faith. Jesus ordinarily healed only when his healing power was requested or sought. (See *Luke 8:48*.) In some cases, healing took place not because of the faith of the person healed, but because of another's faith. (See *Luke 7:20*.) Some who are healed by Jesus become his disciples.

Just as not everyone who heard Jesus' words believed in him, not everyone who witnessed Jesus' miraculous deeds understood them to be a sign of the glory of God. Yet the power of Jesus' miracles showed him to be the Son of God and proved the presence of the kingdom.

Miracles occur when we have faith. God's love and forgiveness heal us from sin and its effects. Through the Church's faith, those who are powerless and oppressed can find hope and welcome in our communities. Then healing miracles can occur. Miracles of healing can be physical, spiritual, emotional, or psychological. God's healing presence leads us from death to new life.

Development of the Gospels and the New Testament

The four Gospels of the New Testament provide much of our knowledge and understanding of Jesus.

The Gospels

The Gospels comprise the heart of the Scriptures; they are the definitive source for learning about the life and lessons of Jesus Christ. God revealed the truth of Jesus Christ to the biblical authors, but the authors used their own words when writing the Gospels and all the other books of the Bible.

Gospels	Approximate Date Written
Matthew (Mt)	A.D. 70–85
Mark (Mk)	A.D. 65–70
Luke (Lk)	A.D. 70–85
John (Jn)	A.D. 90–100

The Gospels of Matthew, Mark, and Luke are referred to as the **synoptic Gospels**. The word synoptic is taken from the Latin *syn,* which means "together" and *optic,* which means "seen." This term expresses the idea that these Gospels have a similar vision.

From the chart above, you will notice that the Gospel according to Mark was written first. Luke and Matthew employed most of the Gospel according to Mark in their Gospels. In fact, 631 of Mark's 661 verses were used either in the Gospel according to Luke or in the Gospel according to Matthew. In addition, Matthew and Luke share similar material that does not appear in Mark.

Scholars suggest that Matthew and Luke used another common source, referred to as the *Q* document. The name for this document is derived from the first letter of the German word *quelle,* meaning "source." *Q* is a hypothetical source believed to consist mainly of the sayings of Jesus.

The Gospel of John, however, is very different from the synoptic Gospels. Using symbolism and powerful imagery, the Gospel according to John emphasizes the divinity of Jesus.

Acts of the Apostles

Approximate date written, A.D. 80–100

The Acts of the Apostles is an account of the growth of the Church under the guidance of the Holy Spirit.

- Acts is the second part of the Gospel according to Luke and covers Christian expansion in the Roman world.

- In Acts Luke describes the activity of the early Church, including the preaching of Peter and the Apostles, the growth of the first Christian community, the missionary journeys of Paul, and the Council of Jerusalem. This council emphasized the importance of the leadership of the Apostles and their successors in the Church.

Letters

The New Testament Letters	Approximate Date Written
Romans (Rom)*	A.D. 57–58
1 Corinthians (1 Cor)*	A.D. 54–57
2 Corinthians (2 Cor)*	A.D. 55–57
Galatians (Gal)*	A.D. 54–57
Ephesians (Eph)+	A.D. 61–63 or A.D. 80–100
Philippians (Phil)*	A.D. 54–58
Colossians (Col)+	A.D. 61–63 or A.D. 70–80
1 Thessalonians (1 Thess)*	A.D. 50
2 Thessalonians (2 Thess)+	A.D. 52+
1 Timothy (1 Tm)☆	A.D. 63–67
2 Timothy (2 Tm)☆	A.D. 67
Titus (Titus)☆	A.D. 63–67
Philemon (Philem)*	A.D. 61–63
Hebrews (Heb)	A.D. 65 or A.D. 90–100
James (Jas)	A.D. 63–70
1 Peter (1 Pet)	A.D. 64
2 Peter (2 Pet)	early second century
1 John (1 Jn)	early second century
2 John (2 Jn)	early second century
3 John (3 Jn)	second century
Jude (Jude)	A.D. 90

* Written by Paul
+ Attributed to Paul, but not commonly agreed upon. Letters attributed to Paul which scholars believe were actually written by disciples of Paul are referred to as *deutero-Pauline*.
☆ Attributed to Paul, but virtually all scholars believe he did not write them.

Twenty letters, or Epistles, follow the Acts of the Apostles. The letters were written to a Christian community or to individuals, and generally took the form of letter writing in the ancient world. The letters open with a greeting that identifies the sender and recipients, followed by a prayer. The body of the letter usually contains an account of Jesus' life, teachings on how to grow in the Christian life, and advice and encouragement to the community. The letters conclude with a brief personal remark and a farewell.

The letters of Paul, or the Pauline Letters, are the letters from Romans to Philemon, with the Letter to the Hebrews added at the end. The other seven letters of the New Testament are called the Catholic Epistles. They are called *catholic*, or "universal," because they were written to the general public instead of to a specific Christian community.

Revelation

Approximate date written, A.D. 95–96

The final book in the New Testament, the Revelation to John, offers poetic imagery and challenges the reader to grasp the truth of Jesus.

- The author wrote in the style of apocalyptic literature, a form popular with both Christian and Jewish communities at this time. *Apocalyptic* means "revealed" or "unveiled."

- In apocalyptic writings the secrets of heaven or the future are revealed by an angel or by the Risen Christ. Much of the imagery of Revelation comes from the Old Testament books of Ezekiel, Zechariah, and Daniel.

- The book also contains the symbolism of numbers, colors, and images used to hide messages from the Romans, who were actively persecuting the Christians. During this time of crisis, these writings were meant to comfort and give hope to a suffering people. They also exhorted Christians to remain faithful to their mission.

▲ The Last Judgement by Michelangelo, 1535–1541.

THE GOSPELS

ave you ever seen a large crystal ball hanging from the center of a ceiling in a ballroom? As you move around the crystal ball, the light reflects different colors of the spectrum. Looking at the Gospels is similar in that the Gospels offer different reflections of one story.

Although different in many ways, all the **Gospels** tell the Good News, which is the meaning of the word *Gospel*. They present the story of Easter faith rooted in the life, death, and Resurrection of Jesus Christ, the incarnate Son of God. They were written in a particular time and culture to convey the truth about Jesus. We learn that Jesus is the Son of God who has become man. He is true God and true man. Written by people of faith for people of faith, the Gospels tell of God's kingdom, love, forgiveness of sins, redemption of the human race, and promise of eternal happiness for his faithful people.

The Gospels tell the story of the religious life of people on a spiritual journey. As in all stories, there are major characters, plots, a drama, and a climax. The **Evangelists**—the Gospel writers Matthew, Mark, Luke, and John—told these stories to uncover what was at the center of the religious encounter of the community with God.

Sometimes the Gospels according to Matthew, Mark, Luke, and John are referred to as the *four faces* or *four portraits* of Jesus. They are, in fact, four versions of the same story. Each writer developed a somewhat different perception of Jesus because he wrote his Gospel to benefit the needs of the community he was addressing. While each is unique, all helped lead their communities of faith on a journey to God.

Note: None of the Evangelists clearly stated his identity. The general belief today is that many authors wrote the Gospels, and the Lord worked through each of them. Additionally, the dates when the Gospels were written are approximate.

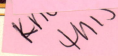

Gospel According to Matthew

Who was the author? Unknown author, probably a Jewish Christian of Palestinian origin

Approximate date written: A.D. 70–85

Location where written: Syria (Antioch)

Written for: Jewish Christians

Image of Jesus: Jesus as Teacher

Genealogy: Traced back to Abraham, the first ancestor of the Jews. Jesus, as promised Messiah, is King of the Jews.

Theological themes: Five teaching sections like the Torah; Jesus as the new covenant who fulfills the old covenant   *Messiah*

Symbol: Human figure—recording of Jesus' human ancestors in Gospel's beginning

Gospel According to Mark

Who was the author? Unknown, but linked by Tradition to John Mark (appears in Acts of the Apostles 12:12, 25 and 15:37); probably a friend or disciple of Peter

Approximate date written: Before A.D. 62–70

Location where written: Probably Rome

Written for: Gentile Christians

Image of Jesus: Jesus as the Suffering Servant/Unrecognized Suffering Messiah

Genealogy: None given; Jesus presented as a servant, who were not required to have a genealogy

Theological themes: Jesus on a journey—more actions than words; Jesus as servant

Symbol: Desert lion; John the Baptist, the voice of one "crying out in the desert" in Gospel opening

Gospel According to Luke

Who was the author? A Greek convert (Gentile) and companion of Paul

Approximate date written: A.D. 70–85

Location where written: Greece

Written for: Christians of Greek background (Gentiles)

Image of Jesus: Jesus as the Compassionate Savior

Genealogy: Traced back to Adam. Jesus is Savior of everyone (universal).

Theological themes: Stresses prayer, Holy Spirit; concerned with outcasts and sinners

Symbol: Ox, which is a sacrificial animal; Zechariah offering sacrifice in Temple in Gospel opening

Gospel According to John

Who was the author? Unknown, possibly John the Apostle; probably a disciple of John's (Apostle John may be source of testimony.)

Approximate date written: A.D. 90–100 or A.D. 110

Location where written: Ephesus (Asia Minor)

Written for: Christians of all backgrounds

Image of Jesus: Jesus—God Incarnate; Life-Giving Divine Savior

Genealogy: Traced back to God (Jesus the Word eternally begotten); never a time the Son of God did not exist

Theological themes: Jesus is fully God; emphasizes use of symbolism

Symbol: Eagle; starts with a hymn of praise to Jesus who uniquely looks on the face of God, just as the eagle looks on the sun

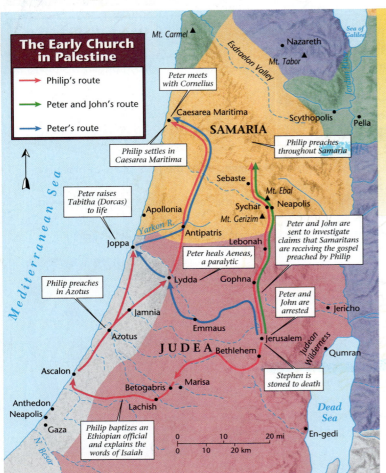

The Early Church in Palestine

→ Philip's route
→ Peter and John's route
→ Peter's route

Mt. Carmel ▲
Nazareth
Mt. Tabor ▲
Sea of Galilee
Esdraelon Valley
Jordan River

Peter meets with Cornelius

Caesarea Maritima
Scythopolis
Pella
SAMARIA

Philip settles in Caesarea Maritima

Philip preaches throughout Samaria

Sebaste
Mt. Ebal ▲
Sychar
Neapolis
Mt. Gerizim ▲

Peter raises Tabitha (Dorcas) to life

Apollonia
Yarkon R.
Antipatris
Lebonah

Peter and John are sent to investigate claims that Samaritans are receiving the gospel preached by Philip

Joppa

Peter heals Aeneas, a paralytic

Lydda
Gophna

Peter and John are arrested

Philip preaches in Azotus

Jamnia
Emmaus
Jericho

Mediterranean Sea

Azotus
JUDEA
Bethlehem
Jerusalem
Judean Wilderness
Qumran

Ascalon

Stephen is stoned to death

Betogabris
Marisa
Lachish

Anthedon
Neapolis
Gaza

Philip baptizes an Ethiopian official and explains the words of Isaiah

N. Besor

Dead Sea
En-gedi

0   10   20 mi
0   10   20 km

Explore the Land

Early Growth of the Church

The Apostles and the early Evangelists traveled throughout the Mediterranean region, spreading the Good News. *How far from their homes did the Apostles travel? In Acts of the Apostles, read about the main cities where the Apostles stopped and about the difficulties of their travels.*

Written Records of Early Christianity

Scripture and Tradition are the major sources of our knowledge and understanding of Jesus. Other non-Christian sources have limited recorded information about the life of Jesus and the early Christians. Although these sources give historical evidence of the life of Jesus, they do not provide details about his life.

Josephus (A.D. 37–101) Josephus was born in Jerusalem at a time when his Jewish homeland was occupied by Roman forces. Josephus was an eye-witness to the destruction of Jerusalem and the Temple. He became a Roman citizen and spent the remainder of his life writing volumes of books on the war and on Jewish culture and faith. Many passages attributed to Josephus may not have been written by him, but were added to the manu-script at a later time by Christian scribes who preserved his writings. Regardless, the work of Josephus remains a reliable reference to Jesus. It alludes to Jesus' wisdom, his teaching, his miracles, the many conversions he made, his death and Resurrection, and the continuation of the Christian movement.

Tacitus (A.D. 56–120) One of Rome's most famous historians, Tacitus moved through the ranks of the Roman government as a senator, a consul,

Interpret the Art

The Persecution of Christians Nero's cruelty and persecution of Christians was outrageous, even by the standards of his contemporaries. He took great pains to mock and deride Christians even as he tortured and executed them. Those killed by Nero or by others for their Christian beliefs and faith are called martyrs.

and finally, the Roman governor of Asia. Because Tacitus was a pro-Roman official, his writing is a surprising source of how Nero blamed the Christians for the fire that destroyed most of Rome in A.D. 64. Because Nero was blamed for the fire—or for not putting it out fast enough—he used the Christians as a scapegoat to divert the anger directed at him. Tacitus further wrote that the originator of the Christian movement was Christ, therefore providing a solid reference to the role of Jesus Christ as the one whom the early Christians followed.

Pliny the Younger (A.D. 61–115) Another Roman official was Pliny the Younger. Pliny was originally a Roman orator who became the governor of Bithynia. He was known for his literary and oratorical skills. While in office, he wrote to Emperor Trajan for advice on the treatment of the Christians. Pliny often asked people brought before him if they were, in fact, Christians. They would say that they were, knowing the punishment was execution. Trajan responded that he was in agreement with Pliny's course of action toward Christians.

Suetonius (A.D. 69–120) A contemporary of Tacitus, Suetonius was a Roman historian who served as a court secretary. Suetonius had access to imperial records and recorded the expulsion of the Jews in Rome who followed Jesus. Suetonius' accounts also establish that Nero punished the Christians for professing their beliefs.

Faith Activity

A Panel Interview
Form a panel to portray eyewitnesses—Mary, the Apostles, disciples, and those who witnessed the words and actions of Jesus. Add a second group of non-eyewitnesses to the panel—Josephus, Pliny the Younger, Suetonius, and Tacitus. Each person on the panel, who will be interviewed by the class about the life of Jesus and her or his experience of him. The remainder of the class should prepare questions to ask members of the panel.

Sister Thea Bowman, FSPA

(1937–1990)

Sister Thea Bowman exhibited a relationship with the Spirit that we should all share. Sister Thea's relationship with God was shaped through her family, religious community, prayer, and reading of the Scriptures. Scripture provided her nourishment in life and as she faced death. Relationships are at the center of our lives and faith. Relationships with God can help us discover "who we are and whose we are," as Sister Thea would say.

It would be a great challenge to embody the Spirit the way Sister Thea did. The granddaughter of slaves, she was born Bertha Bowman on December 29, 1937, in Mississippi. She was raised a Methodist until, at age nine, she asked her parents if she could become a Catholic. At age ten, after becoming Catholic, she was enrolled in Holy Child Jesus School staffed by the Franciscan Sisters of Perpetual Adoration. The life and work of the sisters impressed her so much that at age fifteen, she joined them by entering Saint Rose Convent in LaCrosse, Wisconsin. There she was given the name Thea.

The gifts of the Holy Spirit are shown in everything that Sister Thea did in her life. Her courage, knowledge, and right judgment guided her in sharing of the message of God's love through a teaching career. After sixteen years of teaching at various institutions, she became the consultant for intercultural awareness in the Diocese of Jackson, Mississippi. In that role Sister Thea gave presentations across the country—gatherings that combined Gospel preaching, prayer, storytelling, and singing. Sister Thea particularly enjoyed singing as a method to bring everyone together. Her programs were directed toward breaking down racial and cultural barriers. She encouraged people to communicate with one another so they could understand other cultures and races.

In 1984 Sister Thea was diagnosed with terminal cancer. She prayed "to live until I die—to live fully." Her prayer was answered. Thea was able to continue her gatherings while seated in a wheelchair. The U.S. Catholic Bishops invited her to be a key speaker at a 1989 conference on Black Catholics. At the end of the meeting, at Sister Thea's invitation, the bishops stood and enthusiastically sang "We Shall Overcome."

During an interview, Sister Thea stated, "I think one difference between me and some other people is that I'm content to do a little bit. Sometimes people think they have to do big things in order to make a change, but if each one of us would light the candle, we'd have a tremendous light." One of Sister Thea's favorite songs was "This Little Light of Mine."

Thea had a full life; she fought evils that drive people apart—prejudice, suspicion, and hatred. She fought for God and for all people. She died in 1990.

Abstracted from information given by Franciscan Sisters of Perpetual Adoration, LaCrosse, Wisconsin.

Renewal of Baptismal Promises

Begin by praying the Sign of the Cross.

Leader: Do you reject Satan and all his works and all his empty promises?

All: I do.

Leader: Do you believe in God the Father almighty, creator of heaven
and earth?

All: I do.

Leader: Do you believe in Jesus Christ, his only son, our Lord,
who was born of the Virgin Mary,
was crucified, died, and was buried,
rose from the dead,
and is now seated at the right hand of the Father?

All: I do.

Leader: Do you believe in the Holy spirit,
the Lord, the giver of life,
who came upon the apostles at Pentecost?

All: I do.

Leader: Do you believe in the holy catholic Church,
the communion of saints, the forgiveness of sins,
the resurrection of the body, and life everlasting?

All: I do.

Leader: This is our faith. This is the faith of the Church.
We are proud to profess it in Christ Jesus our Lord.

All: Amen.

End by praying the Sign of the Cross.

Review

1. What are the differences between the baptisms given by John the Baptist and sacramental Baptism?

2. What prayer accompanies the ritual of Baptism?

3. Who are the three Persons of the Holy Trinity? How can you develop a greater relationship with each Person of the Trinity?

4. How did Pentecost transform or change those who were present? Why is Pentecost important to the Church?

5. What is the role of the Holy Spirit in the life of the Church? And the difference between the Jewish and the Christian understanding of the Spirit of God and the Holy Spirit.

6. List the seven gifts of the Holy Spirit. Discuss their connection with the Old Testament.

7. What role did the house church have in early Christianity? What did the house churches leave as a lasting legacy for the Church today?

8. Which Gospels are referred to as *synoptic*? Why are these Gospels called synoptic?

9. Identify and describe the three stages of development of Scripture.

10. Describe the key audience of each of the Gospels.

11. How does the location where the Gospel was written help you identify the key audience?

12. List four sources other than Scripture that provide historical information about Jesus and the early Christians. Give a one-sentence summary of what each source said.

Key Words

apostolic succession (p. 45)—The uninterrupted succession of bishops, from the Apostle Peter to each of his legitimate successors. The continuity of shepherding responsibility given by Christ to the Church leadership is realized in this line of authority.

Baptism (p. 37)—Baptism is the first of the Sacraments of Initiation. In Baptism, the infant has holy water poured on his or her head and is anointed with chrism. He or she is then forgiven of Original Sin and united with Jesus.

Evangelists (p. 54)—The Gospel writers: Matthew, Mark, Luke, and John. They told the stories of Jesus to uncover what was at the center of the religious encounter of the community with God.

Gospels (p. 54)—All the Gospels tell the Good News, which is the meaning of the word *Gospel*. They present the story of Easter faith rooted in the life, death, and Resurrection of Jesus Christ, the incarnate Son of God. There are four Gospels: Matthew, Mark, Luke, and John.

Holy Trinity (p. 36)—The three Persons in one God. The Holy Trinity comprises the Father, the Son, and the Holy Spirit.

miracles (p. 51)—Signs of wonder that can be attributed to God only.

parables (p. 48)—metaphors or similes drawn from common life experiences or nature to illustrate moral or spiritual truths.

Pentecost (p. 34)—The fiftieth day following Easter when the Holy Spirit is made present, given, and communicated as a divine Person of the Trinity.

Sacrament (p. 37)—An effective sign that conveys grace and which was established by Jesus and given to the Church.

synoptic Gospels (p. 53)—The Gospels of Matthew, Mark, and Luke; so labeled because of their similar vision.

Teen to Teen

It's very easy to become negative in a world full of problems. You may find yourself saying, "It's impossible," or "Nobody really loves me," or "I feel all alone," or "I don't have enough self-confidence." The Holy Spirit is alive in you and in the sacred words of Scripture. Jesus is always with you. You can turn to him with all your thoughts, joys, worries, and concerns. What saying of Jesus do you turn to when you are feeling down? Here's what some teens had to say about this:

"John 13:14–15. When my mom tells me to do my chores and I really don't want to, I think about these verses because Jesus says that he has set an example that we should follow."

Angel G.

"Luke 5:20. When I received first Reconciliation, the priest told me to pray this verse to remember that Jesus always forgives me. Now, when I am feeling really bad about something I've done, I go do penance and pray this verse."

Frank P.

"John 16:32. I moved around a lot when I was a kid, so I never really got to know people in school. I always felt so lonely because I didn't have a lot of friends. God the Father was with Jesus in his times of need, and God was with me too."

Teri A.

Personal Challenge

Living according to the Ten Commandments and the Law of Love can be challenging. It is particularly difficult—given the temptations in the world around us—to avoid the many false idols that are present in society. The gifts of the Holy Spirit aid you in your journey with Christ, and they can grant you wisdom or right judgment to do the right thing when facing a difficult decision. Over the next week, consider the gifts of the Holy Spirit when making decisions, read the verses associated with the gifts, and find more to help you in your journey. Listen to the Holy Spirit, and let him motivate you to do what is right.

Break Open the Word

Praying to God "This is my Son, the Beloved, with whom I am well pleased" (*Matthew 3:17*). These are the words spoken by the Father after Jesus was baptized. This event is one of only a handful of times in the Gospels when we hear the Father's word spoken aloud. On the other hand, Jesus often speaks with his Father through prayer in the Scriptures.

1. Find at least five instances where Jesus speaks with God his Father through prayer.
2. Read Ephesians 6:18. How does this relate to how Jesus prays?

A.D. **14–37**
Tiberius ruler
over Roman Empire

A.D. **28–29**
John the Baptist's active ministry

A.D. **33**
Crucifixion, death, and
Resurrection of Jesus

A.D. **54**
Nero's rise to
power as emperor
of Roman Empire

A.D. 14-37

A.D. 47

A.D. **26–36** Pontius Pilate
the Roman procurator
over Judea and Samaria

A.D. **29**
Jesus' baptism; beginning
of his public ministry

C. A.D. **50**
First Pauline Letters written

Called to Be Like Jesus

"For where your treasure is, there your heart will be also."

Matthew 6:21

Chapter Goals

In this chapter, you will:

- learn about the background and the main themes of the Gospel according to Matthew.

- explore the Incarnation, Jesus' message about God's kingdom, and the Infancy Narratives in the Gospels.

- increase your knowledge of the Beatitudes and the parables as religious and moral lessons.

- explore Jesus' vision for the Church and for just actions toward all people.

- learn about Sister Dorothy Stang.

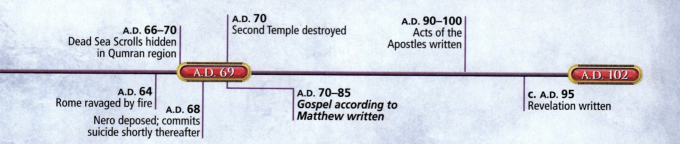

A.D. 66–70 Dead Sea Scrolls hidden in Qumran region

A.D. 70 Second Temple destroyed

A.D. 90–100 Acts of the Apostles written

A.D. 69

A.D. 102

A.D. 64 Rome ravaged by fire

A.D. 68 Nero deposed; commits suicide shortly thereafter

A.D. 70–85 *Gospel according to Matthew written*

C. A.D. 95 Revelation written

The Gospel According to Matthew

Your values and those things you treasure shape your attitude, influence the choices you make, and affect the way you live your life. Your values motivate and guide you as you journey through life. As Christians, we are called to live in a relationship of faith and grace with Jesus Christ. Jesus models the eternal values that should motivate and guide our lives. You share with others your personal relationship with Jesus when you live your Christ-centered values in the outside world of family, friends, and society.

Many of Jesus' Jewish contemporaries believed that God would send a Messiah to save and deliver them. This belief was their greatest hope, what they treasured most. We read in the Gospel according to Matthew that Jesus is the promised Messiah who saves and delivers all people. This Gospel describes how the followers of Jesus are called to be like him and to be directed toward an awareness of Jesus' eternal values. In this chapter we will identify these values and consider how Jesus calls us to live in a relationship of faith and grace with him.

Overview of the Gospel

From the late second century until the eighteenth century, biblical scholars and researchers considered the Gospel according to Matthew to be the first Gospel written. In addition, the traditional belief held that the Apostle Matthew wrote this Gospel. Hence, when choosing the order of placement of Gospel texts, the Church placed Matthew first. As we learned in chapter two, most modern biblical scholars believe that the Gospel according to Mark was written first.

Authorship and Date We do not know who wrote the Gospel according to Matthew. Most biblical scholars agree that the author was probably from Palestine and of Jewish Christian background, and that he wrote the Gospel between A.D. 70 and 85.

The author of the Gospel according to Matthew drew material from the Gospel of Mark and from a large body of other material—principally the sayings of Jesus—not found in Mark. This material, also found in the Gospel according to Luke, is called *Q*. In addition to the content drawn from Mark and Q, the Gospel according to Matthew contains unique material found in that Gospel only. Many scholars designate this content as *M*.

The Gospel according to Matthew is a bridge between the Old and New Testaments. Beginning with Jesus' genealogy, this Gospel traces Jesus' roots

Faith Activity

Reflect on Values
Silently consider the following questions:

1. What does your family treasure or value the most?
2. What do your friends value?
3. What does society place a value on?
4. What do you treasure or value most in life?
5. What treasures within yourself can you offer for the betterment of your family, friends, and society?

back to Abraham and David. Because it opens with the ancestry of Jesus, the Gospel according to Matthew has the face of a human being as its symbol.

Audience and Location The Gospel's author wrote to Jewish-Christians, but he also invited Gentiles into his accounts. Early in the Gospel, Magi from different nations seek the child Jesus. The Gospel ends with the Apostles being sent forth to make disciples of all nations.

Most biblical scholars believe that the Gospel according to Matthew was written in Antioch, the capital of the Roman province of Syria and a prominent city at that time. Antioch was one of the largest cities in the Greco-Roman Empire in the first century A.D., and it had a large mixed population of Jews and Gentiles. According to the Acts of the Apostles, Antioch was the first place where the disciples were called Christians, and the community at Antioch was the first to allow uncircumcised Gentiles to join. We also learn from Acts that Paul began his missionary journeys from Antioch. Also, tradition holds that Saint Peter served as the bishop of Antioch before he moved to Rome.

Theological Perspectives and Themes Although the author's thoughts and feelings are not known, his desire to explain to his audience that Jesus is the Christ and the culmination of God's unfolding plan of creation and salvation is apparent.

CAPPADOCIA

GALATIA

Tyana

PAMPHYLIA

CILICIA
Tarsus
Olive Oil

Zeugma

PARTHIAN EMPIRE

Tigris River

Myra
32°N

Antioch

Laodicea

SYRIA

Euphrates River

Cyprus

Emesa

Mediterranean Sea

Beirut

Syrian Desert

Silk from China

Tyre

Damascus

ARABIA

Ptolemais

Bostra

JUDEA

Gerasa

Jerusalem

Grain

Antioch

— Transportation Routes

▨ Agricultural resources for trade

0   100   200 mi
0   100   200 km

Explore the Land

Antioch Antioch was a flourishing city largely because of its location: It was situated along the trade route from China and India to the rest of the world. The people of Antioch also benefited from sea trade, desert trade, and river trade.

How do you think these trade routes affected the spread of Christianity? Compare this map with the map on page 181. How do the trade routes correspond with the travels of the early missionaries?

▲ Early Christian floor mosaic showing Jesus Christ as the Good Shepherd.

Faith Activity

Prayer When you pray, what do you call Jesus? Why do you call Jesus what you do? Does the title you use have any special significance to you? Discuss with your classmates the words they use to refer to Jesus.

To call Jesus the **Christ** is a statement of faith declaring who Jesus is. *Christ* is the Greek word for "anointed." *Messiah* is the Hebrew word for "anointed." For the Jews, the term **Messiah** referred to the one that God would send to liberate and lead the Jewish nation. In this Gospel we see that Jesus broadened this notion by offering salvation not only to the Jewish people, but also to the Gentiles. Salvation is offered to all people—to the whole human family. The author of this Gospel emphasized that Jesus of Nazareth is the Christ, the Messiah.

We can find many references in this Gospel to Jesus' speaking of God as his Father. Those references correspond to Matthew's presentation of Jesus as the "Son of God." In this Gospel Jesus also described himself as "servant of God," "shepherd," "son of David," and "Son of Man." All of these descriptions have their biblical roots in the Scriptures proclaimed and read by Jews. The connection that the Gospel according to Matthew draws to the Old Testament helps connect the audience—Jews and Gentiles— to Jesus.

In addition, Matthew recorded that Jesus' disciples and followers often referred to Jesus as "rabbi," meaning "teacher." By doing so, the author portrays Jesus as the teacher who has come to teach the world about God's plan of salvation. The Gospel portrays Jesus as the new Moses, the teacher of the New Law. His teaching often takes the form of parables and memorable sayings that describe the kingdom of God and its attributes.

The Gospel according to Matthew was written during a time of great loss for the Jewish people. They had lost the war and their spiritual home—the Temple. The author illuminated the minds and hearts of those who heard his Gospel to the realization that in Jesus and his teachings, they could find their new spiritual home.

In his writings the author wove together the Jewish Scriptures and the stories of Jesus. In blending these stories, the author merged Jewish tradition with the new life found in Jesus. More than in any other Gospel, Matthew contains prophecies from Scriptures that the Jewish people would have known to emphasize Jesus as the long-awaited Messiah. In one instance where this technique was used, the author wrote, "But all this has taken place, so that the scriptures of the prophets may be fulfilled" (*Matthew 26:56*).

In some places the Gospel depicts the tension between Jesus' actions and teachings and the practices and philosophies of two groups of Jews: the Pharisees and the scribes. In Matthew 12:1–8 the disciples gather grain on the Sabbath because they are hungry. The Pharisees see them and tell Jesus, "Your disciples are doing what is not lawful to do on the sabbath." Whereupon Jesus recounts an Old Testament story featuring David and his companions who entered the house of God and ate the bread of the Presence, meant only for the Priests. Jesus finishes by telling the Pharisees that "the Son of Man is lord of the sabbath."

Some people—past and present—have mistakenly interpreted scripture passages in which Jesus rebukes the scribes and Pharisees as anti-Semitism. Anti-Semitism is a hostility toward or discrimination against Jews as a religious, ethnic, or racial group. Anti-Semitic attitudes and actions are morally and ethically wrong. They are against the actions of Jesus and the teachings of the Church.

Structure of the Gospel

The Gospel according to Matthew has a five-part structure based on the five major discourses, or collections of Jesus' sayings. The author preceded each of the major discourses with a narrative. The Infancy Narrative and the Passion Narrative stand on their own at the beginning and at the end of the Gospel, respectively.

Matthew's community most likely made a connection between the five major teachings of Jesus and the five books of the Torah—Genesis, Exodus, Leviticus, Numbers, and Deuteronomy. Matthew places emphasis on the discourses of Jesus to present him as a teacher, or rabbi, and as the New Moses, the teacher of the New Law.

The Narratives and Discourses
Infancy Narrative: Birth of Jesus (Matthew 1:1—2:52)
Narrative: Beginning of Jesus' Public Ministry (Matthew 3:1—4:22)   First Discourse: Sermon on the Mount (Matthew 4:23—7:29)
Narrative: Authority of Jesus and the Invitation to Follow Him (Matthew 8:1—9:38)   Second Discourse: Mission Discourse to the Apostles (Matthew 10:1–42)
Narrative: Jesus Rejected (Matthew 11:1—12:50)   Third Discourse: Parables on the Kingdom (Matthew 13:1–52)
Narrative: Disciples Acknowledge Jesus (Matthew 13:53—17:27)   Fourth Discourse: Community Discourse (Matthew 18:1–35)
Narrative: More About the Authority of Jesus and the Invitation to Follow Him   Fifth Discourse: Sermon About Last Days (Matthew 23:1—25:46)
Passion Narrative: Passion, Death, and Resurrection of Jesus (Matthew 26:1—28:20)

A New Rabbi

Those who knew Jesus considered him a teacher. In the Gospels this image is used more frequently than any other to describe Jesus. The repeated use of the word *teacher* and the depiction of Jesus as a teacher show that this word was more than just a title given him. Jesus did not teach with words alone. His actions taught his followers how to love God and serve others. Jesus' words and deeds were examples of living that challenged and rewarded his followers.

The Gospel according to Matthew, in particular, portrays Jesus as a teacher. Matthew's Jewish-Christian audience expected the Messiah to be a teacher who surpassed Moses and the other prophets. Matthew shows Jesus as the New Moses who teaches the New Law.

What Jesus taught and how he taught mirrored the content and style of a teacher of the Law. Jesus would typically begin his teaching with a discussion of a scriptural text. He also quoted the prophets of the Old Testament. Jesus not only explained the old Law, but also proposed a new law—the law of love.

Jesus gathered a group of disciples in the same way a rabbi gathered disciples. His relationship with the disciples was that of a teacher to his students. The uniqueness of his teaching lay in its power. (See *Matthew 7:29*; *Mark 1:22*; *11:18*.) The authority with which Jesus taught astonished some and prompted others to admire him.

Jesus did not teach on his own authority, but on the authority he received from God the Father. John's Gospel says, "My teaching is not mine but his who sent me" (*John 7:16*). Jesus continues to say that the Father has taught him and that "the Advocate, the Holy Spirit, whom the Father will send in my name, will teach you everything, and remind you of all that I have said to you" (*John 14:26*). These words indicate the divine teaching of Christ and remind the readers of the Old Testament concept of God as teacher.

 ## Faith Activity

Teaching by Example Jesus taught through his words and actions. Many parishes plan events that combine teaching and serving. You might know of a parish that welcomes everyone to special topic nights that end with a spaghetti dinner or a meal of bread and fish. In what ways can the members of your parish community serve one another and the members of your wider community? If your parish doesn't host a loaves and fishes meal, find out if you can organize one.

Jesus' Birth and Beginning Ministry

The Evangelists chose certain events and aspects of Jesus' life and mission to communicate to their specific audiences. The author of the Gospel according to Matthew began his narration by describing the circumstances surrounding the birth of Jesus. He showed his audience that Jesus, from the time of his birth, fulfilled the messianic prophecies made in the Old Testament. Jesus is the fulfillment of God's plan.

Jesus' disciples told and retold the stories of Jesus' birth in light of his Passion, death, and Resurrection. In addition, the sacred authors wrote the Gospel parts over a period of time. They first wrote the accounts of Jesus' Passion, death, and Resurrection, and followed these accounts in varied order with Jesus' miracles, his parables and teachings, and the **Infancy Narratives**—stories of Jesus' birth. Therefore, we have to read the Infancy Narratives knowing that the writers and the audience already knew that Jesus was indeed the Messiah. We cannot separate the mystery of Jesus' Resurrection from the mystery of his birth.

▼ The Annunciation to the Shepherds by Laura James.

The Infancy Narratives

Two records of Jesus' birth and early years exist in the Gospels—one in Matthew and one in Luke. These records have similarities, but they also have marked differences. The Gospel according to Matthew begins with a genealogy.

Genealogy of Jesus A genealogy is the record of a person's ancestry. Matthew presents a genealogy for Jesus that traces Jesus' ancestry back to Abraham and David. The audience of the Gospel according to Matthew placed great importance on Jesus being firmly rooted in the history of Israel. The genealogy shows that Jesus is the Messiah. (See *Matthew 1:16*.) He is the king, the son of David, the Messiah of Israel, and the son of Abraham. (See *Matthew 1:1*.)

The genealogy includes the names of five women:

■ Tamar, a woman who disguised herself as a harlot, had two sons fathered by Judah, her father-in-law. (See *Genesis 38*.)

■ Rahab, a harlot, aided Joshua's spies in Jericho. (See *Joshua 2* and *6*.)

■ Ruth, a Moabite woman, was married to Boaz, a Jewish man. (See *Book of Ruth*.)

■ The "wife of Uriah," also known as Bathsheba, was the wife of David and the mother of Solomon. She became David's wife after David planned the death of her husband. (See *2 Samuel*.)

■ Mary, who is mentioned in relationship to her husband, Joseph.

A common element united the first four women across the ages: their foreign nationalities. All except Mary, were Gentiles. By including these women, the author of Matthew indicated that Jesus came for both Jews and Gentiles.

Interpret the Art

Ruth and Naomi Ruth and Naomi by Tim Langenderfer, 2003. Ruth, who was a Moabite, became the great-grandmother of King David. *What do you think David's "impure" bloodline foretells about the coming of Jesus?*

Jesus' Birth The stories of Jesus' birth emphasize his uniqueness from the moment of his conception. The angel Gabriel announced Jesus' conception, which occured through the power of the Holy Spirit. He was named Jesus, as the angel instructed, which means "God Saves." The visitation of angels, shepherds, and Magi greeted Jesus' birth, a source of tremendous joy. Others, such as Herod, considered Jesus' birth a source of conflict. These stories foreshadowed the fact that some people would accept Jesus and his ministry, while others would reject him.

Break open the Word

Magi Foretold Some biblical scholars see allusions to the visit of the Magi in the following scripture passages from the Old Testament. Read the passages, and discuss in small groups how you think they relate to the Infancy Narratives:

Micah 5:1
Isaiah 60:6
Hosea 11:1
Numbers 24:17
2 Samuel 5:2
Psalm 72:10–11
Jeremiah 31:5

Work with the Chart

Infancy Narratives in Matthew and Luke This chart on the Infancy Narratives indicates what parts of the Infancy Narratives are found in each Gospel.
What similarities and differences do you see? Why do you think different Gospel authors stressed different aspects of Jesus' birth and early years?

Infancy Narrative Comparisons		
Aspects of Infancy Narratives	**Matthew**	**Luke**
Genealogy	✔	✔
Annunciation of the birth takes place	✔ To Joseph	✔ To Mary
Angel announces that child will be Messiah	✔	✔
Mary and Joseph are engaged but not married	✔	✔
Joseph descended from David	✔	✔
Mary conceived through power of Holy Spirit	✔	✔
Angel tells Joseph to name the child Jesus	✔	✔
Mary and Joseph go to Bethlehem for census	✘	✔
Jesus wrapped in swaddling clothes in a manger	✘	✔
A star appears	✔	✘
Visitors come to adore and worship Jesus	✔ Magi, or Wise Men	✔ Shepherds
Jesus' rejection referred to	✔ Rejection by Herod, scribes, and Pharisees	✔ Simeon says Jesus will be opposed
Children in Bethlehem massacred	✔	✘
Holy Family flees to Egypt	✔	✘
Jesus presented in the Temple	✘	✔
Jesus raised in Nazareth	✔	✔
Jesus found in the Temple	✘	✔

THE HISTORY OF THE CRÈCHE

Christians have many customs for celebrating the Advent and Christmas seasons. Nativity scenes are perhaps the most popular of family and parish customs. Historians have traced the practice of creating nativity scenes to the early years of the Church. Many churches built mangers of gold, silver, and jewels that were much more ornate than the simple manger that held Jesus. However, in the thirteenth century, Saint Francis of Assisi was among the first to create an entire scene.

Francis thought it was important for Christians to recall and celebrate the fact that Jesus had been born in a humble stable. During December of 1223, in a cave in the town of Greccio, Francis and some friends gathered a manger, some straw, a donkey, and other animals. On Christmas Eve he and the townspeople celebrated Mass in the cave. They also reenacted the story of Jesus' birth.

The word *crèche* comes from the French word for manger. The French word is derived from the Italian word *Greccio,* the name of the town in Italy where Saint Francis first had a live nativity scene.

Connect to the Past

Crèches Three different crèches and nativity scenes are pictured here. Each represents a different style of art, but all share similarities.
What similarities do you see among all of the crèches? What similarities and differences are there between these crèches and others you have seen?

The Incarnation

The Infancy Narratives profess the mystery whereby the Son of God, while remaining God, became man through the **Incarnation**. *Incarnation* means to become flesh or to take on a human body. The Incarnation of the second Person of the Holy Trinity is a great and awesome mystery. In Jesus the human and divine natures are united, yet fully whole and distinct. Jesus Christ is true God and true man.

The divine Son of God became man for several reasons:

- Jesus became man "*in order to save us by reconciling us with God.*" Jesus is our mediator, restoring us to friendship with God the Father.

- "The Word became flesh *so that thus we might know God's love.*" Through the life and teachings of Jesus, we learn the meaning of God's unconditional love.

- Jesus became incarnate "*to be our model of holiness.*" Jesus taught us what it means to have a loving relationship with God and others.

- The Son of God became man in order to make us "*partakers of the divine nature*[9]." We are able to partake in Jesus' divinity. We share his divinity when we live in God's grace, participate in the Church's sacraments, and experience moments of oneness with God.

Catechism of the Catholic Church, 457–460

Through the grace of Baptism, we also share in the divine nature.

The Temptation of Jesus

Temptation is part of everyone's life. It can lead to sin. Sin is a turning away from God and a refusal to participate in God's plan of salvation.

However, when we are faithful to God, we receive from God the power to fight temptation and sin. In fact, to fight the power of evil, the only sure force we have is God within us. This grace and strength come from being centered in God. We are reminded of this fact when we read the story of Jesus' temptation by the devil. (See *Matthew 4:1–11.*) Each temptation of Jesus was toward a different form of power. The first temptation was toward material power, the second to miraculous power, and the third to political power. Each temptation shows the distortion between living by the powers of the world and living by the power of God. Jesus answers the devil by quoting Scripture.

Faith Activity

Scripture Aids In the Temptation Narrative Jesus counters all of Satan's temptations with scripture passages. Scripture can also aid us when we are tempted to do something wrong. Search the Bible for passages you can remember to pray when temptations come into your life. Write down one or two of the passages you find. Here is an example: "I have the strength for everything through him who empowers me" (*Philippians 4:13*).

The Temptation Narrative

Good Versus Evil

Narrator: Then Jesus was led up by the Spirit into the wilderness to be tempted by the devil. He fasted forty days and forty nights, and afterwards he was famished. The tempter came and said to him,

Satan: If you are the Son of God, command these stones to become loaves of bread.

Narrator: But he answered,

Jesus: It is written, "One does not live by bread alone, but by every word that comes from the mouth of God."

Narrator: Then the devil took him to the holy city and placed him on the pinnacle of the temple, saying to him,

Satan: If you are the Son of God, throw yourself down; for it is written,
  "He will command his angels concerning you,"
    and "On their hands they will bear you up,
  so that you will not dash your foot against a stone."

Narrator: Jesus said to him,

Jesus: Again it is written, "Do not put the Lord your God to the test."

Narrator: Again, the devil took him to a very high mountain and showed him all the kingdoms of the world and their splendor, and he said to him,

Satan: All these I will give you, if you will fall down and worship me.

Narrator: Jesus said to him,

Jesus: Away with you, Satan! for it is written,
  "Worship the Lord your God,
    and serve only him."

Narrator: Then the devil left him, and suddenly angels came and waited on him.

Based on Matthew 4:1–11

Interpret the Art

Temptation of Jesus Painting of the Temptation of Christ located in Axum, Ethiopia. Jesus responded to all of Satan's temptations with scriptural quotes.

In a small group, find other quotes from Scripture that counter the temptations.

Resisting Temptation The temptation narrative would have reminded Matthew's audience of the time their ancestors were in the desert. God tested the Israelites to see what was in their hearts and whether they would keep the commandments. (See *Deuteronomy 8:1–5*.) The Israelites often failed to follow God's commandments. Ultimately they realized that trusting God instead of turning from him was the only way they would complete their journey.

The first instance of temptation that we read in the Scriptures is that of the first humans. They were unable to resist Satan's temptations. By abusing their freedom, giving in to temptation, and disobeying God and thereby sinning, they lost the original holiness that God had given them. As a result of this original sin, all humankind has been weakened. We are prone to suffering and inclined to sin.

Jesus, however, obeyed God the Father through all of the temptations Satan presented, and Jesus refused to compromise with evil. He did not succumb to the false promises of Satan. He chose instead to trust in his Father's will and to trust his Father's plan of salvation.

Like Jesus, we might find ourselves in a desert—alone, hungry for direction, isolated, and tempted towards sin. We need to realize that when we are at our lowest, the power of evil can creep into our lives in strong and varied ways. Realizing our vulnerability is a first step toward fighting temptations. Admitting our weakness and relying on God's strength can help us recognize when we are tempted to mask our problems and our pain in unhealthy ways. Resisting evil as Jesus did strengthens us against future trials.

Jesus Begins His Public Ministry

Soon after his temptation in the desert, Jesus began to travel and to preach to the crowds, "Repent, for the kingdom of heaven has come near" (*Matthew 4:17*). Jesus proclaimed that the saving intervention of God was close at hand and, in a certain sense, was already present. Jesus' message had a note of urgency in that he demanded a decision involving the whole person. Jesus told his followers that if they search for the treasure—the kingdom—they must be prepared to give all that they have and all that they are. If they seek the kingdom, they should renounce whatever will keep them from a complete response to the call of Christ.

In the synoptic Gospels the coming of God's kingdom is the central theme in Jesus' ministry and teaching. The New Testament writers used **kingdom of heaven**, kingdom of God, and reign of God interchangeably; however, you will not find the term "kingdom of God" in the Gospel according to Matthew. For the Jews, God is the Holy One, so holy that one must not utter God's name, rendered in Hebrew as **YHWH**. Biblical texts often record YHWH as *Yahweh*. By using the term "kingdom of heaven," the author of Matthew reflected a tendency among some Jews not to use the word *God*.

Break Open the Word

Present and Future Reality

1. How do the following passages describe the present reality of the kingdom? Matthew 3:2; 4:17, 23; 9:35; 10:7; 12:28

2. How do the following describe the future reality of the kingdom? Matthew 5:3, 10; 7:21; 8:11; 13:43; 18:3; 25:34

3. How do the following relate to eternal life? Matthew 5:19 and 7:21

Faith Activity

In Your Own Words

Complete the following phrase: The kingdom of heaven is like . . . Compare your response to responses of others in your class. Compare your response to what the author of the Gospel according to Matthew wrote about the kingdom.

What Is the Kingdom? To understand what Jesus meant by *kingdom,* we need to consider the Old Testament concept of God as king. Many psalms refer to God as king:

> "God is king over the nations;
> God sits on his holy throne. . . .
> he is highly exalted"
>
> *Psalm 47:8–9*

These phrases mean God takes possession of his kingdom and establishes his rule in it.

God establishes his kingship through a powerful intervention aimed at salvation. God overcomes his enemies and those of his people, whose care he takes upon himself, to bring them salvation. We read of such powerful interventions in the Old Testament: the Exodus event, the conquest of Canaan, and the return from exile.

The kingdom of God is the gift of salvation (See *Matthew 25:34*.), life (See *John 11:25*.), and eternal life (See *Mark 10:17*.). In a world that was a slave to sin, Jesus' followers understood the gift of salvation as, above all, the overthrow of evil and the universal offer of pardon.

Those who hear the offer of pardon and salvation must take it seriously, for the offer is accompanied by a call to conversion and a threat of judgment on those who allow grace to pass them by.

The Coming of the Kingdom When will the kingdom of God come? This question asked of Jesus touches on one of the more controversial points in his whole message. The kingdom is present and active in Jesus. Contemporaries of Jesus witnessed in his miracles the graces and blessings resulting from the presence of the kingdom active in the world. However, the full and perfect realization of the kingdom is still in the future and an object of hope and prayer as reflected in the Our Father: "Your kingdom come" (*Matthew 6:10*).

The coming of the kingdom of God is intimately connected with the person of Jesus. Jesus does not merely announce the coming of the kingdom, as did the prophets of the Old Testament. He is the person through whom God establishes his reign. (See *Mark 3:27*; *Matthew 12:28*; *Luke 11:20*; and *Matthew 11:1–5*.) The progress of the kingdom coincides with the destiny of Jesus, whose triumph is the kingdom's triumph and establishment.

The Christian Life

Jesus sometimes preached in the synagogues as other teachers did. Although Jesus associated with those who attended the synagogue, he also chose to be with many people the rabbis seemed to avoid—sinners, children, women, tax collectors, and those who were suffering or ill. Jesus especially preached the good news of the Sermon on the Mount, particularly the Beatitudes, to those people so often ignored by others.

The Sermon on the Mount

The Sermon on the Mount is the first of Jesus' five major discourses recorded in the Gospel according to Matthew. As the Gospel verses begin, Jesus goes up to the mountain to teach the Beatitudes, just as Moses went to the mountain to receive the Ten Commandments. Jesus sat and taught, as did the rabbis of his day. On the mountain, regarded as a place of revelation, Jesus—the *new* Moses—brought to light the value system of the New Law.

The Beatitudes As the value system taught and lived by Jesus, the **Beatitudes** express how God expects people to live in relationship with one another. The word *beatitude* means "blessed" or "happy." In the Beatitudes Jesus taught about the meaning and path to true happiness. The Beatitudes express the values of the kingdom of heaven, and they describe the way to attain eternal blessedness, or holiness, to which God calls all of us.

When Jesus saw the crowds, he went up to the mountain, and his disciples came to him. Then he taught them, saying:

 scripture

"Blessed are the poor in spirit,
　for theirs is the kingdom of heaven.
"Blessed are those who mourn,
　for they will be comforted.
"Blessed are the meek,
　for they will inherit the earth.
"Blessed are those who hunger and
　thirst for righteousness,
　for they will be filled.
"Blessed are the merciful,
　for they will receive mercy.
"Blessed are the pure in heart,
　for they will see God.

"Blessed are the peacemakers,
　for they will be called children of God.
"Blessed are those who are persecuted for
　righteousness sake,
　for theirs is the kingdom of heaven.
"Blessed are you when people revile you and persecute you and utter all kinds of evil against you falsely on my account. Rejoice and be glad, for your reward is great in heaven,
　for in the same way they persecuted the prophets who were before you."

Matthew 5:1–12

Faith Sharing

Beatitude Values In your faith-sharing group, consider the values represented in the Beatitudes in Matthew 5:1–12: dependence on God, compassion, humility, righteousness, mercy, honesty, peace or service, and standing up for the truth.

Then make a list of five ways you spend your free time and five ways you can integrate the Beatitudes into that time. Discuss with your group what you can do to follow the Beatitudes in your thoughts and actions.

An Expression of Law The Beatitudes do not negate the law of the Ten Commandments; rather, they are an expression of that law. Both the Beatitudes and the Ten Commandments offer guidance for living in faithfulness to God and his kingdom.

> "The Beatitudes take up and fulfill God's promises from Abraham on by ordering them to the Kingdom of heaven. They respond to the desire for happiness that God has placed in the human heart."
> *Catechism of the Catholic Church, 1725*

While the Ten Commandments express the fundamental duties of humans, the Beatitudes yield an understanding of the law of love that promotes attitudes of justice and compassion. The Beatitudes are a key teaching in Jesus' Sermon on the Mount, which expresses the New Law of "the grace of the Holy Spirit received by faith in Christ" (*CCC*, 1983) and lived out in love. We receive this grace in the sacraments.

Almsgiving, Fasting, and Prayer The teachings of the Sermon on the Mount include three religious practices important to Jews at the time of Jesus: almsgiving, prayer, and fasting. (See *Matthew 6:1–18.*) Jesus also cautioned his followers to avoid public display of these spiritual disciplines.

The Torah gave guidelines for feeding the poor and for fasting. Prayer was also integral to the religious life of a Jewish person. These three practices remain central to Jews and Christians alike. While these practices have an important role in the Christian life year-round, they take on special meaning during the season of Lent. We often refer to prayer, almsgiving, and fasting as Lenten practices or Lenten observances.

◄ The Sermon on the Mount by Fra Angelico, c. 1438–1445.

Living the Beatitudes	
the poor in spirit	You depend on God rather than on things, and you believe that helping others is more important than acquiring things.
those who mourn	You are aware of the sufferings of others and walk with them in their grief; your grieving is not dominated by selfishness.
the meek	You are humble, patient, and gentle with yourself and with others.
those who hunger and thirst for righteousness	You stand up for what is right and for the rights of others; you work for a more just world and for the fullness of God's kingdom.
the merciful	You readily forgive others from the heart, refusing to hold a grudge, and you forgive yourself as you seek God's forgiveness and the forgiveness of those you have hurt or harmed.
the pure in heart	You recognize God's image in yourself and in those around you, and you treat others with reverence.
the peacemakers	You live peacefully with others and promote peace between people and groups.
those who are persecuted for righteousness' sake	You make a stand for what you believe in, even when you suffer emotional or physical pain as a result of your decision.

Work with the Chart

The Beatitudes Today In small groups, review the meanings for living the Beatitudes listed above.

■ Make a list of people or events in the news that depict the Beatitude in action.
■ Then rewrite the Beatitudes as if Jesus were giving them to us today. Keep the meanings the same, but use words and sentence structure that would appeal to today's teens.
■ Share your Beatitudes with the class.

◀ Rabbi Schneerson reads the Torah with a young boy in Brooklyn, New York.

Faith Activity

Materialism Read Matthew 6:19–34 for insights on materialism. Find current magazine ads and label each ad with the craving that the advertiser is trying to have you buy into (for example: competition, success, beauty, health, success, superiority, security, consumerism, sexuality, youth, or individualism). Discuss how such false treasures compare with the values taught by Jesus.

The Lord's Prayer We learn from all four Gospels that Jesus prayed often. He prayed with his family and friends, he prayed alone, he prayed at his death. He offered thanks and praise to God his Father; he asked his Father to bless his followers and make them one as he and the Father are one. Jesus went to the Temple and traveled to Jerusalem for important Jewish feasts. Jesus taught his followers to pray by his example and by giving them the words to say.

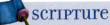

Scripture

"Pray then in this way:
Our Father in heaven,
   hallowed be your name.
   Your kingdom come.
   Your will be done,
      on earth as it is in heaven.
         Give us this day our daily bread.
   And forgive us our debts,
      as we also have forgiven our debtors.
   And do not bring us to the time of trial,
      but rescue us from the evil one."

Matthew 6:9–13

In this prayer that Jesus taught the Apostles, which Christians refer to as the Lord's Prayer or the Our Father, we have a glimpse into the spirituality of Jesus. The word *Our* shows Jesus' connectedness to God the Father, to us, and to the world. In this prayer, we are called to share in the forgiveness and compassion of God by the way we live our lives and respond to those who hurt us. The Lord's Prayer has the greatest importance of all Christian prayers, for it sums up the entirety of Jesus' teaching and stirs in us the desire to rely on and become more like God the Father.

The Lord's Prayer begins with praises for the glory of God the Father and ends with numerous petitions in which we ask for the Father's assistance. By calling God "our" Father, we acknowledge that we are his people through the loving action of his Son. We are united to him and one another, and this belonging is a gift only God can give. We praise him for being both transcendent and present among us, and we long for being with him forever. After we have shown our desire to adore and praise God the Father, we focus on his glory: on his holy name, on his coming kingdom, and on doing his will for us. Only after this do we turn to ask for the things we need.

The Missionary Discourse

Many scholars call the second discourse in the Gospel according to Matthew the missionary discourse. We find in Jesus' words and actions recorded here the foundation of the Church. In this discourse, which begins in Matthew 9:35, we read of Jesus' compassion for those to whom he preaches, and those he heals and cures. Jesus had compassion for the large crowds who seemed lost. In this context Jesus compelled his disciples, "The harvest is plentiful, but the laborers are few; therefore ask the Lord of the harvest to send out laborers into his harvest" (*Matthew 9:37*). Jesus then commissioned twelve of his disciples to share in his mission to preach and, in his authority, to heal and cure the sick. Jesus instructed them, "As you go, proclaim the good news, 'The kingdom of heaven has come near'" (*Matthew 10:7*).

Jesus instructed his Apostles not to take money, provisions, or unnecessary clothing; their lodging and food would be provided by those who received them. Jesus also warned his Apostles of the coming persecution because of their association with him. He encouraged them—in the face of persecution—to remain strong for the sake of the kingdom of heaven because God would be their protector and their strength. Jesus told them, "Everyone therefore who acknowledges me before others, I also will acknowledge before my Father in heaven" (*Matthew 10:32*).

Just as Jesus called the Apostles and the disciples to share in the proclamation of the kingdom, he calls us to bring his message to all of those we meet. We do not need to fear being rejected or misunderstood, for God is with us. Can we follow Jesus as his first followers did? Are we willing to stand up for what is right and just and fair? Through prayer and worship within the Church, the Holy Spirit will help us grow in our trust of God the Father. God will give us the words to say and the courage to do the things we must do for the sake of his kingdom.

▼ A lone worker harvests a wheat field.

The Community and Just Actions

Faith Activity

Forgiveness Think about forgiveness in your own life. Whom do you need to forgive? Who needs forgiveness from you? How can you work toward showing forgiveness to others and accepting the forgiveness of others?

Biblical scholars sometimes refer to the fourth discourse in the Gospel according to Matthew as the "community" or "church order" discourse. However, you will not find details about specific roles and responsibilities of the different orders or ministries within the Church. In this discourse Jesus discussed the way in which members of the community should relate to one another.

In Matthew 18:1–14 Jesus taught his disciples that greatness in the kingdom of heaven is measured not by rank or power, but by childlikeness. He continued to tell the disciples that they must take care not to cause "one of these little ones who believe in me to sin" or to neglect a member of the community who has strayed. Jesus further instructed his Apostles on the proper way to correct members of the community who sin, giving the Apostles the authority to forgive sin in his name. He also emphasized the power of community prayer. Jesus told them that when they gather together in prayer, he is with them. (See *Matthew 18:19–20*.)

The Parable of the Unforgiving Servant completes the discourse and makes very clear the importance attached to forgiveness that must be repeatedly extended to all community members and to those who repent.

Scripture

"Then Peter came and said to him, 'Lord, if another member of the church sins against me, how often should I forgive? As many as seven times?' Jesus said to him, 'Not seven times, but, I tell you, seventy-seven times. For this reason the kingdom of heaven may be compared to a king who wished to settle accounts with his slaves. When he began the reckoning, one who owed him ten thousand talents was brought to him; and, as he could not pay, his lord ordered him to be sold, together with his wife and children, and all his possessions, and payment to be made. So the slave fell on his knees before him, saying, 'Have patience with me, and I will pay you everything.' And out of pity for him, the lord of that servant released him and forgave him the debt. But that same slave, as he went out, came upon one of his fellow slaves who owed him a hundred denarii; and seizing him by the throat, he said, 'Pay what you owe.' Then his fellow slave fell down and pleaded with him, 'Have patience with me, and I will pay you.' But he refused, then he went and threw him into prison until he would pay the debt. When his fellow slaves saw what had happened, they were greatly distressed, and they went and reported to their lord all that had taken place. Then his lord summoned him and said to him, 'You wicked slave! I forgave you all that debt because you pleaded with me. Should you not have had mercy on your fellow slave, as I had mercy on you?' And in anger his lord handed him over to be tortured until he would pay his entire debt. So my heavenly Father will also do to every one of you, if you do not forgive your brother or sister from your heart."

Matthew 18:21–35

Peter, the Rock

Saint Peter's Basilica in Rome.

We learn from the Gospels that Peter's original name was Simon. He lived in Galilee where he worked as a fisherman. We read about his mother-in-law, whom Jesus cured, in Matthew 8:14. This suggests that Peter was married at the time Jesus called him to be one of his followers.

The Gospels mention Peter more than any other disciple, indicating his special position among the Twelve known as the Apostles. Peter had a close association with Jesus not always shared by the others. He had a special committed responsibility as the leader and spokesman of the Apostles.

In Matthew 16:16–18, after Simon recognized Jesus as the Messiah, Jesus gave him the name Peter, meaning *Rock*. Jesus promised to build his Church upon this rock, and gave Peter the keys of the kingdom of heaven. Jesus instituted Peter as the shepherd of the whole flock and gave him the power to loose and to bind.

Ironically, Peter denied Jesus three times during Jesus' Passion, but Jesus forgave Peter after his Resurrection and entrusted the care of his followers to Peter.

Peter appears as the leader of the Christian community in Jerusalem immediately after the Ascension of Jesus. He proposed the election of a successor to Judas in the Twelve. (See *Acts 1:15–26*.) He was the spokesman of the disciples at Pentecost and thereafter. More than anyone else, Peter shared the healing power of Jesus with others. (See *Acts 3; 5:15; 9:32–43*.) He was the first to preach the Gospel to the Gentiles. (See *Acts 10*.) Mention of Peter in the Scriptures disappears after his important leadership role at the Council of Jerusalem. (See *Acts 15*.)

Peter's final residence, death, and burial were in Rome. He was executed during the reign of Nero between A.D. 64 and 67 on Vatican Hill. Today historians believe the site of Peter's grave is in an old Roman cemetery under Saint Peter's Basilica in Rome.

Connect to the Past

The Chair of Peter The Chair of Saint Peter by Giovanni Lorenzo Bernini, 1665. The Chair of Saint Peter is supported by four fathers of the Church: Saints Augustine, Ambrose, Athanasius, and John Chrysostom. The Holy Spirit is represented as a bright dove surrounded by angels above the chair. *Why do you think Jesus chose Peter as the Church's leader, even though Peter denied him?*

Break Open the Word

Judged by Actions

Read Matthew 25:31–46.
Record your answers to the
following questions:

1. Who does the king in this
   passage symbolize?
   Whom do the sheep sym-
   bolize? The goats?
2. What is required for
   entrance into eternal life?
3. What challenges do this
   passage present to you?

The Judgment

Good and evil exist together in the world. However, evil does not negate the presence of the kingdom of heaven. The presence of the kingdom reverses the power of sin and evil. The kingdom gives new life to human nature, which has been wounded by Adam's sin. The kingdom manifests God's love, action, and presence in the world. Christians cooperate with the kingdom when they are faithful to Christ and perform their earthly tasks with uprightness, patience, and love.

The kingdom calls us to growth and to conversion—a call to believe and to repent—a call to choose a new life. When we welcome God's reign in our lives, God rules our minds and hearts. Our actions become actions for the kingdom and actions of justice, equality, and peace. We can discover the joy and treasure of finding and following Jesus when we say "yes" to living the values of the kingdom.

We read about the importance of saying "yes" in the fifth discourse of the Gospel according to Matthew, specifically in the passage known as the "Judgment of Nations." (See *Matthew 25:31–46.*) We hear a challenging message that demands we change our inner selves and work with others to change the injustices in the world.

Jesus offered his teaching on the judgment of nations in response to the question, "Who will enter the Kingdom of God?" The judgment scene described in this passage involves all the "nations." Jesus summarized his teachings about the kingdom and stated the requirements for entering the eternal kingdom. The passage describes a judge and all humankind before him awaiting judgment. It reveals to those being judged the truth of how they have lived. Each individual is judged on how they have practiced works of mercy. In this passage, unique to the Gospel according to Matthew, Jesus made it very clear that the love of God and the active love for others cannot be separated.

Eternal Life

The Judgment of Nations passage in Matthew provides the basis for the Church's teaching on Jesus' second coming and what happens at the end of time. At the end of time, when Christ the judge comes, all people will appear in their own bodies before Christ to account for their actions in life and their state in death. Then God's kingdom will be complete. The just—those who have lived a life of grace and have been purified in death—will be glorified as Christ is glorified and will have a place with him.

We do not know when the second coming will take place. But we do know that each person will also be judged at the moment of our death based upon the way he or she has lived. This is known as particular judgment.

If a person has lived in God's friendship, accepted his grace, and sought forgiveness for sin, he or she will surely know the joy of heaven. Heaven is not some great city floating in the sky with pearly gates at the entrance. In fact, heaven is not a geographical location at all. It is the state of living in eternal happiness with God. The New Testament letters lead us to the understanding that heaven is the experience of God in the beatific vision, seeing God "face to face," "as he is." (See *1 Corinthians 13:12* and *1 John 3:2*.)

However, not everyone who dies in God's friendship is ready to be received into heaven. They experience purgatory, the state of purification between death and heaven. They need to be made holy before they can enter full communion with God in heaven. This time removes any personal obstacles keeping them from heaven, such as punishment for sins for which they had been forgiven or for venial sins not confessed before death. This is why prayers for the dead are important, for through them we can intercede for those who are in purgatory.

Not everyone embraces God's love. Those people who have rejected God's love and grace even at the final moment of life will be separated from God forever. This eternal separation is known as hell. Like heaven, hell is not a geographical place. It's important to remember that this eternal separation is human choice, not God's. It results from a person's refusal to accept God's grace and continual love. Each and every human is created to have life and happiness beyond our understanding. This comes with life forever with God, and we know that God desires all of his children to experience this. The forever separation from God is truly a sad reality.

How we live our lives is really a means to our ultimate end, the end for which God created us: to know him completely and to live with him forever in happiness. If we make good choices based upon Jesus' teachings in the Beatitudes, if we seek his forgiveness, if we follow his example in what we say and do, we will be preparing for life forever.

Works of Mercy The passage from Matthew on the judgment of nations might sound familiar to you. The Church forms its **Works of Mercy** on the actions Jesus described in that passage. The Works of Mercy are charitable acts by which we care for the physical and spiritual needs of others. It is possible to work for mercy and justice in the world. We can take action in simple ways to begin the process of making the kingdom of heaven present in our own time. Practicing the works of mercy reflects the presence of the kingdom.

Works of Mercy	
Corporal Works of Mercy	**Spiritual Works of Mercy**
Feed the hungry.	Teach the ignorant.
Give drink to the thirsty.	Counsel the doubtful.
Shelter the homeless.	Comfort the sorrowful.
Clothe the naked.	Bear wrongs patiently.
Visit the sick.	Forgive injuries.
Visit the imprisoned.	Warn the sinner.
Bury the dead.	Pray for the living and the dead.

There are many ways you can perform both Corporal and Spiritual Works of Mercy in your community and in the world. You can feed the hungry by participating in the Heifer Project, a project which allows you to donate an animal or group of animals—such as buffalo, sheep, or chickens—to a family that will allow them to become self-sufficient. You can shelter the homeless by participating in a Habitat for Humanity new-home construction in your area.

You can comfort the sorrowful through your kind words and actions by creating an "essentials kit" for those in need—women, men, or children—at homeless shelters. By including some new essential items and a personal note, you can help bring light into someone's life.

Requesting that prayers be said at Mass for loved ones, as well as including all those who you care for in your every day prayers is an easy and meaningful way to pray for the living and the dead.

Justice We are reminded that the message of the Gospel and the mission of the Church is to proclaim the Word of God by becoming living witnesses to it. Injustice and suffering must be opposed by word and deed. We will be judged according to the way we actively love God and our neighbor. Jesus calls us to act with justice—to give to each person what is his or her due. The Church has a rich tradition of social justice teaching based upon Jesus' teachings and the belief in the human dignity of all people.

God makes every person in his image and likeness. Every person possesses the human dignity that comes from being made in God's image. Therefore, all people are united and connected as children of God, and all are one another's neighbor. All humans share a bond as children of God. Because all of us are God's children, God calls us to share the fruits of the earth and of our labor. Furthermore, all people should have access to the water and food the earth produces, not just those living in wealthy countries. Being made in God's image and sharing human dignity is the foundation for all just action.

Faith Activity

Make a Difference

The wealthiest 20 percent of the world's people hold 83 percent of the world's wealth, while the 20 percent who are most impoverished hold only 1.4 percent of the wealth.

1. List and discuss several changes in attitude, lifestyle, and governmental policies that are needed to shift these percentages toward a just distribution of resources.
2. How can you change your priorities in order to become more sensitive and responsive to the needs of others?

Sister Dorothy Stang, SNDdeN

(1931–2005)

Witnesses testified the last words uttered by Sister Dorothy before she was martyred were, "Blessed are the peacemakers, for they shall be called the children of God." As two gunmen had approached her, she opened her Bible and read this Beatitude. They shot her and left her to die on a muddy road. Sister Dorothy died as she lived—standing with the poor in her efforts to bring peace and justice to the Amazon region of Brazil.

Her journey of faith led her to become a member of the Sisters of Notre Dame de Namur, whose mission is to educate and stand with the poor. In the early years with her religious congregation, Sister Dorothy was a school teacher for several different Catholic elementary schools. While a teacher in Arizona, she and other Sisters would spend free time traveling to the outskirts of urban areas to teach religion to children of migrant workers.

During this time, Pope John XXIII asked religious communities from around the world to give members of their communities to service in Latin America. The SNDdeN responded by sending Sister Dorothy and several other Sisters to Brazil in the 1960s. There they worked with people in villages giving them religious instruction, training them to be faith leaders and catechists, assisting men in building houses and school rooms, and teaching women to sew and sell clothing to finance the building of a dam to provide electricity to the community.

As the Sisters continued their ministry with the poor, they learned how the farmers had suffered and been oppressed by their landowners. The Sisters taught people about their rights and dignity as human beings and showed them how to live by farming without deforestation. Sister Dorothy worked with the Pastoral Land Commission, a Catholic Church organization that advocates and fights for the rights of rural peasants and workers as well as defends land reform in Brazil. She was unafraid to speak on behalf of the environment and to advocate for the poor.

As Sister Dorothy continued to defend the rights of the poor, she began to receive death threats. Some thought she should leave Brazil. Her response, "I am grateful to Notre Dame for not asking me to leave. . . This shows they are aware of the needs of the poor. The Sisters have said they are worried about my safety. It is not my safety, but that of the people which matters." "I don't want to flee, nor do I want to abandon the battle of these farmers who live without any protection in the forest. They have the sancrosanct right to aspire to a better life on land where they can live and work with dignity while respecting the environment." She was killed on February 12, 2005, within a week after meeting with Brazil's human rights officials about threats to local farmers from landowners and illegal loggers.

Prayer

Begin by praying the Sign of the Cross.

Leader: Holy Spirit, give us the courage and perspective to sincerely reflect on our successes and failures as we try to embrace the Beatitude values in our daily living. Amen.

After each reading, let us pause for silent reflection.

Reader 1: "Blessed are the poor in spirit."

Do I let pride stand in the way of my being dependent on others or on God?
Do I take responsibility for the choices I make?

Reader 2: "Blessed are they who mourn."

Is it difficult for me to let go of past hurts?
Have there been times when I have walked away from the pain of others and refused to be compassionate?

Reader 3: "Blessed are the meek."

Do I feel that I have to be in control of certain people or situations?
Do I thank God for all the gifts and talents I have been given?

Reader 4: "Blessed are they who hunger and thirst for righteousness."

Am I "possessed" by my possessions or my desire to have them?
Do I stereotype others because of their gender, race, or ethnic background?

Reader 5: "Blessed are the merciful."

Am I able to forgive those who have hurt me?
Have I ever really thought about all the times God has forgiven me?

Reader 6: "Blessed are the clean of heart."

Am I sincere in my relationships with others? In my relationship with God?
Do I see God's image in myself? In others?

Reader 7: "Blessed are the peacemakers."

Am I silent when I see others being persecuted or treated unjustly?
Do the stands I take at home and at school promote or undermine peace?

Reader 8: "Blessed are they who are persecuted for the sake of righteousness."

Do I persecute those who do not think or act as I do?
Do I try to become informed about social issues happening in the world?

Leader: Holy Spirit, bless us with your gifts so that we can better live out the Beatitudes in our daily lives. Amen

End by praying the Sign of the Cross.

Review

1. Describe the audience to whom the author of the Gospel according to Matthew wrote. What perspective did the author use to capture his audience?

2. What images or titles of Jesus occur frequently in the Gospel according to Matthew? Why do you think the author focused on those images?

3. What are the important truths conveyed in the Infancy Narratives? Identify two similarities and two differences between the Infancy Narratives in Matthew and in Luke.

4. What is the Incarnation, and why did it take place?

5. What does the temptation of Jesus teach us about trusting in God the Father?

6. What does the term *kingdom of heaven* mean? Why isn't the term *kingdom of God* ever used in the Gospel according to Matthew?

7. What are the values Jesus taught in the Beatitudes?

8. How did the Apostles share in Jesus' mission?

9. What do the parables invite us to do? How should we respond to the message contained in the parables?

10. Describe the role of Peter among the disciples.

11. What is the Judgment of Nations? How should we respond to Jesus' teaching?

12. Describe the Spiritual and Corporal Works of Mercy. Why are they important?

Key Words

Beatitudes (p. 77)—Jesus' teachings about the meaning and path to true happiness; descriptions of the way to attain eternal blessedness, or holiness, to which God calls all of us.

Christ (p. 66)—The Greek word for "anointed" and "Messiah." Jesus, as Messiah, restored all people to communion and friendship with God through his life, death, and Resurrection.

Incarnation (p. 73)—The second Person of the Holy Trinity, who, while remaining God, assumed a human nature and became man.

Infancy Narratives (p. 69)—Recorded stories in the Gospels of Jesus' conception, birth, and early years.

kingdom of heaven (p. 75)—Also known as the kingdom of God or the reign of God; the gift of salvation and eternal life; God's rule of justice, love, and peace.

Messiah (p. 66)—The Hebrew word for "anointed"; a savior sent by God to redeem his people from the power of sin and everlasting death and to restore them to his friendship.

Works of Mercy (p. 86)—Charitable acts by which we care for the physical and spiritual needs of others.

YHWH (p. 75)—Hebrew name for God, sometimes translated "I AM," or "the One Who Is," or "The One Who Causes to Be What Is."

Personal Journey

Teen to Teen

Do you have enough faith in the Lord to rely upon the Beatitudes in times of trouble or even times of violence and personal danger? Can you react as Saint Clare of Assisi did when her order was attacked—with peace and prayer? Describe a time when you responded with prayer to a time of trouble.

"My grandma got the flu my freshman year of high school and she had to be put in the hospital. I prayed with my family and faith sharing group, and that helped me get through my time of trouble. When I told grandma later about all the prayers that were said for her, she was overwhelmed and thankful that so many people reacted with peace, love, and prayer."

Toni B.

"The most troubling times that I have encountered are tests and exams. I'm a solid C student and I'm tempted to cheat off other students. I have always managed to resist, though. I pray before every test . . . sometimes during the test, that I have the courage to resist temptations. Praying always calms me down during the test and gets me through it."

James H.

"By 15 I was in prison and serving a two-year sentence for car theft. In prison I joined a prayer group and started turning my life around. I found myself turning more and more to God as I finished out my sentence. I was baptized about a month after I left prison. If I hadn't joined the prayer group, I don't know how I would have turned out. Prayer gave me hope and a reason to wait for my two years to be over."

Will N.

Personal Challenge

Choose one group who is addressed in the Beatitudes. Identify who they are in your community. If there is an organization that helps these people, join them for at least a day, and help them administer aid. If there is not an organization, gather with other students and try to administer help to a group mentioned in the Beatitudes who needs help.

BREAK OPEN the Word

Jesus' Teachings

Read the quote at the beginning of the chapter from Matthew 6. Then read verses 19–21 in your Bible in their entirety. What do you think Jesus is telling you in these verses? How can you apply Jesus' teachings from these verses to the groups of the Beatitudes and their needs?

A.D. **14–37**
Tiberius ruler
over Roman Empire

A.D. **28–29**
John the Baptist's active ministry

A.D. **33**
Crucifixion, death, and
Resurrection of Jesus

A.D. **54**
Nero's rise to
power as emperor
of Roman Empire

A.D. 14-37

A.D. 47

A.D. **26–36** Pontius Pilate
the Roman procurator
over Judea and Samaria

A.D. **29**
Jesus' baptism; beginning
of his public ministry

C. A.D. **50**
First Pauline Letters written

Called to Believe

"If any want to become [Jesus'] followers, let them deny themselves and take up their cross and follow [him]."

Mark 8:34

Chapter Goals

In this chapter, you will:

- learn about the background and the main themes of the Gospel according to Mark.

- learn about Jesus' public ministry and the call of the first disciples.

- explore the Messianic Mystery and learn how to overcome obstacles to discipleship.

- consider the Paschal mystery as the central mystery of our faith.

- learn about Padre Pio.

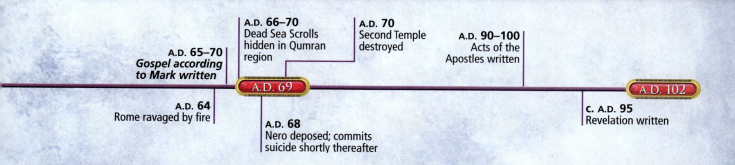

A.D. 65–70
*Gospel according
to Mark written*

A.D. 64
Rome ravaged by fire

A.D. 66–70
Dead Sea Scrolls
hidden in Qumran
region

A.D. 69

A.D. 68
Nero deposed; commits
suicide shortly thereafter

A.D. 70
Second Temple
destroyed

A.D. 90–100
Acts of the
Apostles written

C. A.D. 95
Revelation written

A.D. 102

The Gospel According to Mark

We often use the word *believe* casually—such as when we say, "I believe our team is better than their team" or "Can you believe she likes that movie?" These examples obviously do not carry the same weight as a statement of belief or faith. Beliefs of faith are so strong that they shape who we are and what we will become. When our convictions lead us to public speech and actions, we become witnesses to what we believe.

The author of Mark emphasized that following Jesus is a choice we make. Focusing our minds and hearts on following Jesus leads to discipleship. A disciple lives out his or her faith commitment within the Church community. The Catholic Church is our faith community, the living Body of Christ.

The Church's faith makes our faith possible, supporting and strengthening us in our belief.

Overview of the Gospel

Authorship and Date For centuries, biblical scholars believed that the Gospel according to Mark was a shortened version of the Gospel according to Matthew. However, during the nineteenth and the twentieth centuries, scripture scholars offered strong evidence that the author of the Gospel according to Mark wrote this Gospel first, probably between A.D. 65 and A.D. 70.

Traditionally, biblical scholars thought John Mark, a companion of Paul mentioned in Acts 12:12, was the author of the Gospel according to Mark. While some still hold this belief, others believe Mark to be an unknown writer, probably a Gentile Christian who might have been a disciple of Saint Peter.

Audience and Location The author of the Gospel according to Mark wrote approximately thirty years after the death of Jesus and shortly before and during the fall of Jerusalem and the Temple. By that time, Peter, Paul, and James had already died. The early Christians living in Jerusalem were experiencing the brutality of Nero's rule and living under the eye of Rome in an occupied territory.

Christians at that time had to decide whether to fight with the Jews to defend the Temple. Most chose not to fight because they fervently believed that the new temple was the Body of Christ. The Gospel according to Mark has sometimes been called the Gospel of nonviolence because despite the fighting around them, the Christians refused to be part of it. Other titles

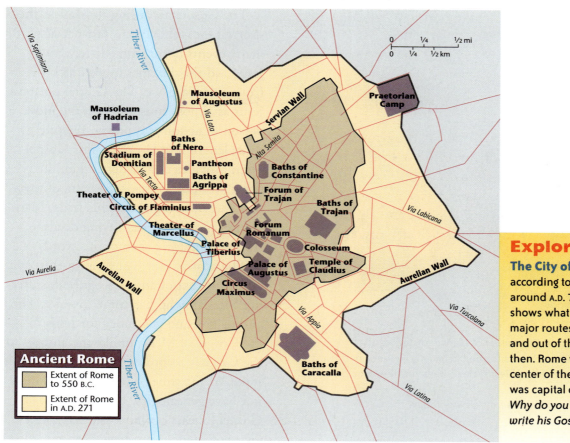

Explore the Land

The City of Rome The Gospel according to Mark was written around A.D. 70 in Rome. This map shows what Rome—along with the major routes of transportation in and out of the city—looked like then. Rome was considered the center of the Western world and was capital of the Roman Empire. *Why do you think Mark chose to write his Gospel from Rome?*

for this Gospel include the Gospel of Conversion, the Gospel of the Cross, and the Gospel of "the Way."

People in Mark's community followed "the Way" of Jesus during a time when many others persecuted and martyred Christians. Written to an audience that included Gentile Christians, this Gospel contains few references to the Old Testament, something to be expected if an audience did not have knowledge of the Scriptures. The Gospel according to Mark has an urgent message to the community to model their lives after Jesus'. This commitment required disciples who were willing to serve others and to suffer for them. The author wrote that believing in Jesus wholeheartedly meant following in his footsteps.

Theological Perspectives and Themes From the beginning, the author presents the Gospel of Mark as an interactive story. We are drawn into the mystery of who Jesus is and into the action of the events. We are encouraged to see ourselves in the personalities and lives of Jesus and his followers. This Gospel helps us understand what it means to believe in Jesus. It challenges us to become part of the story, make choices, commit our lives to Jesus, and become his disciples.

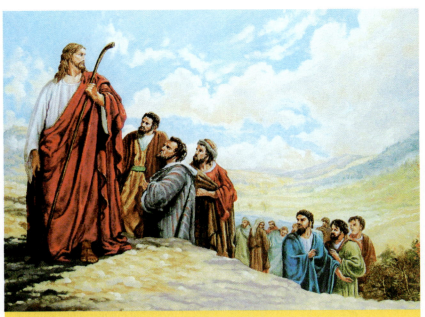

The Gospel according to Mark is the shortest Gospel. Mark is fast-paced—many events occur immediately, and Jesus and the disciples move quickly from place to place. The Gospel portrays Jesus as almost constantly on the move, a person of action and power. Despite its short length and fast pace, this Gospel often provides clearer detail than the other synoptic Gospels. An aura of mystery and suffering surrounds Jesus. Mark focuses more on Jesus' saving deeds through suffering than on his words.

The central image of Jesus in this Gospel is that of an unrecognized, suffering Messiah who has come to serve. The author gives no genealogy for Jesus in the Gospel of Mark, unlike the authors of the Gospels according to Matthew and Luke. At the time of Jesus, servants did not have genealogies. Because this Gospel focuses on Jesus as a servant, a genealogy would not have been recorded.

One of the themes throughout this Gospel is the portrayal of Jesus' followers and his opponents. This Gospel begins with a clear distinction between Jesus' followers—the enthusiastic crowds, the disciples, and the people who are healed—and his opponents—the people with hardened hearts, the chief priests and scribes, and the political authorities. As the Gospel progresses, the distinction blurs. Some of Jesus' followers misunderstand or betray him because he does not meet their messianic expectations. Even some of his enemies, like the Roman centurion at the cross, later acknowledge Jesus as the Son of God.

The author of Mark filled the events recorded in the Gospel with conflict, tension, and challenge. Some people attempt to destroy Jesus, while others suffer along with him. In the end, Jesus suffers and dies to save all people. The Gospel according to Mark is a journey with Jesus from the beginning of his public ministry and ultimately to his Passion, death, and Resurrection.

Structure of the Gospel of Mark

The Gospel according to Mark has three major sections, with a short introduction preceding each section:

Prologue: teaching of John; baptism and temptation of Jesus

The Galilean Ministry (Mark 1:14—6:6a)
Capernaum and the surrounding district (Mark 1:14–45)
Conflict of Jesus and the Jews: five controversial discourses (Mark 2:1—3:6)
Success of Jesus and further conflicts (Mark 3:7–35)
The parables (Mark 4:1–34)
Four miracles at the Sea of Galilee (Mark 4:35—5:43)
Conclusion of Galilean ministry; rejection at Nazareth (Mark 6:1–6a)

The Journeys of Jesus (Mark 6:6b—10:52)
The mission of the Apostles (Mark 6:6b–29)
Journey and return, feeding of the 5,000, controversy (Mark 7:1–23)
Journey and return, miracles, controversy (Mark 7:24—8:12)
Journey and return, cures, confessions of Peter, predictions of the Passion, Transfiguration (Mark 8:13—9:50)
Journey to Jerusalem, controversy, instructions, cure of blind man (Mark 10:1–52)

Ministry in Jerusalem, Passion and Death, Resurrection (Mark 11:1—16:8)
Messianic activity (Mark 11:1–26)
Messianic teaching (Mark 11:27—12:44)
Apocalypse (Mark 13:1–37)
Jesus and His disciples (Mark 14:1–42)
Jesus tried by the Jews (Mark 14:43–72)
Jesus tried by Pilate and crucified (Mark 15:1–47)
The risen Jesus (Mark 16:1–8)

Prominent Figures in the Gospel of Mark This Gospel features several people or groups.

Jesus: Jesus practiced what he asked of his followers: total commitment to the will of God the Father, who had sent him. As Jesus personifies this way of living, Mark reveals Jesus' relationship with his followers, the crowds, and the Jewish religious authorities.

Jewish and political authorities: The Jewish religious authorities included the Pharisees, the Sadducees, the Sanhedrin, the chief priests, the scribes, and the elders. The political authorities were the Herodians, the supporters of King Herod and his political position. From the beginning, they questioned, accused, and rejected Jesus. Opponents from these two groups conspired against Jesus in Mark 3:6. Jesus debated them and ultimately reduced them to silence. (See *Mark 12:34*.)

Faith Activity

Women in Mark's Gospel Mark's Gospel records women who had faith in Jesus and chose to serve and follow him. Read the scripture verses indicated below, and list the women who were disciples of Jesus. In small groups, discuss the importance of each of the women listed here:

Mark 5:25–34
Mark 7:24–30
Mark 14:3–9
Mark 15:40–41
Mark 15:47
Mark 16:1–7

Writing Techniques

When Jesus began his public ministry, he was on the move. He surprised many people. Jesus' identity was revealed through his public ministry.

Read the following passages to discover why people were, and are today, astounded, amazed, and in awe of him:

Mark 1:22

Mark 1:23–27

Mark 2:3–12

Mark 4:35–41

Mark 6:2

Mark 7:37

Mark 11:18

Followers: Jesus' followers were people whose final actions showed their desire to journey with him. The followers included his mother, Peter and the other Apostles, women, sinners, tax collectors, those who suffered, and many other unnamed disciples. Some of Jesus' followers continued to struggle with the real identity of Jesus and did not truly recognize and follow him until after his Resurrection.

Crowds: Crowds are mentioned thirty-eight times in this Gospel. The crowds initially responded with enthusiasm to Jesus' words and deeds but did not make a commitment to follow him.

Mark's Techniques

The author of Mark used several writing techniques in formulating his Gospel. In several cases he framed one incident within another. For example in Mark 11:11 we read that Jesus is in Jerusalem and in the Temple, where he "looked around at everything." Later in the same chapter, Jesus departs with his disciples to the village of Bethany. As Jesus leaves Bethany, he passes a fig tree that bore no fruit. And even though it is not the season for figs, Jesus places a curse on the tree saying, "May no one ever eat fruit from you again" (*Mark 11:14*). The story of Jesus cleansing the Temple area of the buyers and sellers is then found in verses 15 through 18. The fig tree, now withered, returns to the story in verses 20 and 21. The fig tree reminds the reader of the prophets of the Old Testament who previously used this image to designate Israel. Jesus' cursing of the fig tree represents

his judgment of barren Israel and the fate of Jerusalem for failing to receive his teaching. The story symbolizes the fate of the Jewish people and the Temple, which would come to the same end as the fig tree because they did not produce the fruit they were supposed to. The author prompts his readers to see the tension between the story used as a frame and the story inserted into the frame.

Another technique used in Mark is the **threefold pattern**. The Gospel contains

- three seed parables (See *Mark 4:3–32.*)
- three popular opinions about who Jesus really is (See *Mark 6:14–15.*)
- three popular opinions about Jesus (See *Mark 8:27–28.*)
- three failures of the disciples to stay awake in the garden (See *Mark 14:32–42.*)
- the three denials of Jesus by Peter (See *Mark 14:66–72.*)

On a larger scale, this threefold pattern seems to encompass the whole of the Gospel according to Mark, which contains three declarations of Jesus as the Son of God. These declarations are interspersed from beginning to end. (See *Mark 1:11*; *9:7*; and *15:39.*) The tension shows Jesus as the beloved Son of God and Jesus as the executed criminal.

The Beginning of Jesus' Ministry

The Gospel of Mark includes events at the beginning of Jesus' public ministry that revolve around discovering his identity by answering the question, "Who is Jesus?" In these events, Mark presents the true nature of Jesus as the Messiah.

Jesus Christ, the Son of God   Mark 1:1–8:26

The Gospel according to Mark opens by proclaiming, "The beginning of the good news of Jesus Christ, the Son of God" (*Mark 1:1*). This statement immediately reveals Jesus' identity to the readers. The author applies the title Son of God to Jesus to convey the intimate and eternal relationship that exists between Jesus and God the Father. The remainder of the Gospel describes how this revelation unfolds.

The author of this Gospel also uses the term Son of Man to describe Jesus. In the Old Testament, this term refers to the prophet Ezekiel, who brought Israel a renewed life, a restored city, and a magnificent Temple. The Son of Man terminology continues in the prophecies of Daniel and reveals the Son of Man as a glorious, god-like figure. This figure's appearance is a judgment against the corrupt kingdoms of the world and vindicates Israel. In Jesus' time, the title Son of Man referred to the glorious manifestation of divine power.

The terms Son of God and Son of Man in Mark identify Jesus and the purpose of his mission. That Jesus is the divine Son of God is revealed through his mission and, ultimately, through his Resurrection.

The Baptist and the Baptized
The baptism of Jesus is recorded in all four Gospels. In Mark, as in the other Gospel accounts, Jesus' baptism revealed who he is.

The Gospel according to Mark makes it clear that Jesus' mission began with his baptism. John the Baptist, the messenger sent before Jesus to prepare the way, baptized Jesus and pointed to Jesus as the Messiah. John was prophesied by Isaiah: "See, I am sending my messenger ahead of you, who will prepare your way; the voice of one crying out in the wilderness: 'Prepare the way of the Lord, make his paths straight'" (*Mark 1:3*).

When the voice of God pronounced Jesus as his beloved Son, Jesus' eternal preexistence was confirmed. Jesus is the only Son of the Father. He is God himself. The descent of the Holy Spirit upon Jesus indicated that from the beginning Jesus was one with the Father and the Holy Spirit. Jesus then led his public ministry by doing the will of God the Father and in union with the Holy Spirit.

Faith Activity

God's Presence Like Jesus, you have faced times in your life when you began something new. Like Jesus, you have the assurance that God the Father and the Holy Spirit are always with you on your journey. Draw, write a poem, or write a song about one of these new beginnings in your life. How were you aware of God's presence during that time in your life? How did that time help you learn more about yourself and about God's plan for you?

This event closes with the arrest of John the Baptist. John's arrest is a warning that the struggle between good and evil prevails throughout the Gospel. The shadow of the cross follows Jesus until it becomes the symbol of his victory over evil.

The Catholic Church celebrates the Feast of the Baptism of Jesus on the last Sunday of the Christmas season. This celebration marks the end of the proclamation in the liturgy of the accounts surrounding the birth and early life of Jesus, and the beginning of his public life and ministry.

Discipleship: A Life Rooted in Jesus

Discipleship is a life rooted in Jesus—a life expressed in union with his Church. Caring for others and living in harmony with our fellow human beings is linked directly with our living, loving relationship with God. We become true disciples of Jesus by responding to his call and by living in a community of faith.

In his first ministerial act, Jesus called disciples to follow him and join in his mission. He continued to invite followers, and soon a small group had gathered to serve the kingdom of God on earth. Those followers also sought the fullness of the kingdom in eternity.

The Gospel according to Mark has three call narratives, which describe how Jesus summoned others to hear and respond to the word and the power of God.

Discipleship The following scripture passages specifically relate to being a disciple of Jesus. Look up the passages and express in writing how they connect to ideas of discipleship:

Mark 9:33–37

Mark 10:35–45

Mark 12:41–44

Mark 14:3–8

Jesus Calls and Commissions the Twelve As Jesus began his ministry, he recruited four ordinary people to help him proclaim the message of the kingdom of God. Jesus expected an immediate and total commitment to serve God. In similar ways, he invited others to follow him, too.

scripture

"As Jesus passed along the Sea of Galilee, he saw Simon and his brother Andrew casting a net into the sea—for they were fishermen. And Jesus said to them, 'Follow me and I will make you fish for people.' And immediately they left their nets and followed him. As he went a little farther, he saw James son of Zebedee and his brother John, who were in their boats mending the nets. Immediately he called them; and they left their father Zebedee in the boat with the hired men, and followed him."

Mark 1:16–20

Faith Activity

Follow Me The first and third "call narratives" required Jesus' followers to leave things behind.

1. What are the "nets," "boats," and "baggage" that people in today's world need to leave behind to follow Jesus?

2. What are the things you need to leave behind to follow Jesus?

After Jesus called the first disciples, he went up on a mountain. In Scripture, the mountain is a special place for meeting God. On the mountain, Jesus chose his twelve Apostles, from the Greek word *apostolos,* which means "one who is sent." Although the Apostles were a diverse group of people, their relationship with Jesus bound them as a community. Jesus called them to be with him. Through spending time with Jesus, their minds, hearts, and attitudes were transformed so that they could go forth to preach the Gospel.

scripture

"He called the twelve and began to send them out two by two, and gave them authority over the unclean spirits. He ordered them to take nothing for their journey except a staff; no bread, no bag, no money in their belts; but to wear sandals and not to put on two tunics."

Mark 6:7–13

▼ The Great Catch by John August Swanson.

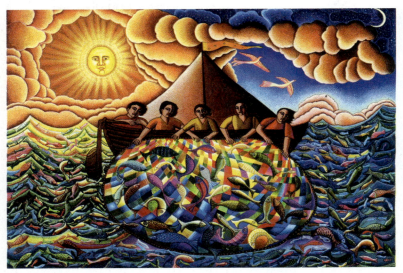

In this third call narrative, Jesus called his chosen Apostles and sent them on a journey. He sent them out "two by two" to minister together. When we follow Jesus and become part of his Church, we share the journey with others. Jesus asked his Apostles to trust in God and others to meet their needs. We too are called to trust totally in God for all we need. All three call narratives in the Gospel according to Mark remind us to put God first in our lives.

Confronting Evil Immediately after each call narrative, the power of evil shows itself in different forms: Jesus confronts evil in the form of a man with an unclean spirit after the call of the disciples. (See *Mark 1:21–28*.) Jesus and Beelzebul, a demon, have a confrontation after the commission of the Twelve. (See *Mark 3:20–30*.) The murder of John the Baptist is recounted after the mission of the Twelve. (See *Mark 6:14–29*.)

When we say "yes" to becoming disciples of Jesus, we are also asked to confront evil. The kingdom of God demands our response and requires our ongoing commitment. Our response and commitment must be strong, especially in the presence of evil or in the face of obstacles. These obstacles can come from the outside world, from our closest friends, or even from within us.

Invitation Being a disciple is an invitation to journey with Jesus and follow his example. As disciples, we respond to the call each of us receives from God and live our vocation in the Church community, in our families, in our schools, and in the world. Being a disciple requires a choice to accept God's grace, to turn away from sin, and ask God's forgiveness for our sins and mistakes. It also involves rejecting evil and standing up for what is good and right. Discipleship leads to a growth process of self-fulfillment, as we hear and respond to Jesus' teachings and invite others to do the same. Being a disciple involves a life of prayer, action, and trust in God the Father, the Son, and the Holy Spirit.

Faith Sharing

Obstacles Even though we desire to follow Jesus, birds, rocks, and thorns along the way distract us from our purpose. Answer the following questions with your group and think about how God's grace has prepared you for a life rooted in Jesus:

1. Consider a recent decision you made. On what did you base your decision?
2. Think of a time you made a poor choice or decision. What was the result?
3. What can you do to have healthier "soil"? How can you grow in God's grace?

Following Jesus and Our Call to Discipleship The Gospel of Mark teaches us about the conditions and the consequences of choosing to follow Jesus and live in his community, the Church. As members of the Church, we are called by Jesus to proclaim by the way we live that we are followers of Jesus. Even though we, like the Apostles, are a diverse group, our relationship with Jesus and the grace of the Holy Spirit bind us together as a community. Through our personal lives at home, school, work, and even at leisure, we can fulfill the call to holiness we received at Baptism.

The Parable of the Sower offers us insight into how ready the soil of our life is for becoming a follower of Jesus. As he told a crowd of followers:

Faith Activity

Symbolism in Mark

After reading the "Parable of the Sower," read the explanation of the parable in Mark 4:14–20. Create a chart naming each following symbol from the parable and give an explanation for each symbol:

- Sower
- Seed
- Birds
- Seed on the path
- Seed on the rocky ground
- Seed in the thorns
- Seed on the good soil

SCRIPTURE

"'Listen! A sower went out to sow. And as he sowed, some seed fell on the path, and the birds came and ate it up. Other seed fell on rocky ground, where it did not have much soil, and it sprang up quickly, since it had no depth of soil. And when the sun rose, it was scorched; and since it had no root, it withered away. Other seed fell among thorns, and the thorns grew up and choked it, and it yielded no grain. Other seed fell into good soil and brought forth grain, growing up and increasing and yielding thirty and sixty and a hundredfold.' And he said, 'Let anyone with ears to hear listen!'"

Mark 4:3–9

In this parable, Jesus teaches us that the way we respond to the word of God illustrates the kind of person we are. Jesus also described the type of "soil" that hinders us from responding to God's word. In spite of our imperfect soil, Jesus remains with us and can work through our imperfections. Jesus continually invites us to a life rooted in him.

TRAVELING IN THE TIME OF JESUS

In outlining the mission of the Apostles, Jesus listed several items they were not to take with them on their journeys. Each one was to take only his stave, his sandals, and a single tunic. During the time of Jesus, the items he ordered the Apostles to leave behind were considered necessities.

To travel on the dusty—and potentially dangerous—roads from city to city without money, food, a change of clothes, or any other travel materials was unwise and possibly harmful. The lack of those items likely precluded the Apostles from traveling any more than a day without stopping. In this manner, the Apostles preached of Jesus' work while also resting in a safe home. Jesus frequently stopped during his travels and used nature to provide for himself and his followers—such as in the feeding of the 5,000.

Read the parable of the Good Samaritan to learn more about the dangers of traveling in the time of Jesus. The Apostles placed their trust in Jesus and God the Father, whom they knew would provide for their needs.

Connect to the Past

Travel in the Time of Jesus The well-developed roads of the Roman Empire allowed trade and commerce to reach the farthest corners of the empire in short amounts of time. In the area surrounding and connected to the capital city of Rome, the roads were paved. However, in Galilee and Judea, the roads that led from city to city were unpaved. Pictured here are foot coverings from that era. *What items do you think you would need to make the journey that the early disciples did?*

The Misunderstood Messiah

Break Open the Word

Predictions of the Passion Study the following scripture passages for three predictions Jesus makes about his Passion, predictions that his disciples fail to understand. What clouds their understanding?

Mark 8:31–33

Mark 9:30–32

Mark 10:32–45

The readings from Mark 1:1—8:33 contain what some scholars call the Messianic Secret. This refers to the fact that as Jesus heals, preaches, and teaches, he instructs his followers not to tell others about his miraculous works, but then they go out and, disregarding his instructions, share what they have witnessed. The Gospel according to Mark emphasizes the messianic mystery from 8:27 to Jesus' death in 15:37. Within these passages, we read about the paradox that as the Messiah, Jesus must suffer, die, and then be raised in glory—a mystery his followers were unable to understand because their Messiah was supposed to establish a glorious kingdom, not die and disappear.

The Messianic Mystery   Mark 8:27–15:37

As Jesus journeyed with his disciples, he was aware of the forces mounting against him. As a good teacher, he wanted to test what his students had learned—for they would become the teachers someday. He posed two questions. First, he asked, "Who do people say that I am?" They answered, "John the Baptist; and others, Elijah; and still others, one of the prophets" (*Mark 8:27–28*). Then Jesus asked the crucial question, "But who do you say that I am?" (*Mark 8:29*) Although in his answer, Peter correctly hailed Jesus as the Messiah, he did not understand the nature of Jesus' messiahship. Peter and the disciples hoped for a hero-messiah, not a prophet-messiah. As Jesus began to prophecy his own death and Resurrection, Peter spoke up and rebuked Jesus. Jesus silenced Peter and compared him to Satan for worrying about human, rather than divine, concerns. (See *Mark 8:31–33*.)

Why did he do this? Throughout the Gospel of Mark, there are times when Jesus silences demons that recognize him. Peter acted like a demon because, although he recognized Jesus as the Messiah, he did not accept the necessity of Jesus' suffering and death. Peter and the disciples continued to misunderstand and even deny Jesus—especially as the journey became more difficult.

Faith Activity

Timeline of Your Life In Mark 8:33—10:52 Jesus is journeying from Galilee to Jerusalem. Similarly, our lives are a journey. Record the journey of your life on a timeline. Draw one timeline that represents major events in your life. Then draw another overlapping timeline that represents your relationship with God during each of those times.

Can you detect any patterns in what was happening in your life and where your relationship was with God?

The Suffering Servant

Las Posadas are part of the Mexican traditions of Christmas in which there is a reenactment of Joseph and Mary seeking lodging in Bethlehem. This is a piñata from a latter part of the reenactment.

The mystery of God is revealed in the image of Jesus who is "the image of the unseen God" (*Colossians 1:15*). Jesus is the Son of God, the Father's gift to us. He became flesh and dwelt among us. United with Jesus through the Holy Spirit and as members of the Church, we experience the liberating power of God's grace.

We celebrate the life of Jesus in a special way during two great seasons in the Church—Christmas and Easter. Love of God is made incarnate in Jesus, and the Church celebrates the mysteries of life and death in the liturgy, just as death marks our own lives on earth. The reality of death does not leave us without hope, for by Jesus' redeeming actions, death can lead to resurrection for each of us too.

The Old Testament frequently pictures God as a warrior. But in the prophecies of Isaiah, God saves not by strength or force, but by suffering—that of the Suffering Servant. Isaiah prophesied the coming of a suffering servant Messiah, using graphic imagery and very distinct language. Isaiah tells the reader that the one who "by his bruises we are healed" will be "struck down by God, and afflicted," "a man of suffering," and "despised and rejected by others." (See *Isaiah 53:3–5*.)

Even in the Infancy Narratives, suffering had already entered into the story of Jesus' birth: there was no room for him in the inn. Mary and Joseph had to wrap him in bands of cloth and lay him in a manger—the feeding trough for animals. Herod the Great slaughtered innocent children to try to kill Jesus after his birth. Mary and Joseph fled with Jesus into exile in Egypt. At Jesus' presentation in the Temple, Simeon said to Mary, "This child is destined for the falling and the rising of many in Israel, and to be a sign that will be opposed . . ."

Jesus is the suffering Messiah whose life—from the beginning—points to the cross. Jesus died so his true identity would be made known: "for the Son of Man did not come to be served but to serve and to give his life a ransom for many" (*Mark 10:45*).

The Transfiguration of Jesus

After the first prediction of the Passion, Jesus was transfigured before the disciples Peter, James, and John. For a moment Jesus disclosed his divine glory, confirming what Peter had said—that Jesus was the Messiah. During the **Transfiguration**, Jesus' disciples were told to "listen to him."

scripture

"Six days later, Jesus took with him Peter and James and John, and led them up a high mountain apart, by themselves. And he was transfigured before them, and his clothes became dazzling white, such as no one on earth could bleach them. And there appeared to them Elijah with Moses, who were talking with Jesus. Then Peter said to Jesus, 'Rabbi, it is good for us to be here; let us make three dwellings, one for you, one for Moses, and one for Elijah.' He did not know what to say, for they were terrified. Then a cloud overshadowed them, and from the cloud there came a voice, 'This is my Son, the Beloved; listen to him!' Suddenly when they looked around, they saw no one with them any more, but only Jesus. As they were coming down the mountain, he ordered them to tell no one about what they had seen, until after the Son of Man had risen from the dead."

Mark 9:2–9

Interpret the Art

Transfiguration During the Transfiguration, Jesus' face shone like the sun and his clothes became bright white. The prophets Elijah and Moses appeared beside him and God the Father spoke to the present disciples.

Why were Moses and Elijah the figures who appeared?

Jesus also revealed to Peter, James, and John that he would have to endure the suffering of the cross to enter into glory. In the Transfiguration, Jesus' disciples witnessed the transformation of his appearance. They also saw the two great figures many of Jesus' followers thought he was. The two figures were Moses, the great liberator of Israel, who led the Israelites out of slavery and gave them the Torah; and Elijah, the powerful prophet of those who were poor and oppressed. The prophet who brought forth the Law and the prophet who announced the coming of the Messiah appeared with Jesus at the Transfiguration.

Jesus' Transfiguration strengthened the Apostles and their questioning faith as his Passion and death approached. Leading them up a mountain prepared them for the ascent to Calvary for his crucifixion. The cloud indicated the presence of the Holy Spirit, and the voice was that of God the Father. This event gave witness to the Trinity: the Father in the voice, Jesus the Son, and the Holy Spirit in the cloud.

Just as the baptism of Jesus began his public life, the Transfiguration of Jesus began his Passion, death, and Resurrection. "Jesus' baptism proclaimed 'the mystery of the first regeneration,' namely, our Baptism; the Transfiguration 'is the sacrament of the second regeneration': our own Resurrection.[10] From now on we share in the Lord's Resurrection through the Spirit who acts in the sacraments of the Body of Christ" (*Catechism of the Catholic Church, 556*).

The Transfiguration of Jesus appears in Matthew and Luke, the other synoptic Gospels. The Gospel reading the assembly hears on the Second Sunday of Lent is the Transfiguration of Jesus. This reading prepares the Church for the celebration about five weeks later of Jesus' Passion, death, and Resurrection during the most holy days of the Church year, the Easter Triduum. The Church also commemorates this event on the Feast of the Transfiguration of Jesus on August 6. In these liturgies, the Church remembers and celebrates Jesus' Transfiguration and its central message of salvation.

Challenges to Discipleship

During the first half of the Gospel according to Mark, we read that Jesus experienced numerous confrontations with Jewish religious authorities. However, in the second half of the Gospel, Jesus encountered resistance from an unexpected source—his own disciples. Although they had witnessed his teachings and healings, the disciples did not really understand who Jesus was or what he expected of them.

As Jesus traveled from Galilee to Jerusalem on the road toward his cross, the disciples' lack of understanding continued. In an attempt to encourage their understanding before his final journey, Jesus asked his disciples a series of questions: "Why are you talking about having no bread? Do you still not perceive or understand? Are your hearts hardened? Do you have eyes, and fail to see? Do you have ears, and fail to hear? And do you not remember? . . . Do you not yet understand?" (*Mark 8:17–19, 21*). While these questions were harsh, they served as a prelude to the frustration Jesus experienced when his disciples did not completely understand or accept his journey toward Calvary.

In the middle chapters of the Gospel according to Mark, several stories involve the restoration of sight and hearing to those in the crowds who truly believe. The author of Mark used those stories to describe times when Jesus' disciples did not have faith, when they were blind, deaf, or had a hardened heart to his presence and message. Those events became a gradual process of healing—physical healing, spiritual healing, or both—and offered hope that the disciples would come to understand and accept Jesus in faith. These stories serve as reminders of obstacles that can separate us from Jesus.

Faith Activity

Keeping Your Faith

Sometimes certain events in life can shake or weaken our faith. Like the disciples whose faith was in question before the Transfiguration, we have moments in our lives that challenge our faith. Think of a time when your faith was shaken or weakened by some event. How did God strengthen your faith at that time? Take time this week to pray to God in thanks for your faith. Ask God to rekindle your faith and to make you stronger in your faith.

Faith Activity

The Parable of the Wealthy Man The young man in the story could be said to be possessed by his very possessions. The young man's desire for wealth kept him from the richness of the treasures of heaven.

1. Make a list of the different ways you follow Jesus. Remembering Jesus' love for you, what could you do or give up to follow him more closely?

2. How does wealth show itself in our society? How can society keep wealth in a proper perspective so people can follow Jesus more closely?

Wealth Mark describes a man who seemed to have faith. However, a roadblock prevented him from following Jesus. That man is a reflection of many of us. The wealthy man in Mark 10:17–22 claimed to have held true to the Commandments since his youth, and sought to inherit eternal life. But Jesus proclaimed that this is not enough to inherit eternal life. Jesus tells him, ". . . go, sell what you own, and give the money to the poor, and you will have treasure in heaven . . ." (*Mark 10:21*). This both shocked and saddened the man, for he was very wealthy. The proclamation of Jesus echoes the Beatitude "Blessed are the poor in spirit, for theirs is the kingdom of heaven" (*Matthew 5:3*). A person need be poor in all aspects—having given to God all he or she has in spirit, mind, and body—to inherit eternal life and enter the kingdom of heaven.

Blindness At times, distractions blind us and prevent us from truly seeing Jesus. The Gospel of Mark gives this example of the blindness of ambition: "James and John, the sons of Zebedee, came forward to him [Jesus] and said to him, 'Teacher, we want you to do for us whatever we ask of you.' And he said to them, 'What is it you want me to do for you?' And they said to him, 'Grant us to sit, one at your right hand and one at your left, in your glory'" (*Mark 10:35–37*). This story shows what discipleship is not.

Remarkably, the one who could "see" Jesus and understand what Jesus was asking was a blind man. Discipleship is going from "blindness to seeing the light." Faith is believing in, trusting in, and surrendering to God, who is revealed in Jesus. At the same time, faith is a free, unmerited gift from God. We must choose to believe, but we cannot believe without God's grace, which he freely offers to all.

scripture

"They came to Jericho. As he and his disciples and a large crowd were leaving Jericho, Bartimaeus son of Timaeus, a blind beggar, was sitting by the roadside. When he heard that it was Jesus of Nazareth, he began to shout out and say, 'Jesus, Son of David, have mercy on me!' Jesus stood still and said, 'Call him here.' And they called the blind man, saying to him, 'Take heart; get up, he is calling you.' So throwing off his cloak, he sprang up and came to Jesus. Then Jesus said to him, 'What do you want me to do for you?' The blind man said to him, 'My teacher, let me see again.' Jesus said to him, 'Go; your faith has made you well.' Immediately he regained his sight and followed him on the way."

Mark 10:46–52

For Bartimaeus, faith cured his blindness. The gift of faith can do the same for us. After Jesus cured Bartimaeus, he followed Jesus. Bartimaeus understood that he could not separate having faith from practicing that faith.

The times when we finally "see the light" are **conversion experiences**. Conversion is a prompting of the Holy Spirit, a turning toward God to seek forgiveness and to understand what he desires of us. Jesus called each of his Apostles and disciples to conversion. He preached conversion when he proclaimed the coming of the kingdom. "The time is fulfilled, and the kingdom of God has come near; repent, and believe in the good news" (*Mark 1:15*). Jesus also calls each of us to conversion. Our first and fundamental conversion takes place in Baptism. Throughout our lives, Christ encourages and invites us to conversion, challenging us to welcome and allow his grace to work in our lives.

Conversion strengthens us to search, to understand, and to do what God wants us to do. These moments come in various ways—in our joys, sorrows, disappointments, failures, insights, and changes in our lives. Conversion is a lifelong process. Moments of conversion can happen at any time, to anyone, and at any age.

Interpret the Art

Conversion Study for St. Philip Baptising the Eunuch of the Queen of Ethiopia by Theodore Chasseriau. *What ritual actions do you see in this work of art that are similar to those you are familar with in the Sacrament of Baptism?*

The Paschal Mystery

The Gospel of Mark records three separate instances of Jesus' predicting his own Passion and death. His followers did not understand what he told them. The third instance occurred as Jesus and his disciples traveled toward Jerusalem to celebrate Passover, the feast that celebrated the Jewish liberation from slavery and death in Egypt. Jerusalem is where he died and rose from the dead. The **Paschal mystery** is Christ's work of redemption through his Passion, death, Resurrection, and Ascension. "The Paschal mystery of Christ's cross and Resurrection stands at the center of the Good News that the apostles, and the Church following them, are to proclaim to the world. God's saving plan was accomplished 'once for all'[11] by the redemptive death of his Son Jesus Christ." (*Catechism of the Catholic Church, 571*).

The term Paschal mystery comes from the Pasch (in Hebrew, *pesah*), the Passover event of the Exodus. (See *Exodus 12—13:16*.) Just as God delivered the ancient Hebrews from slavery and death in Egypt, so Jesus saves us from the power of sin and eternal death. God the Father sent his Son to redeem all humanity. Jesus freely offered himself for the salvation of all through his suffering, death, Resurrection, and sending of the Holy Spirit.

A Recounting of His Last Days

Entry into Jerusalem Mark 11:1–11 The crowds greeted Jesus' entrance to Jerusalem with great excitement. They recognized Jesus as the Messiah and celebrated with song his triumphant return to Jerusalem.

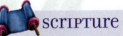
scripture

"Many people spread their cloaks on the road, and others spread leafy branches that they had cut in the fields. Then those who went ahead and those who followed were shouting,
'Hosanna!
 Blessed is the one who comes
  in the name of the Lord!
 Blessed is the coming kingdom
  of our ancestor David!
Hosanna in the highest heaven!'
Then he entered Jerusalem and went into the temple; and when he had looked around at everything, as it was already late, he went out to Bethany with the twelve."

Mark 11:8–11

The Church remembers Jesus' entry into Jerusalem in a special way on the Sunday before Easter Sunday. Passion Sunday—formerly known as Palm Sunday because people receive blessed palm branches in Church—begins the celebration of the Holy Week—the holiest week of the Church year. The events of this week recount the saving acts of Jesus and lead to the greatest feast of the Catholic Church—the feast of Easter.

Jesus' Passion and Crucifixion Mark 14:43–15:33

The Last Supper The chief priests and scribes joined with the Pharisees and Herodians to further the plot against Jesus. Their plan culminated during Passover. The new Passover, initiated by Jesus at the Last Supper, is our liberation from the slavery of sin. Every celebration of the **Eucharist** is a memorial of Christ's Passover.

Jesus and his disciples made preparations for Passover after their entry to Jerusalem. During the Passover meal, Jesus referred to himself as "Teacher"—the only time he did so in this Gospel. That event was also the only time Jesus referred to the Apostles as "my disciples." He taught them that the bread and wine offered at that meal would become his Body and Blood. We call that meal the Last Supper, as it was the last time Jesus would eat with his Apostles.

scripture

"While they were eating, he [Jesus] took a loaf of bread, and after blessing it he broke it, gave it to them, and said, 'Take; this is my body.' Then he took a cup, and after giving thanks he gave it to them, and all of them drank from it. He said to them, 'This is my blood of the covenant, which is poured out for many.'"

Mark 14:22–24

Break Open the Word

The Passion Compare the stories of Jesus' agony in the garden and his betrayal and arrest found in the following passages:

Mark 14:32–50

Matthew 26:36–56

Luke 22:39–53

John 18:1, 3–11

Who are the principal characters? What occurs in each Gospel in the agony scene and in the arrest scene? How does Jesus respond in each scene to what is happening? How do those present respond? In what ways are the accounts similar and different?

The bread and wine, blessed by Jesus at the Last Supper and given to his disciples, are a sharing in the life and death of Jesus—they are his Body and Blood. The Gospel passages Matthew 26:27–28 and Luke 22:20 also make it clear that the Last Supper actions of Jesus initiated the new and everlasting covenant. God made this covenant with his people for the forgiveness of sins and to save them from everlasting death.

The account in Luke also includes the following passage: "Then he [Jesus] took a loaf of bread, and when he had given thanks, he broke it and gave it to them, saying, 'This is my body, which is given for you. Do this in remembrance of me'" (*Luke 22:19*). The Church honors Jesus' command at the celebration of the Eucharist. In the same manner as Jesus at the Last Supper, the priest, through the power of the Holy Spirit, takes the bread and wine, blesses and breaks it, and it becomes the Body and Blood of Christ. As participants in this sacrament, we share in this covenant. The Church remembers the Last Supper in the evening Mass of the Lord's Supper on Holy Thursday.

Gethsemane and the Betrayal of Jesus

After completing their Passover observance for the evening, Jesus and his disciples went to the Mount of Olives. Jesus spoke to his disciples about what was going to happen and told them that they would betray him. Then Jesus went to Gethsemane, a garden on the Mount of Olives, to pray for God's will to be done. He asked his disciples to keep watch while he prayed. Instead, they fell asleep. Judas arrived and betrayed Jesus with a kiss. The religious authorities arrested Jesus.

▶ A Franciscan monk reads in the Garden of Gethsemane in Jerusalem.

Faith Activity

Prayerful Reflection Sometimes, when we think of the death of Jesus, we focus on what others did to Jesus rather than on how he faced death.

1. Jesus' reaction to his suffering and death was to pray. He prayed in the garden of Gethsemane as he awaited his arrest. How do you respond to suffering?

2. Divide into groups and research topics such as AIDS, domestic violence, and war. Discuss how Christians are answering the call to ease the suffering of others in the world.

Jesus Before the Sanhedrin Jesus willingly entered into his Passion, but those who were with him fled. Jesus was not the passive victim of a series of tragic circumstances. Rather, Jesus intentionally gave his life for others. The authorities brought Jesus to the Sanhedrin for questioning. In Jesus' time, the Sanhedrin was a group of seventy-one men that consisted of chief priests, scribes, and elders. These men made decisions regarding the Jewish community. They called witnesses to testify against Jesus, but their claims against him conflicted. Jesus did not respond to the allegations leveled against him.

The Jewish high priest demanded to know who Jesus was. Initially Jesus was silent. After the high priest asked again, "Are you the Messiah, the Son of the Blessed One?" Jesus answered him: "I am; and 'you will see the Son of Man seated at the right hand of the Power,' and 'coming with the clouds of heaven'" (*Mark 14:62*).

For the first time in this Gospel, Jesus actually stated that he is the Messiah. If he had continued to remain unresponsive to the questions and the accusations of the Jewish religious authorities, he might not have been charged. Knowing this, Jesus answered, "I am" to fulfill the prophesies and his mission on earth.

The high priest then tore Jesus' clothes and charged him with **blasphemy**. The Sanhedrin affirmed the high priest's condemnation, spat on Jesus, blindfolded him, struck him, and mocked him. The guards beat him as well. (See *Mark 14:61–65*.)

Jesus' reply of "I am" began his final journey toward the cross. The Sanhedrin regarded Jesus' claim of being the Son of Man as an insult to God. Jesus claimed to have the attributes of God by referring to himself as the Son of Man—he was, in their judgment, a blasphemer.

Jesus Before Pilate Though they could condemn Jesus, the Sanhedrin did not have the power to crucify him. Only the Romans, who ruled the country, could actually carry out a crucifixion. So the Sanhedrin took Jesus before Pilate, the procurator of Judea and the visible authority of Roman rule. This time the charge against Jesus had to be different, because the Romans did not involve themselves in religious concerns. The Sanhedrin had to devise a crime that Jesus would have committed against the Roman government. In the Gospel according to Luke, Jesus' accusers said, "We found this man perverting our nation, forbidding us to pay taxes to the emperor, and saying that he himself is the Messiah, a king" (*Luke 23:2*). Pilate turned to Jesus and asked, "Are you the king of the Jews?" Jesus answered, "You say so" (*Luke 23:3*). Because of his answer, Jesus was charged with **treason** for claiming to be a king, a crime punishable by crucifixion. In the Gospel according to Mark, we read that Pilate traditionally offered to release one prisoner during the feast. Pilate suggested the release of the "King of the Jews." Three times Pilate tried to convince the crowd to demand Jesus' release, for he knew that the chief priests had handed Jesus over out of envy. However, the crowds demanded Jesus' crucifixion, so

Break Open the Word

Jesus and Pilate When Jesus was brought to trial, Pontius Pilate attempted in several ways to release Jesus. Read the following accounts of Pilate's actions with Jesus in each of the four Gospels:

Mark 15:6–15
Matthew 27:15–26
Luke 23:13–25
John 18:28–40

What does Pilate do in each account? What other characters are involved? How does Jesus respond? How do the crowds and the other characters respond? How is Jesus' fate ultimately determined?

Comparing the Gospels

Two events associated with the final hours of Jesus' life before the crucifixion are unique to the Gospels in which they appear. In Matthew 27:3–10, the story of the death of Judas is told, and in Luke 23:6–12, Jesus is taken before Herod. Read each narrative. Reflect on the significance each event adds to the total picture of the Passion and death of Jesus. What lessons can you learn from each event?

Pilate commanded it to be done and directed that an inscription be placed on the cross to read, "Jesus, the Nazarene, King of the Jews."

Peter's Denial of Jesus The author of Mark used the framing technique to recount Peter's denial of Jesus. Jesus before the Sanhedrin and Jesus before Pilate frame Peter's denial and enhance its significance. In a courtyard, Peter denied knowing Jesus to a servant girl of the high priest and then again to bystanders. After being accused a third time of knowing Jesus, "he began to curse, and he swore an oath, 'I do not know this man you are talking about.' At that moment the cock crowed for the second time. Then Peter remembered that Jesus had said to him, 'Before the cock crows twice, you will deny me three times.' And he broke down and wept" (*Mark 14:71–72*). Peter's denial appears in all four Gospels. He expressed sorrow immediately upon realizing what he had done, but he had still betrayed Jesus.

The Crucifixion of Jesus After his Jewish and Roman trials, Jesus was whipped. Weakened by the physical and psychological pain he endured, Jesus carried the heavy crossbeam of his cross on the ripped flesh of his shoulders.

Jesus was taken to Golgotha, a hill outside the city, where he was nailed to a cross. As he hung on the cross in excruciating pain, the crowds taunted him. Jesus afforded hope to others even in the midst of his own suffering. He was between two criminals, one of whom continually shouted at Jesus, "Are you not the Messiah? Save yourself and us!" The other criminal chastised the first saying, "Do you not fear God, since you are under the same sentence of condemnation? And we indeed have been condemned justly, for we are getting what we deserve for our deeds, but this man has done nothing wrong." The latter criminal repented and said, "Jesus, remember me when you come into your kingdom." To which Jesus replied, "Truly I tell you, today you will be with me in Paradise" (*Luke 23:39–43*).

Jesus did not die alone. Several times during the crucifixion Jesus called upon God, his Father. Jesus asked God to forgive those who crucified him: "Father, forgive them; for they do not know what they are doing" (*Luke 23:34*). And "then Jesus, crying with a loud voice, said, 'Father, into your hands I commend my spirit.' Having said this, he breathed his last" (*Luke 23:46*). The Church remembers these final hours of Jesus' life in a special way in the Good Friday liturgy.

Jesus Recognized as Promised Messiah As Jesus was dying on the cross, darkness enveloped the land. This darkness symbolized the power of evil that Jesus overcame through his death. As Jesus took his last breath, the centurion, a Roman soldier whose duty it was to ensure that Jesus died, said, "Truly this man was God's Son!" (*Mark 15:39*) This Gentile soldier recognized the identity of Jesus. The author of Mark wrote to a Gentile audience, and his message conveyed that Jesus is the savior of the world.

When light dawned the day after the Sabbath, the women who had witnessed Jesus' death went to the tomb where his body was laid. The Gospel according to Mark says that the Resurrection of Jesus had occurred before the women risked their safety in going to anoint his body at the tomb.

The women found the tomb empty, except for a young man sitting on the right side; the young man told them,

scripture

"Do not be alarmed; you are looking for Jesus of Nazareth, who was crucified. He has been raised; he is not here. Look, there is the place they laid him. But go, tell his disciples and Peter that he is going ahead of you to Galilee; there you will see him, just as he told you."

(Mark 16:6–7)

Over the next days, the women and the other disciples encountered the risen Jesus. They gave testimony to the Resurrection, and through their belief and proclamation, others came to call Jesus Lord, a sign of their belief in his divinity. From the time of the first disciples to the present, the Church marks Sunday as The Lord's Day, the day of Jesus' Resurrection and the principle day for celebrating the Eucharist.

Interpret the Art

Women of the Cross Salome, Mary Magdalene, and Mary the younger were present at the crucifixion of Jesus, for the other disciples had fled in fear.

How can you stand tall, despite your fears, when you are faced with a difficult decision or situation, as did the women present at the crucifixion?

Saint Pio of Pietrelcina

(1887–1968)

Born as Francesco Forgione to an Italian farming family, Padre Pio has become one of the most well known saints of the twentieth century. Padre Pio was devout, reserved, and ever aware of the suffering that goes on in the world and in the hearts of all people. He had an uncanny gift for knowing and understanding exactly what someone was about to confess to him during Reconciliation. He responded with kindness and gentleness to set hearts at ease. Padre Pio was so devoted to helping both sinners and devout souls alike that he often heard confessions for up to twelve hours a day.

Padre Pio would not only know the suffering of man, but also of the suffering of the Lord, Jesus Christ. Padre Pio received the stigmata—outward signs of the suffering of Jesus Christ during the crucifixion—when he was only 31 years old. He was praying one morning in 1918 when suddenly he was pierced as Christ was. The pain and suffering felt by Padre Pio from the pains in his hands, feet, and side reminded him daily of the suffering Christ endured on the cross. Many other saints throughout the ages have also had the stigmata, among them: Saint Francis of Assisi, Saint Catherine of Siena, and Saint John of God. Among all those who have received the stigmata—over sixty saints or blessed—Padre Pio is the only one who is also a priest.

The first response of Padre Pio when he received the stigmata was actually embarrassment. He never sought to draw undue attention to himself. In a short time, he became overjoyed that he could feel the true suffering of Christ in his life and come closer to understanding the mystery of the Passion and Resurrection of Christ. Padre Pio understood that the stigmata were a gift of suffering that he was to endure, and he accepted it unconditionally.

Padre Pio endured the stigmata for fifty years. What makes the stigmata received by Padre Pio all the more amazing is that when he died, there were no marks upon his body. The five locations—his hands, feet, and side—where Christ had been pierced by nail or lance were completely healed. This can be interpreted as a sign of the Resurrection that follows the crucifixion.

There are many things we can learn from Padre Pio: grace and humility when presented great suffering, peace and gentleness with those seeking forgiveness, and prayer as an answer to all problems.

Prayer

Begin by praying the Sign of the Cross.

Leader: We read about the image Mark presents of Jesus as the Suffering Servant. This image was prophesied by Isaiah. Let us read together Isaiah 53:7–8.

All: He was oppressed, and he was
afflicted,
    yet he did not open his mouth;
like a lamb that is led to the
    slaughter,
    and like a sheep that before its
        shearers is silent,
    so he did not open his mouth.
By a perversion of justice he was
    taken away.
    Who could have imagined his
        future?
For he was cut off from the land
    of the living,
    stricken for the transgression
        of my people.

Leader: I now invite the first reader to come forward.

Reader: (Read aloud John 1:29–32.)

Leader: I now invite the second reader to come forward.

Reader: (Read aloud Mark 15:1–5.)

Leader: We see how the Lord suffered in silence for our sins. Now we ask, silently, that our sins be forgiven.

Leader: Now we pray together . . .

All: Lamb of God, you take away the
    sin of the world:
    have mercy on us.
Lamb of God, you take away the
    sin of the world:
    have mercy on us.
Lamb of God, you take away the
    sin of the world:
    grant us peace. Amen.

End by praying the Sign of the Cross.

Review

1. What is the focus of the Gospel according to Mark? Describe the similarities between the followers and the opponents of Jesus.

2. Describe the difference between a believer and a disciple.

3. Describe the two writing patterns in Mark that convey the story of the life of Jesus.

4. How does the parable of the sower relate to the call of discipleship?

5. What can we learn from the call narratives of Jesus? What is the mission Jesus calls us to continue?

6. What were the professions of the first four disciples? What did Jesus tell the disciples he wanted them to do if they followed him?

7. Describe the messianic mystery.

8. How was the Transfiguration of Jesus a moment of calming and explanation in the midst of confusion among the disciples? What does the Transfiguration ultimately point to?

9. Why is the story of Bartimaeus a true example of what discipleship is? What roles do wealth, power, and position play in discipleship? How do these rank in the kingdom of God?

10. Describe the events in which Jesus initiated the new and everlasting covenant.

11. What was the response of the crowd as Jesus entered Jerusalem? What was the response of the crowd when Pilate asked what to do with Jesus?

12. At the time of Jesus' death, who were the only ones who did not desert him? Who recognized Jesus' true identity? Why was that significant to Mark's audience?

Key Words

blasphemy (p. 115)—To falsely proclaim oneself as God, to falsely claim to have the attributes of God, or to insult God or his name.

conversion experience (p. 111)—An experience that turns us toward God and away from sin and encourages us to search to understand and do what God desires of us.

discipleship (p. 101)—A life rooted in Jesus, also a life rooted in the Church.

Eucharist (p. 113)—The sacrament of Jesus' Body and Blood, truly and really present under the appearances of the bread and wine.

Paschal mystery (p. 112)—Christ's work of redemption through his Passion, death, Resurrection, and Ascension.

threefold pattern (p. 99)—A writing technique, notably used by Mark, to emphasize particular subjects, such as the declarations of Jesus as the Son of God.

Transfiguration (p. 108)—The culminating moment in the public life of Jesus. Jesus' appearance changed in the presence of his disciples, and Elijah and Moses appeared beside him to reveal him as the true Messiah. This event points toward the Resurrection of Jesus.

treason (p. 115)—An attempt or desire to overthrow and replace the head of the government to which one owes allegiance.

Teen to Teen

When people don't understand who you really are inside, they assume certain things about you. This happened with Jesus through his life. The crowds did not know how to react to Jesus—they either rejoiced in his miracles or feared and reviled him when he was finally arrested and crucified. Those who knew him—his disciples and followers—were slow to understand him, but even in knowing him, they had their doubts. How do you show who you really are to people who don't know you by your actions and words?

"I don't think there's anything special or out of the ordinary that I do. I try to just be myself, be the person that the Beatitudes teach us to be."

Ricardo B.

"I think the best way to show who I really am is to help people I don't know any way I can. There was a new guy who came to our school about half way through the year, so he really didn't know where to go, and I showed him around. I helped him get caught up with class work, too."

Heather P.

Personal Challenge

Share the identity of Jesus with your classmates. Create wristbands that feature a verse from the Gospel of Mark in which Jesus is identified. Share your wristbands with your parents or friends in other classes to let them truly know Jesus.

Break Open the Word

Identifying Jesus Read Mark 8:29. The disciples name several prophets, but none are correct. Peter finally correctly identifies Jesus as the Messiah. Identify the verses in Mark that you would share with someone who has never read the Bible to show the identity of Jesus.

A.D. 14–37
Tiberius ruler
over Roman Empire

A.D. 28–29
John the Baptist's active ministry

A.D. 33
Crucifixion, death, and
Resurrection of Jesus

A.D. 54
Nero's rise to
power as emperor
of Roman Empire

A.D. 14–37

A.D. 47

A.D. 26–36 Pontius Pilate
the Roman procurator
over Judea and Samaria

A.D. 29
Jesus' baptism; beginning
of his public ministry

c. A.D. 50
First Pauline Letters written

Called to Justice

"[L]ove the Lord your God with all your heart, . . . soul, . . . strength, . . . and mind; and your neighbor as yourself."

Luke 10:27

Chapter Goals

In this chapter, you will:

- learn about the background and unique features of the Gospel according to Luke.

- consider the role of love, forgiveness, and prayer in being a disciple.

- explore Jesus' compassion for those who are poor, sick, sinners, and outcasts.

- examine the importance of table fellowship.

- learn about Blessed Kateri Tekakwitha.

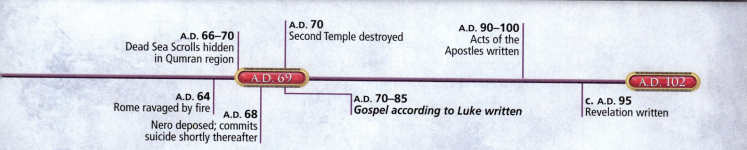

A.D. 66–70
Dead Sea Scrolls hidden in Qumran region

A.D. 70
Second Temple destroyed

A.D. 90–100
Acts of the Apostles written

A.D. 64
Rome ravaged by fire

A.D. 68
Nero deposed; commits suicide shortly thereafter

A.D. 70–85
Gospel according to Luke written

c. A.D. 95
Revelation written

A.D. 69

A.D. 102

The Gospel According to Luke

The Gospel according to Luke stretches us to open our hearts, souls, and minds to see the presence of God. The author of the Gospel challenges us to identify anything that keeps us from seeing God's presence and to remove it from our attitudes and behaviors. This Gospel reminds us that the natural response to loving God is loving our neighbor. From love of God and love of neighbor stem justice—giving people what is their due: respecting their rights, honoring their dignity as human beings, and working to ensure that the needs and rights of all people are met. This message of justice is fundamental to understanding the Gospel according to Luke.

The commandment to love God with all one's heart, soul, and might makes up part of the **Shema**, the Jewish profession of faith. (See *Deuteronomy 6:4–9*.) Many faithful Jews of Jesus' time recited this statement of faith at least twice daily; many Jews do the same today. Although the Shema is an easy passage to remember and pray, we read in the Gospel according to Luke that it is not an easy verse to live. However, Jesus made this Scripture come alive—he embodied its meaning. For Jesus, it was a Scripture he lived out.

Overview of the Gospel

The same author wrote both the Gospel according to Luke and the Acts of the Apostles. Some now believe that the Acts of the Apostles might have been written first. Comprising more than a quarter of the New Testament, these two books form the largest contribution by any one author. However, sometime during the second century, what was one body of work was split into two books. Because of this, many do not fully appreciate the interrelationship between the writings and how issues raised in the Gospel according to Luke are continued in the Acts of the Apostles.

Authorship and Date As with the Gospels according to Matthew and Mark, the author of the Gospel according to Luke remains anonymous, although the work is attributed to Luke the Evangelist. Most biblical scholars agree that the author of this Gospel was a well-educated Gentile who wrote the Gospel between A.D. 70 and 85.

The name Luke does not appear in either the Gospel according to Luke or the Acts of the Apostles. However, three references to someone named Luke exist in other books in the New Testament. Colossians 4:14 refers to "Luke, the 'beloved physician.'" In Philemon, verse 24, Paul refers to Luke as one of his "fellow workers." In 2 Timothy 4:11, Paul again alludes to Luke as one of his companions. Is this Luke the Evangelist, who wrote the

Faith Activity

Love of Neighbor

1. How do you show your love for God?
2. Who do you consider to be your neighbor?
3. Have you ever had to stretch yourself to accept a person?
4. What are the risks involved in accepting those people who are different from you or who have different opinions or ideas than you have?

Gospel and Acts of the Apostles? While the early Church and some today hold this belief, others say we cannot know for certain that this Luke authored the Gospel.

Audience and Location The author of the Gospel of Luke probably wrote in Greece. People who heard this Gospel were mostly Gentiles who did not face the same problems as the people in the communities associated with Mark and Matthew. Where many of the struggles in Mark and Matthew concerned outside forces, the struggles the community faced in Luke were from within. The Gentile community had to confront the inner obstacles that kept them from being a true community of faith.

The author of Luke-Acts, as most scholars refer to the two books when discussing them as a single composition, addressed his writings to Theophilus, which means "Beloved of God." We do not know whether the author was writing to an actual person or to a group of people—a community of faith. The symbol of the Gospel of Luke is an ox because the Gospel opens with Zechariah performing his priestly duties in the Temple; an ox was one of the animals that priests sacrificed in the Temple.

Explore the Land

Greece This map shows the Greek peninsula and its many islands, including Crete. The author of Luke likely wrote from one of the larger cities in Greece.

What advantages were present for the author of Luke by writing from a central location such as Greece? By which route do you think Luke arrived in Greece?

SHEMA

The Shema is the greatest expression of Jewish faith. We cannot directly compare it to any prayers in Christianity. The Apostle's Creed is a strong expression of our faith, but we generally do not repeat it when we rise in the morning and when we go to sleep. Nor do we pray it in the moments that precede death. From an early age, Jews are expected to know and to pray the Shema at least twice daily. Jesus, as a Jew, prayed the Shema as well. The Shema reads:

scripture

"Hear, O Israel: The LORD is our God, the LORD alone. You shall love the LORD your God with all your heart, and with all your soul, and with all your might. Keep these words that I am commanding you today in your heart. Recite them to your children and talk about them when you are at home and when you are away, when you lie down and when you rise. Bind them as a sign upon your hand, fix them as an emblem on your forehead, and write them on the doorposts of your house and on your gates."

Deuteronomy 6:4–9

The synoptic Gospels record Jesus' references to the beginning of the Shema. (See *Matthew 22:34–40, Mark 12:29–33, Luke 10:25–28*.) These references appear in different settings in each Gospel, but the message is always the same. Jesus reaffirms that love of the Lord is the greatest commandment and is required to inherit eternal life. He states: "You shall love the Lord your God with all your heart, and with all your soul, and with all your strength, and with all your mind; and your neighbor as yourself" (*Luke 10:27*). Jesus expands upon this teaching in the Gospel of Luke with the parable of the Good Samaritan.

In Mark and Matthew, scribes, Sadducees, or Pharisees ask Jesus which commandment is the greatest. In these instances, as with many other challenges from these groups, Jesus responds by citing the Old Testament and then expanding upon the teaching.

Connect to the Past

Hear, O Israel Because the Shema is among the oldest prayers in Judaism, it is found on handwritten parchment scrolls that are thousands of years old.
Try to find out where the oldest copy of the Bible is in your community; see if you can organize a trip to see it.

Theological Perspectives and Themes

Luke is the only non-Jewish Evangelist—a Gentile writing to Gentiles. He traced Jesus' birth back to Adam to portray Jesus as the Savior of all, Jews and Gentiles alike. The author regarded salvation history, the saving action of God through time, as the *ongoing* work of the Holy Spirit, and Luke-Acts portrays Jesus' journey through history. Beginning with Jesus in Mary's womb and ending with his death in Jerusalem, the story continues into Acts. Led by the Holy Spirit, the Church—the Mystical Body of Christ—spreads Jesus' message to Rome, and then to the ends of the earth.

Because Gentiles from around the Roman Empire comprised his audience, the author of Luke seemed concerned about connecting the story of Jesus to the broader historical context of the empire. In Luke the Infancy Narrative of Jesus is connected to world leaders—King Herod, Emperor Augustus, Emperor Tiberius, Pontius Pilate—perhaps to indicate that Jesus' actions affect all of world history. (See *Luke 1:5*; *2:1–2*; *3:1–2*.) The author of the Gospel according to Luke also connects historical events to events in Jesus' life. For example, in Luke 2:3–4, 6, he writes that the world census ordered by the Roman Emperor Augustus was the reason Mary and Joseph were in Bethlehem when Jesus was born.

The Holy Spirit plays a major role in the Gospel of Luke. The author constantly alludes to the gift and the role of the Holy Spirit. He writes that Jesus, Mary, and John the Baptist are all filled with the Holy Spirit. (See *Luke 4:1*; *1:41*; *1:15, 80*.) The Holy Spirit also has the same importance in Acts. Luke makes it clear that the Holy Spirit continues in our midst as we live the mission of Jesus and the mission of the Church in our daily lives. The Holy Spirit in and through the Church continues the work of salvation.

At the time Luke was written, many believed that the **Parousia** was about to happen. The Parousia is the second coming of Christ at the end of time, when God's plan for salvation is accomplished and humanity is glorified. At this time, the Last Judgment will take place. The Gospel according to Luke takes up this theme of the Parousia and cautions readers to be aware that the end is coming, although not as soon as some expected. The author tells readers to concentrate on the importance of living every day in this world in the manner of Jesus.

break open the Word

Jesus' Travels Read the following scripture verses. List the names of places or the general locations that Jesus visited while on the way to Jerusalem:

Luke 13:22

Luke 17:11

Luke 19:1

Faith Activity

Discussion How can you live every day in this world as Jesus did? Who are the outcasts of society that need your help most? Find three verses in Luke where Jesus cares for those who are the outcasts of society, and then apply what he does to your life and your mission in the world.

The unique perspective of Jesus in Luke concentrates on Jesus' attributes of prayer, mercy, forgiveness, compassion, and joy. Jesus is shown to be the savior of those who need him most—the outcasts of society, or those who are poor, rejected, sinners, persecuted, or sick. Luke thus reverses the expectations of the world—those who are humble and powerless are chosen and used to bring about salvation. Luke's stories and parables instruct the reader on the importance of a complete generosity—one that wipes out the evils of poverty, sickness, sin, and death.

Throughout the Gospel of Luke, the author lays out a key part of being a follower of Jesus—a person who cares for the needs of others, especially those who were rejected by society.

Structure of the Gospel The action in the Gospel according to Luke moves the reader toward the city of Jerusalem. Why is Jerusalem so central to this Gospel? The city and its Temple had significant historical importance for Judaism and later for Christianity. Jesus died and rose from the dead in Jerusalem. Christianity was born in Jerusalem.

The Eight Sections of Luke
The Prologue (Luke 1:1–4)
The Infancy Narrative (Luke 1:5—2:52)
The Preparation for the Public Ministry (Luke 3:1—4:13)
The Ministry in Galilee (Luke 4:14—9:50)
The Journey to Jerusalem: Luke's Travel Narrative (Luke 9:51—19:27)
The Teaching Ministry in Jerusalem (Luke 19:28—21:38)
The Passion Narrative (Luke 22:1—23:56)
The Resurrection Narrative (Luke 24:1–53)

The "journey to Jerusalem" theme in the Gospel of Luke begins with the Infancy Narrative. Even though Jesus was born in Bethlehem, Mary and Joseph took Jesus "up to Jerusalem to present him to the Lord" in the Temple (*Luke 2:22*). When Jesus was twelve years old, Jesus, Mary, and Joseph went to the Temple in Jerusalem as was their custom to celebrate the feast of Passover. After he had been lost for several days in Jerusalem, Mary and Joseph found Jesus in the Temple "sitting among the teachers, listening to them, and asking them questions" (*Luke 2:41–51*).

Further, in Luke 9:51, the author solemnly announces that the journey toward Jesus' death in Jerusalem is beginning. Throughout later chapters in Luke, the author makes a number of references to Jesus' working his way toward Jerusalem where he will fulfill his mission. Jesus' journey ends when he arrives in Jerusalem. (See *Luke 19:28*.) After Jesus' Resurrection, all his appearances are within or near Jerusalem.

The Response of Love

The Gospel according to Luke includes several famous passages that challenge our concept of love. Jesus requires his followers to love God and neighbor as he does—to go beyond their own needs and to care for the needs and the well-being of others.

We rely on the power of God for strength and courage in situations where it is difficult to help someone—especially if we find the person difficult to love. However, prayer and the guidance of the Holy Spirit can strengthen us to love. Love also demands forgiveness. We can find all aspects of love in the parable of the prodigal son.

Model of Forgiveness and Love

Only the Gospel according to Luke includes the parable of the prodigal son, also known as the parable of the forgiving father. This parable is part of a pattern of three stories: the lost sheep, the lost coin, and the lost son. All three share a theme: there is a loss, something is found, and there is a celebration.

Jesus told these parables to the scribes and the Pharisees to teach them valuable lessons about human life and God the Father's forgiveness, acceptance, and love. Each story expresses the joy of finding something or someone who is lost. God embraces the lost sinner with loving and forgiving arms. Jesus challenged the religious leaders to show great compassion and forgiveness to the people— their neighbors—whom they had not cared for, had rejected, and had been prejudiced toward.

Faith Activity

Group Discussion Form small groups, read Luke 15:11–32, and discuss the following questions:

1. Select a character from the parable of the prodigal son. What is the pain and hope in this character?

2. Recall and share a time when you felt overwhelming forgiveness.

3. Recall and share a time you forgave someone.

▶ The Prodigal Son, Albert Museum, London, Great Britain.

A Lesson Learned Like the older brother in the parable of the prodigal son, we often have our minds made up about how things ought to be done. We have our own ideas about the treatment of others and about who deserves our love and respect. To really love our neighbors, we have to go beyond our prejudices.

This story also reminds us of the nature of sin in our lives. **Sin** is an offense against God—any word, action, or thought contrary to God's law. Sin weakens, and at times can even break, our relationship with God. Sin often results when we act out of selfish desires and cannot resist the temptation to disobey God's will. The process of acknowledging our sin, expressing sorrow for our sin, and being open to receiving God's loving forgiveness can lead us to a new life with God and others. Just as the father in the parable totally and unconditionally forgave his son, God the Father totally and unconditionally forgives our sins, failings, and shortcomings if we are truly sorry. We can seek and receive this forgiveness in the Sacrament of Penance and Reconciliation. We receive grace, are restored to relationship with God and others, and are strengthened to choose the good.

Just as God forgives our sins, we are called to forgive others. God's grace gives us the courage to forgive others just as we have been forgiven. Can we show the same love and forgiveness to our neighbors that the father showed to his son? Or will we react like the older brother who questioned the unconditional love and forgiveness of the father?

Mary: Model of Perfect Love

In the Gospel according to Luke, we learn about Mary as the perfect disciple—not only because she is the Mother of Jesus, but also because of her faith in God. Mary is the model of perfect love as she responds completely to God the Father's love and to his call. God chose an ordinary, poor, and very young woman to be the Mother of the Son of God. "Mary is truly 'Mother of God' since she is the mother of the eternal Son of God made man, who is God himself." (*Catechism of the Catholic Church, 509*) Mary responds to God's call with self-surrender and trusting faith in him.

The Unexpected Scholars believe Mary was between the ages of fifteen and seventeen when she received the announcement that she was to be the Mother of Jesus. Both she and Joseph must have been confused about the turn their lives had taken. Yet they were willing to be open to the divine will of God, despite the questions and the ridicule it might bring.

When the angel Gabriel announced to Mary that she would give birth to the Son of the Most High, she responded, "How can this be, since I am a virgin?" (*Luke 1:34*). The Holy Spirit made this possible. And Mary, through her entire life, remained a virgin. Mary's acceptance of the Lord's will at the Annunciation shows how she actively participates with the work of her Son, Jesus.

Faith Activity

Taking Risks Mary took risks to follow God's will. The life of faith can be risky at times. As you look at your own life, answer the following questions:

1. What part of following your faith involves risk?
2. What fears keep you from taking risks?
3. For whom would you risk everything?
4. What is God asking you to do that is risky?

▼ Statue of Mary

Honoring Mary

Mary loved Jesus with a mother's love. Mary is also our mother and the Mother of the Church. She understands when we are confused and uncertain about the unexpected experiences of our lives. We can turn to her in prayer, for she understands our struggles. The example of her life can teach us how to trust in and love God. Mary was centered on doing God's will. Her life invites us to do the same.

The Church honors Mary as the most special and first saint. We celebrate many feast days for Mary throughout the Church, and we have numerous prayers to venerate her, especially the Hail Mary. The first two lines of the Hail Mary come from the words the Angel Gabriel spoke to Mary. In doing so, Gabriel ministered God's favor to Mary, the mother of God and announced salvation to all people through the fruit of her womb, Jesus. Angels are spiritual creatures who give glory to God and bring news of salvation.

Many parish churches and family homes have statues of Mary, and some parishes honor Mary in a special way during May and October.

Praying the rosary—and the accompanying blessed rosary beads—is perhaps one of the most popular Marian devotions. The rosary consists of praying decades of Hail Marys, along with the Lord's Prayer and the Gloria Patri, while meditating on a different mystery of the rosary. See page 253 for a full description of how to pray the rosary. Historical records do not give us a clear picture of when this practice began, but in the thirteenth century, Saint Dominic preached a form of the rosary in France. Evidence appears to connect the modern rosary to a Dominican priest in the late fourteenth century.

Connect to the Past

The Rosary Throughout the ages, artisans and craftspeople have crafted rosaries out of many materials: ceramic, crystal, glass, wood, and even plastic in modern times. Most rosaries are blessed by a bishop or a monsignor.
Look at the rosary beads pictured here. In what ways do they differ from the rosary beads you own?

 *Faith* **Activity**

God's Plan God had a special plan for Mary. What do you think God the Father's plan is for you? How can you trust God's plan and follow Jesus? How has the Holy Spirit empowered you to say "yes" to God's plan?

Source of Courage and Strength

The Gospel of Luke refers to the Holy Spirit more than the other synoptic Gospels do. The Holy Spirit was with Jesus from conception through infancy, childhood, baptism, temptation, and the beginning of his public ministry. The following passages from the Gospel according to Luke are examples of the emphasis placed on the Holy Spirit:

The Holy Spirit in the Gospel of Luke	
Luke 1:15	Before birth, John the Baptist is filled with the Holy Spirit.
Luke 1:35	Jesus is conceived by the power of the Holy Spirit.
Luke 1:41	John's mother, Elizabeth, is filled with the Holy Spirit.
Luke 1:67	John's father, Zechariah, is filled with the Holy Spirit.
Luke 2:26	The Holy Spirit reveals to Simeon that he will see the Messiah before his death.
Luke 3:16	John the Baptist announces that someone more powerful than he is will baptize with the Holy Spirit and fire.
Luke 3:22	At Jesus' baptism, the Holy Spirit descends as a dove.
Luke 4:1–14	Jesus, "full of the Holy Spirit," is led by the Spirit into the wilderness to be tempted for forty days; Jesus resists the devil's temptations and returns to Galilee with the "power of the Spirit."

As the nature of Jesus' mission unfolds, he preaches that God's plan is being fulfilled among his listeners. His mission does not focus on himself, but on others. So it must be for those who choose to follow him.

scripture

"When he came to Nazareth, where he had been brought up, he went to the synagogue on the sabbath day, as was his custom. He stood up to read, and the scroll of the prophet Isaiah was given to him. He unrolled the scroll and found the place where it was written:

'The Spirit of the Lord is upon
     me,
  because he has anointed me
     to bring good news to the
     poor.
He has sent me to proclaim
     release to the captives
and recovery of sight to the
     blind,
     to let the oppressed go free,
to proclaim the year of the
     Lord's favor.'

And he rolled up the scroll, gave it back to the attendant, and sat down. The eyes of all in the synagogue were fixed on him. Then he began to say to them, 'Today this scripture has been fulfilled in your hearing.'"

Luke 4:16–21

With these words, Jesus began his public ministry. The Holy Spirit was with Jesus at the beginning and throughout his ministry. The work of these two persons of the Holy Trinity cannot be separated. Where one is, so is the other.

Our Guide The Holy Spirit remains with us always, too. He gives us courage and strength to do the will of God. He empowers us to show the love and forgiveness that the followers of Jesus are called to bring to the world. The Holy Spirit guides us in the ways and times of prayer, helping us to hear and act on his word. The gifts of the Holy Spirit that we received in the sacraments of Baptism and Confirmation continue to guide us on our journey as followers of Jesus Christ. Each gift helps us grow more deeply in our love for God and for others and respond in love to the needs of others.

The Holy Spirit guides and empowers the Catholic Church. As members of the Church we receive the Holy Spirit who enables us to proclaim the Good News of Jesus and to do great works of love and forgiveness. Jesus said in Nazareth, "The Spirit of the Lord is upon me, . . ." (*Luke 4:18*). As members of the Catholic Church, we know that the Holy Spirit has come upon us. We are challenged to do the will of God and respond in love to our neighbors.

Faith Activity

Discussion
1. Share a story of a time when you took a risk in accepting a person or how you took a risk in forgiving or loving another person.
2. How does the Church show forgiveness and love in the world?

The Trinity and the Church Throughout the New Testament, the authors refer to what the Church came to call the Trinity—the Father, Son, and Holy Spirit working in the lives of the people in the early Church. Guided by the power of the Holy Spirit, the Church grew and spread the Good News of Jesus Christ, the Son of God. The people of the early Church came to a fuller understanding of God's presence among them and his works through them.

Being called into relationship with God means finding God, being one with him. It means living in communion with the Blessed Trinity in mutual love. It also means developing a relationship with God the Father, God the Son, and God the Holy Spirit. Finding God helps us find our purpose, or meaning, in life.

The Church defined itself as being one with God the Father, Son, and Holy Spirit, and the Trinity is still central to the Church's belief and practice today. At Mass we affirm our belief in the Trinity when we profess the Nicene Creed: "We believe in the Holy Spirit, the Lord, the giver of life, who proceeds from the Father and the Son, with the Father and the Son he is worshiped and glorified. He has spoken through the Prophets." In the Glory to the Father—or lesser doxology—we say, "Glory to the Father, and to the Son, and to the Holy Spirit." Each time we bless ourselves with the Sign of the Cross, we pray, "In the name of the Father, and of the Son, and of the Holy Spirit." We are blessed with the sign of the cross at our Baptism. On the Sunday following Pentecost Sunday, the Church celebrates the Feast of the Blessed Trinity.

◀ A teenager paints as part of a program for troubled teens.

Confirmation

The second Sacrament of Initiation is **Confirmation**. Through Confirmation we are sealed with the gifts of the Holy Spirit. In some churches we may choose a Confirmation name—usually that of a saintly person—that reflects a special meaning in our lives.

In the Sacrament of Confirmation, the bishop extends his hands over the candidate—the person who will be confirmed—and invokes the Holy Spirit through prayer. The bishop lays his hand on the forehead of the candidate and anoints it with chrism. While anointing the candidate, the bishop says, "(Name), be sealed with the Gift of the Holy Spirit." Like the anointing in Baptism, this anointing leaves an indelible character, or seal, on the candidate's soul; this character never goes away, no matter what happens in our lives. For this reason, both Baptism and Confirmation cannot be received twice.

On Pentecost the Apostles received the full outpouring of the Holy Spirit. We too receive this outpouring during Confirmation. It strengthens and deepens the grace received during Baptism. Through Confirmation we are united more closely to Christ, rooted more deeply as children of God, and increased in the gifts of the Holy Spirit. Our bond with the Church is perfected, and we receive a special strength of the Holy Spirit to spread and defend the faith. Our actions and our words as true witnesses of Christ help us boldly confess the name of Christ.

Below are the **Gifts of the Holy Spirit**, as well as references to the Spirit of the Lord in the Old Testament.

Wisdom	Proverbs 2:6
Understanding	Psalm 119:34
Wonder and Awe	Isaiah 29:23
Knowledge	Isaiah 11:9
Reverence	Psalm 96:9
Right Judgment	Isaiah 28:29
Courage	Psalm 17:14

Faith Activity

Gifts Alive Today Read the scripture verse for each reference to the Spirit of the Lord in the Old Testament listed on this page. Answer the following questions, and discuss those answers in your group:

1. Which of these gifts is most alive in you at this time? Which needs to be more alive?
2. Which of these gifts is most alive in your family? Which needs to be more alive?

Prayer In the Gospel of Luke, the disciples ask Jesus to teach them to pray. Read the following passages and note what Jesus teaches about prayer:

Luke 11:5–13

Luke 18:1–8

Luke 18:9–14

Jesus in Prayer

We read in Luke that Jesus prayed at each major point in his ministry. He prayed after he was baptized, before he called his disciples, as he predicted his Passion to the disciples, and in the garden the night before he died. He even prayed on the cross. Prayer was central to all that Jesus did. Through prayer Jesus received strength and gave honor and glory to God the Father.

The disciples recognized the power of prayer and asked Jesus to teach them how to pray. On one occasion they asked, "Lord, teach us to pray, as John taught his disciples" (*Luke 11:1–4*). At this time, Jesus taught the disciples the Our Father. In that same prayer, we ask God the Father to give us what we need each day—"our daily bread," to forgive our sins, and to give us the courage and strength to forgive others. (See *Luke 11:3*.) Even without their asking, Jesus taught the disciples "about their need to pray always and not to lose heart" (*Luke 18:1*).

Jesus encouraged his disciples to pray for whatever they needed and to not become discouraged. He taught them to be persistent in their prayer to God and to know that God the Father would give them what they needed.

The Power of Prayer

Prayer was a source of strength for the disciples. While at prayer, the disciples received the gift of the Holy Spirit, who enabled them to do courageous things. Prayer does the same thing for us; it is a source of strength and courage for us. Through prayer we encounter the Trinity. God the Father gives us the Holy Spirit if we ask him. Through the power of the Holy Spirit, we can follow Jesus.

In the Catholic Church, we come to understand and appreciate the fullness of prayer. We activate our sense of mutual belonging and of being part of the Church through personal, communal, and liturgical prayer. Through prayer we learn more about God the Father, God the Son, and God the Holy Spirit. We develop in prayer a deeper relationship with the Holy Trinity. Prayer begins with God's invitation to us. We respond with a desire to listen to God. God is with us when we pray and God helps us to pray. Our prayer begins and ends with God.

Through prayer and the sacraments, we receive the grace and the courage to respond in love to God and others. With God in our midst, we pray with others in petition for what we need, in thanksgiving for what we have already received, in praise for all that God has done, in intercession for God's help, and in sorrow and forgiveness for what we have failed to do.

▼ A worshiper bows his head in prayer near a statue of Christ.

Who Is My Neighbor?

The Jewish people of Jesus' time had clear rules about the ways they interacted with others. They established some of those rules to keep themselves "pure" from the outside culture, and established others within the context of Judaism as dietary laws and laws for ritual purity. By his words and deeds, Jesus established the law of love as the only path to completely loving God and neighbor.

In all of the Gospels we see how Jesus addressed the needs of a diverse group of people. Because of the cultural and religious boundaries of the time, society considered many of the groups outcasts. For Jesus, boundaries did not exist. He considered everyone worthy of love and respect. He calls his followers to treat all people with dignity and justice.

 War often brings poverty, malnutrition, disease, and famine. These people are standing outside of a burned-out building in a shantytown near Albania's capital.

Jesus Welcomes Those Who Are Outcasts

The ancient world had no middle class. Those who were rich and those who were poor divided society, with wealth concentrated in the hands of a few. Widespread poverty was a reality of everyday living. The author of the Gospel of Luke, more than the other Evangelists, challenged the rich. In many ways Christianity had its origins and growth in the poor and lower classes. It changed society not from above, but from below.

Anawim The poorest people of the Jewish population were the *anawim*. **Anawim**, which means "People of the Land," has it roots in the Scriptures of the Hebrew people. The prophets, in particular, condemned the oppression of those who were poor and told people that living in right relationship with God required sharing their resources with those who were poor. For the most part, the anawim could not read or write, which made it challenging for them to follow their religion and its codes. They had menial jobs such as shepherding.

The Gospel according to Luke, however, gives shepherds a significant role at its beginning. They were the first to hear of the birth of Jesus. While the shepherds tended their flocks, an angel of the Lord appeared to them to proclaim the Good News that the Messiah had been born. They "went with haste" to Bethlehem and "found Mary and Joseph, and the child lying in the manger," and then were given the mission to make "known what had been told them" (*Luke 2:8–18*).

Faith Activity

Discussion Discuss the following questions:

1. Why do you think people treat others as outcasts?
2. Whom does today's society consider as outcasts?
3. What do these groups have in common?
4. How can you show respect for those who are mistreated by society?

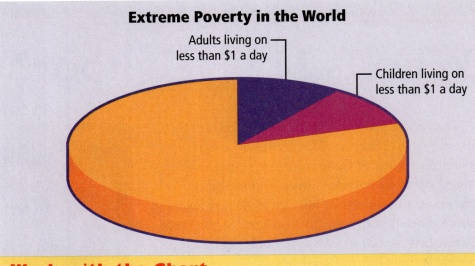

Extreme Poverty in the World

Adults living on less than $1 a day

Children living on less than $1 a day

Work with the Chart

Poverty Each day in the developing world, 30,000 children die from mostly preventable causes such as respiratory infections and measles.
What could you do to alleviate the poverty of one child? What does your church do to alleviate poverty?

The Sick During this time, most people thought that evil caused illness. Thus, healthy people feared those who were sick and did not want to have contact with them. Others believed sickness was a punishment from God for their sins or the sins of their ancestors. Those who were ill were not allowed in the Temple. Jesus challenged those practices. He cured many ailments of the sick and told them their suffering was not a result of sinfulness.

Among the sick, lepers received some of the worst treatment. Leprosy is a bacterial disease that affects the skin, nerves, and muscles. If left untreated, leprosy causes paralysis and eventual death. People in Jesus' time feared contracting this disease, and the New Testament refers to it several times. Lepers were treated as outcasts and believed to be ritually impure. Lepers were forced to live apart from society because people did not want to be near them. Jesus, however, associated with and ate with lepers. On one occasion, Jesus cured a leper by stretching out his hand and touching him. (See *Luke 5:12–16.*)

Slaves The Greco-Roman society at the time of Jesus accepted slavery as an economic and social institution. Any free person had a legal right to own a slave. Even some Jews and Christians owned slaves. Usually, slaves were people captured in war or those who were unable to pay their debts. Slaves performed various tasks, including farming, domestic help, artisan work, and cooking. Although Jesus' teaching did not change the structure of slavery, he used parables to insist on a nonabusive relationship between owners and slaves.

Sinners and Prostitutes Both the Old and the New Testament include references to sinners and prostitutes. Some Gospel passages show prostitution as part of the culture in first-century Palestine. Jewish law detailed severe punishment for prostitution, but the Greco-Roman culture did not. Matthew 21:31 refers to Jesus' view of prostitutes. While Jesus spent time with sinners and prostitutes, he told them to sin no more. It was these sinners who were contrite for their sin, had a firm purpose of amendment, and accepted the forgiveness offered to them by Christ that were entering the Kingdom of God.

Tax Collectors The Romans hired Jews to collect the emperor's taxes. They collected money by taxing goods transported on the roads. Some tax collectors charged additional fees and kept the profits. Most people intensely disliked tax collectors. Jesus, however, invited the tax collector Levi to become one of his disciples. Jesus told the tax collector Zacchaeus that because he was a generous man, salvation had come to his house. (See *Luke 19:9*.)

Samaritans The Samaritans lived in Samaria, an area between Judaea and Galilee. Assyria had conquered the inhabitants of this land and sent them into exile. A few Israelites remained and intermarried with the foreign occupants. Other Jews then considered Samaritans to have "mixed blood" and treated them like outcasts. The Gospel according to Luke recounts the parable of the Good Samaritan. In John 4, Jesus chooses to reveal his identity to a Samaritan woman.

Women Jesus lived in a patriarchal society that marginalized women, who had limited legal rights and no political rights. In Luke, women have a prominence they do not have in other Gospels. By his words and actions, Jesus reversed the cultural norms of his day. He recognized the dignity of women and the importance of their roles in caring for children and providing for the needs of their families.

Faith Sharing

Group Discussion How we treat our neighbors affects our life, our neighbors' lives, and the lives of generations to come. When we die, we will be judged on how we have lived and the effects our lives have had on the world.

Take two sheets of paper; on one sheet, list the names of five people who have caused suffering in the world. On the other sheet of paper, list five people who have done great good in the world.

In your faith-sharing group, discuss the people each person chose to list. We can have a profound effect on others by recognizing suffering and working to ease it. How can your group ease suffering in your community?

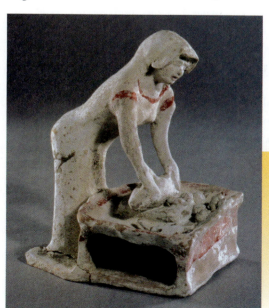

Interpret the Art

Respect Woman kneading bread on top of a square slab, Greek, from Aulis, c. 500–475 B.C. Women usually had the arduous task of preparing and serving meals.
How did Jesus reject the traditional role of women at this time? How can you show respect for people that others have rejected?

Break Open the Word

Women in Luke In the following Scripture quotes, note the names of the women mentioned. Describe their roles:

Luke 1:5–7, 24, 26–38, 57–66
Luke 2:5–7, 36–38
Luke 7:11–17
Luke 8:1–3
Luke 23:27–31, 49, 55–56
Luke 24:1–10

Meeting the Needs of Others

We must put our love for God into action by loving our neighbors. This involves risk and sometimes rejection. The parable of the Good Samaritan illustrates the importance of putting our love for God into action by loving our neighbor.

A lawyer first posed several questions to Jesus. Ultimately, Jesus led the lawyer to answer his own questions. Jesus shocked the lawyer and his listeners because Jesus knew that his listeners hated and distrusted Samaritans, yet this is the person who helped the stranger. How could the enemy they hate turn out to be the hero in this story? Jesus pushed the definition of neighbor far beyond the normal understanding of the term and cast aside restrictions on who their neighbor was. Jesus taught them that the law of love had no boundaries.

The Good Samaritan

Narrator: Just then a lawyer stood up to test Jesus.

Lawyer: Teacher, what must I do to inherit eternal life?

Jesus: What is written in the law? What do you read there?

Lawyer: You shall love the Lord your God with all your heart, and with all your soul, and with all your strength, and with all your mind; and your neighbor as yourself.

Jesus: You have given the right answer; do this, and you will live.

Narrator: But wanting to justify himself, he asked Jesus,

Lawyer: And who is my neighbor?

Narrator: Jesus replied,

Jesus: A man was going down from Jerusalem to Jericho, and fell into the hands of robbers, who stripped him, beat him, and went away, leaving him half dead. Now by chance a priest was going down that road; and when he saw him, he passed by on the other side. So likewise, a Levite, when he came to the place and saw him, passed by on the other side. But a Samaritan while traveling came near him; and when he saw him, he was moved with pity. He went to him and bandaged his wounds, having poured oil and wine on them. Then he put him on his own animal, brought him to an inn, and took care of him. The next day he took out two denarii, gave them to the innkeeper, and said,

Samaritan: Take care of him; and when I come back, I will repay you whatever more you you spend.

Jesus: Which of these three, do you think, was a neighbor to the man who fell into the hands of the robbers?

Lawyer: The one who showed him mercy.

Jesus: Go and do likewise.

Based on Luke 10:25–37

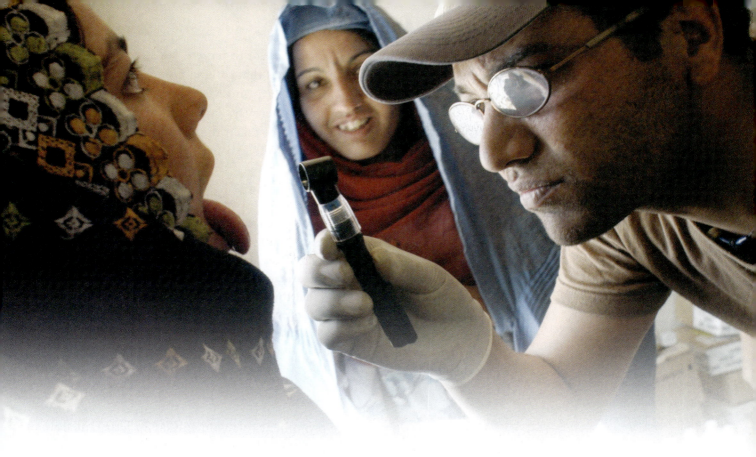

American military doctors work with Afghan doctors outside of the city of Gardez.

The Parable Explained Jesus used this parable to criticize the use of religious excuses to ignore someone in need. The priest and Levite probably passed by the injured man to maintain ritual purity. Because the road went to Jerusalem, they were probably on their way to the Temple. The person lying by the road might have appeared dead, and contact with a dead body made a person ritually impure. This parable taught the listeners that true holiness is found in compassionate love, not ritual piety.

Jesus extended love of neighbor to include everyone—even one's enemies. Jesus challenges us to approach everyone as worthy of love and respect. Only compassion can lead us toward solidarity with others as we respond to the needs and suffering of all. Christian concern for the rights of everyone in society is based on a firm sense of human solidarity.

Like the Good Samaritan, we should be moved to love out of caring and concern for the dignity of another person—even if religious and cultural customs tell us something different. In our society people suffer because they are "passed by," as was the injured person in the parable. People are excluded and discriminated against because of their gender (sexism), race (racism), age (ageism), social class, or disabilities. Such discriminations are examples of social sin—negative attitudes and actions of groups that cause evil in society. Jesus' story challenges us to always see others as our brothers and sisters, and to break the boundaries that keep the children of God separated from one another.

Faith Activity

Discussion

1. Were you ever in a situation similar to that of the injured person in the parable of the Good Samaritan?
2. Who helped you? What was your reaction? Did you thank the person who helped you?
3. What are the rewards of being a Good Samaritan?

Faith Activity

Finding Balance The author of Luke indicates the need for God in one's life in the story of Martha and Mary. The author also shows the difficulty of finding balance in life.

1. What do you need to do to bring more balance into your life?

2. Do you need more time in prayer?

3. Do you need more time to think about and to meet the needs of others?

4. With whom do you identify in the story, Mary or Martha?

Martha and Mary What does it mean to serve God? In the story of the Good Samaritan, the obvious answer is that serving God leads a person to compassionate action. The story of Mary and Martha examines the question of serving God and neighbor in another way, and leads to another question: Can we really serve Jesus if we have not taken the time to listen to him first? Sometimes we can be distracted from the real "work" Jesus asks us to do.

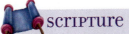

Scripture

"Now as they went on their way, he entered a certain village, where a woman named Martha welcomed him into her home. She had a sister named Mary, who sat at the Lord's feet and listened to what he was saying. But Martha was distracted by her many tasks; so she came to him and asked, 'Lord, do you not care that my sister has left me to do all the work by myself? Tell her then to help me.' But the Lord answered her, 'Martha, Martha, you are worried and distracted by many things; there is need of only one thing. Mary has chosen the better part, which will not be taken away from her.'"

Luke 10:38–42

This story exemplifies the prominent role women play in Jesus' mission and in the Gospel according to Luke. The author illustrates the importance and the value of women by placing a story about a man with that about a woman. For example, the author parallels Simeon and Anna in Luke 2:25–38, and the shepherd with the lost sheep and the woman with the lost coin in Luke 15:1–10.

The story of Mary and Martha reminds us to avoid the distractions and worries that can clutter our lives and keep us from listening to God's guiding presence. While faithful *service* to God is important, we must balance it with *listening* to the word of God and spending time in prayer. By praying daily, reading the Bible, participating in the celebration of the Eucharist and the other sacraments, we place ourselves in God's presence.

The Importance of Table Fellowship

The Gospel according to Luke contains nineteen references to table fellowship. Of these, thirteen are found exclusively in Luke. Understanding the social and religious customs surrounding meals in the ancient Mediterranean world helps explain why they were important.

Jewish people normally did not eat with strangers because if the meal did not meet their dietary laws, they could be made unclean. They would then have to perform prescribed ritual washings before being able to worship in the Temple. They also did not eat with sinners (considered unclean) and Gentiles.

Mealtime was a social event in which those who shared the meal were considered extended family. Sharing food was a sign of acceptance, unity, and closeness. Refusing to eat with someone was treating that person as an outsider.

The community ostracized those who were considered undesirable table companions. Meals and banquets reflected the invisible boundaries of those who were the "fit" and "unfit" in society. In addition, the community followed many laws governing ritual purity. In the Gospel according to Luke, we find that Jesus ignored the laws that governed ritual purity and relationships. Table fellowship was the way Jesus connected to the poorest of the Jewish population.

Unlike those who discriminated against others at mealtime, Jesus included everyone. Jesus ate with Gentiles, sinners, tax collectors, and those who were considered unclean. Those meals became occasions for reconciliation, conversion, and healing. Jesus' actions infuriated the religious authorities who refused to acknowledge or to eat with those who were disadvantaged or outcasts. They were unwilling to offer healing and reconciliation to others.

Break Open the Word

Meals as Inclusive Events and Occasions

Read the scripture passages below. State whom Jesus was with and what the circumstances were. Decide if the meal was an occasion for invitation, healing, conversion, or reconciliation:

Luke 5:29–30

Luke 7:36–50

Luke 14:12–14

Luke 15:1–2

Luke 16:19–31

Luke 19:5–9

Luke 22:26–27

Luke 24:30–35

Faith Activity

Fellowship Today How significant is table fellowship today? How often does your family gather for meals? What are the benefits of gathering with your family for daily meals?

Feeding of the Five Thousand

The only one of Jesus' miracles described in all four Gospels is the multiplication of the loaves and fish (or as Luke titles it, "The Feeding of the Five Thousand"). This miracle, and Jesus' explanation of it, is the promise of the Eucharist.

scripture

"The day was drawing to a close, and the twelve came to him and said, 'Send the crowd away, so that they may go to the surrounding villages and countryside, to lodge and get provisions; for we are here in a deserted place.' But he said to them, 'You give them something to eat.' They said, 'We have no more than five loaves and two fish—unless we are to go and buy food for all these people.' For there were about five thousand men. And he said to his disciples, 'Make them sit down in groups of about fifty each.' They did so and made them all sit down. And taking the five loaves and the two fish, he looked up to heaven, and blessed and broke them, and gave them to the disciples to set before the crowd. And all ate and were filled. What was left over was gathered up, twelve baskets of broken pieces."

Luke 9:12–17

▼ Feeding of the 5000 by Laura James, 1999.

Jesus did not directly interact with the crowd. Instead he showed those who were to continue his mission how to minister to all. As the Twelve served the meal, another social restraint was challenged. In Jesus' time women served meals, not men. Jesus reversed another social reality and taught those gathered that following him required crossing any boundary that separated people from one another. Following Christ involves answering the call to selfless loving service to all of God's family. At a meal for five thousand men and thousands of women and children, as in this miracle story, all the rules for table fellowship had to be disregarded. Barriers of class and economics did not exist, and all were welcome.

The Eucharist An allusion to the Last Supper is present at the Feeding of the Five Thousand. In both, Jesus blesses the bread, breaks it, and gives it to his disciples. However, what happened at these two events is very different. Jesus fed the crowd with bread, but he fed his disciples at the Last Supper with his own Body and Blood. The Last Supper is the institution of the Eucharist.

The Eucharist is the sacrament of Jesus' Body and Blood, truly and really present under the appearances of the bread and wine. The Eucharist is both a meal and a sacrifice. At Mass the Church joins with Jesus in offering his Body and Blood to God the Father. This is accomplished by Christ acting through the priest. The Church commemorates Christ's sacrifice on the cross and makes this sacrifice present. The sharing of the Body and Blood of Christ in holy Communion is a sign of oneness with God and other members of the Church.

The word *Eucharist* means "thanksgiving." Every Sunday Catholics all over the world gather to celebrate the Eucharist and thank God the Father for the many blessings he has given them, particularly the gift of his Son, Jesus. The Eucharist is the opportunity for Catholics to be reconciled with God and with one another. The Eucharist offers healing for the brokenhearted and strength and courage to follow Christ. The Eucharist nourishes us so that we can build the Body of Christ.

Like those who first saw Jesus take, bless, break, and share the bread and wine that became his Body and Blood, we are challenged to continue Jesus' mission in the world, by the grace of God and through the power of the Holy Spirit. As we receive Jesus' Body and Blood in the Eucharist, we are called to bring the healing and reconciliation of Christ to others.

Strengthened for Mission

After the Resurrection of Jesus, the author of the Gospel according to Luke recorded a story in which two followers of Jesus meet the Risen Lord on the road to Emmaus. Even though they do not recognize that it is Jesus who is traveling with them, they invite him to stay with them and to eat with them. At the meal they recognize Jesus.

This was not simply a meal, but also a reference to the Eucharist. The Eucharist was central to the life of the early Church, and it is central to the life of the Church today. In the Eucharist the followers of Jesus come to recognize the Risen Lord. The Eucharist strengthened the followers of Jesus to carry out his mission to the entire world. The Eucharist strengthens us to do the same.

Faith Activity

Ritual Actions Read about the four movements of the Eucharist in Luke 22:19. Answer the questions, and apply the concepts to your life this week.

Take In what ways can receiving the real presence of Jesus in Communion be a source of healing in your life?

Bless How have you been blessed by your family?

Break How have the difficulties in your life made you more aware of what is really important?

Give How have you used the gifts God has given you as a means of serving and transforming the needs of the world?

Connect to the Past

Chalices Throughout the centuries, chalices have been made from a variety of materials. Early churches used chalices of glass, wood, ivory, or clay. Later, chalices were made of precious metals such as gold or silver and set with precious gems.

Why do you think the chalice is considered to be the most important of all vessels in the church?

Blessed Kateri Tekakwitha

(c. 1656–1680)

Kateri Tekakwitha is the first Native American to be nearing canonization. She was the daughter of a Mohawk warrior and an Algonquian woman who was Christian. Kateri was born in New York in 1656 and was baptized twenty years later. Although she couldn't read or write, she told stories and recounted the life, death, and Resurrection of Jesus to any who asked or would listen. Kateri often walked through the forest and fashioned sticks into crosses to mark the path. She used the crosses as constant reminders on her return trip that she should stop and pray.

Kateri devoted her life to prayer, penance, and the care of those who were sick or old. After her first Communion a year after she was baptized, Kateri's devotion to the Eucharist strengthened her faith. She was named Blessed in 1980 by Pope John Paul II. She is the patron saint of the environment

and ecology. Her devotion to the faith was so strong that she arrived at the chapel every morning before it opened—at 4 A.M.—and attended every Mass until the chapel closed in the evening, regardless of the weather.

Kateri showed great care for those who were sick and elderly, as well as for the environment. Her actions illustrated two of the key points in Catholic Social Teaching. We can learn from Kateri that regardless of our abilities, our faith and dedication to the Lord are strong enough to get us through life. We are reminded that we can build a society in which all members live justly, and that we must do whatever we can to protect the rights of all people: rich or poor, slave or free, healthy or sick.

In the ceremony at which Kateri was declared Blessed, Pope John Paul II emphasized the strength that she drew from her faith in the Lord. The Pope closed his address with these words:

"Her beatification should remind us that we are all called to a life of holiness, for in Baptism God has chosen each one of us 'to be holy and spotless and to live through love in his presence.' Holiness of life—union with Christ through prayer and works of charity—is not something reserved to a select few among the members of the Church. It is the vocation of everyone.

"My brothers and sisters, may you be inspired and encouraged by the life of Blessed Kateri. Look to her for an example of fidelity; see in her a model of purity and love; turn to her in prayer for assistance. May God bless you as he blessed her. May God bless all the North American Indians of Canada and the United States."

Address of John Paul II to the Indians of North America, 24 June 1980

Prayer

Begin by praying the Sign of the Cross.

Leader: We read in our chapter about how Jews profess their faith through the Shema. As a Jew, Jesus often prayed and recited the Shema. Together we will hear part of the Shema, and then reaffirm our faith in the Church by praying the Apostles' Creed. I now invite the first reader to come forward.

Reader: (Read aloud Deuteronomy 6:4–9.)

Leader: I now invite the second reader to come forward.

Reader: (Read aloud Deuteronomy 11:13–22.)

Leader: The Lord continually reminds Israel and all of us to keep his commandments, a difficult task, but one that our faith can help us with. We reaffirm our faith in God the Father, God the Son, God the Holy Spirit, and the Church itself as we pray . . .

All: I believe in God, the Father almighty,
creator of heaven and earth.
I believe in Jesus Christ, his only Son, our Lord.
He was conceived by the power of the Holy Spirit
and born of the Virgin Mary.
He suffered under Pontius Pilate,
was crucified, died, and was buried.
He descended into hell.
On the third day he rose again.
He ascended into heaven
and is seated at the right hand of the Father.
He will come again to judge the living and the dead.
I believe in the Holy Spirit,
the holy catholic Church,
the communion of saints,
the forgiveness of sins,
the resurrection of the body,
and the life everlasting. Amen.

End by praying the Sign of the Cross.

Review

1. Describe the groups in the Gospel of Luke who are the chosen ones used to bring about salvation.

2. Why was Jesus' story of the Good Samaritan shocking to his listeners?

3. What is the "better part" that Mary chose in the story of Mary and Martha?

4. Read Luke 15. What do the parables of the lost sheep, the lost coin, and the lost son have in common? How would you describe the love and forgiveness of God the Father?

5. How is Mary the Mother of God a model of love and discipleship for Christians? What are the risks of love and forgiveness?

6. How is the importance of the Holy Spirit shown in the Gospel according to Luke? How does the Holy Spirit empower Jesus, his followers, and each of us?

7. Why is prayer important? What can be gained through the power of prayer? What did Jesus teach his disciples to pray for?

8. Describe the reaction of people to Jesus' miracles. What is necessary in order for a miracle to occur?

9. Describe the ways in which Jesus was a healer of people and of nature.

10. Which of Jesus' miracles appears in all four Gospels?

11. Who are some of the people with whom Jesus shared meals? What was the reaction of Jesus' critics to his sharing these meals with others?

12. What does the Eucharist challenge us to do? How does the Eucharist help the Church and us to accomplish the mission of Jesus in the world?

Key Words

anawim (p. 137)—A Hebrew word referring to those who are materially or spiritually poor and are seeking God.

Confirmation (p. 135)—Through the Sacrament of Confirmation we are sealed with the gifts of the Holy Spirit. Confirmation strengthens the spiritual life received in Baptism.

Gifts of the Holy Spirit (p. 135)—Conveyed through Confirmation, the seven gifts of the Holy Spirit strengthen us to spread and defend the faith.

Parousia (p. 127)—The second coming of Christ at the end of time, when God's plan for salvation is accomplished and humanity is glorified.

Shema (p. 124)—A Hebrew word meaning "hear," the first word of Deuteronomy 6:4, "Hear, O Israel . . ."

sin (p. 130)—An offense against God—any word, action, or thought contrary to God's law. Sin weakens, and at times can even break, our relationship with God.

Teen to Teen

The Catholic Social Teachings call us to be socially Christians. We see the People of Faith. We learn about performing acts of social justice and mercy, but how can we live similarly? Which of the Catholic Social Teachings have you found easiest to follow? Which has been the most difficult? Name an act of social justice you have accomplished through the Catholic Social Teachings.

"The easiest for me to follow is the Care for God's Creation. At first, I didn't know exactly what to do to help the environment—it seemed like there were so many problems. I picked little problems I could help with around my community. I started a club at school that adopted a road nearby. It only takes an hour a week to keep it clean and clear of trash. A couple weeks ago I also participated in a river cleanup. We pulled aluminum cans out of the weeds and cleared out old, used fishing line."

Billy J.

"I know right off which teaching is most difficult for me—the option for the poor and vulnerable. I have never been entirely comfortable working in soup kitchens or homeless shelters. I have gotten better recently, but I know that if I am to be a good Christian, I need to improve on that. So I'm trying hard. By far the easiest for me is the Call to Family and Community participation. My family and I are very involved with community events. We try to be active in the Church functions that help those who are in need around us."

Bob M.

"I sent a petition signed by all my classmates to the state house representatives from our district, our senators, and Supreme Court justices requesting the repeal of the state's death penalty law. Following the Life and Dignity of the Human Person Social Teaching just feels natural. I don't think I have any difficulty following a particular Catholic Social Teaching, but some of them are just harder to take an active role with in my community."

Pat B.

Personal Challenge

Look back at your responses in the Teen to Teen section and see which Catholic Social Teaching you have the most difficulty with. Talk with your classmates and see if anyone else shares your difficulty and work together in the coming weeks to accomplish something in your community that reflects that teaching.

BREAK OPEN the *Word*

Living as Jesus Did

Read the quote from Luke 4 at the beginning of the chapter again. Then read verses 18–19 of chapter 4 in their entirety in your Bible. Catholic Social Teachings call us to make each year a year of the Lord's favor. Find examples in Luke of Jesus living the Catholic Social Teachings.

A.D. **14–37**
Tiberius ruler
over Roman Empire

A.D. **28–29**
John the Baptist's active ministry

A.D. **33**
Crucifixion, death, and
Resurrection of Jesus

A.D. **54**
Nero's rise to
power as emperor
of Roman Empire

A.D. 14-37

A.D. 47

A.D. **26–36** Pontius Pilate
the Roman procurator
over Judea and Samaria

A.D. **29**
Jesus' baptism; beginning
of his public ministry

C. A.D. **50**
First Pauline Letters written

Called to Love

" . . . I am the light of the world. Whoever follows me will never walk in darkness but will have the light of life."

John 8:12

Chapter Goals

In this chapter, you will:

- increase your knowledge of the uniqueness of the Gospel according to John.

- gain insight into the images used and the signs performed by Jesus to convey his role and the action of his Father in the world.

- learn about Jesus' Last Supper discourses and his command to love and serve as he did.

- consider the significance of Jesus' death and Resurrection for our faith and life.

- learn about Dom Helder Camara.

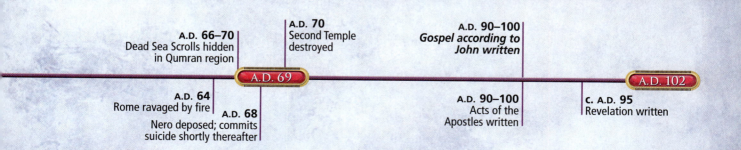

A.D. 66–70
Dead Sea Scrolls hidden in Qumran region

A.D. 70
Second Temple destroyed

A.D. 90–100
Gospel according to John written

A.D. 69

A.D. 102

A.D. 64
Rome ravaged by fire

A.D. 68
Nero deposed; commits suicide shortly thereafter

A.D. 90–100
Acts of the Apostles written

C. A.D. 95
Revelation written

The Gospel According to John

The Gospel according to John is a story of Jesus Christ, the Light of the World, encountering darkness, and the tension that results when those opposing forces meet.

You will find the Gospel of John filled with images and symbols that invite us into the Light of God the Father's life and love. The Light, present from the dawn of creation, came to earth in Jesus to show us how to be the light of love for others. Many have experienced the radiance of this love and have become one with it, while others have chosen to turn away.

Overview of the Gospel

The Gospel of John differs in many ways from the synoptic Gospels. Because this was the last Gospel to be written, the author would have known the story of Jesus through several generations of oral and written tradition. Therefore, the author was not concerned with recording a similar synopsis, or summary, of the life of Jesus because such summaries had already been done in the Gospels of Matthew, Mark, and Luke. Instead, the author of the Gospel of John presented a different perspective on Jesus and his life.

Authorship and Date The literature attributed to the author includes the Gospel according to John, the three Letters of John, and the Book of Revelation. However, only Revelation refers to its author by name—John. (See *Revelation 1:1*.)

The Evangelist refers to himself as "the disciple whom Jesus loved" (*John 21:20*), but the writer never reveals his identity. The Gospel describes the "one whom Jesus loved" reclining next to Jesus at the Last Supper, standing at the foot of the cross, and entering Jesus' empty tomb and believing in his Resurrection (*John 13:23*; and see *John 19:25–27*; *John 20:2–10*).

The Tradition of the ancient Church holds that the Apostle John, the son of Zebedee, is the author of the Gospel and that he wrote it at an advanced age—perhaps while imprisoned on the Greek island of Patmos. However, the Gospels contain no passages that verify this as fact. Therefore, the identity of the author remains unknown. Today most scholars are of the opinion that the Gospel of John was written either by a disciple of John or more probably by a group of disciples connected to John's community. For clarity's sake, we will refer to the author of the Gospel, even if several may have existed.

The author of the Gospel of John wrote sometime near the end of the first century, during a time of great persecution. Scholars speculate that the author composed the Book of Revelation during the time of persecution under the reign of the Roman Emperor Domitian (A.D. 81–96), and they believe the fourth Gospel was written at the end of the first century, followed by the Letters of John.

Audience and Location   Not only did the author's community suffer from the external strife of persecution, but according to the Letters of John, significant internal dissension also caused tension and division. The author and his readers were probably Hellenistic Jewish Christians who had been rejected from the synagogue community in their city. Scholars have traditionally believed that the Gospel was written at Ephesus; however, some now suggest it was written in Syria.

Theological Perspectives and Themes   Biblical scholars often describe the Gospel of John as a theological reflection of the Person and nature of Jesus—God's revelation of the divinity of the one who is the incarnate and living Word. While the synoptic Gospels share similar material, much of the material in John is unique to this Gospel.

John contains no parables; instead, you will find speeches filled with symbolism. In addition, the Gospel of John, unlike the synoptics, has no stories of Jesus' performing exorcisms or casting out demons.

Explore the Land

The Seven Churches of Revelation   This map shows the cities of the seven churches of Revelation. Among them is Ephesus, where the Gospel according to John, as well as the Revelation to John were written.
What kind of community was John writing to in the Gospel and in Revelation? Was the community Jewish, Christian, or pagan? How do you think this affected the style of writing John used?

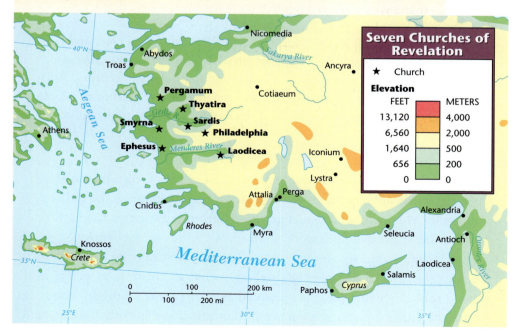

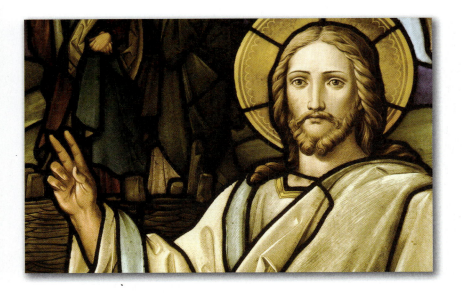

Overall this Gospel has fewer stories about Jesus, but each story is interpreted at greater length through discourse, or dialogue, between Jesus and the other characters. Often the people come to faith only after the dialogue has taken place.

All of the Evangelists believed in the divinity of Jesus, but the Gospel of John begins with a more philosophical or theological presentation of the divinity of Jesus. Only the Gospel of John includes a description of Jesus' preexistence, which is mentioned before the Gospel details his life on earth. And this Gospel's author, more so than the others, depicts Jesus as being more in control of what happened at his trial and crucifixion.

Structure of the Gospel The Gospel of John is divided into two distinct sections. The first section, known as the Book of Signs, presents the deeds and works of Jesus. The second section, known as the Book of Glory, presents the teachings of Jesus and the events surrounding his Passion, death, and Resurrection. Both books convey the message that Jesus is both human and divine and that his mission was to reveal the glory of God the Father.

The Gospel according to John begins with a prologue, a significantly different opening than the synoptic Gospels. Originally, the prologue may have been a hymn about Jesus that was sung when the Johannine community gathered to worship.

Faith Activity

Themes in John Illustrate one or more of the themes in John by drawing a picture, writing a poem, composing the lyrics of a song, or making something out of construction paper or clay.

scripture

"In the beginning was the Word, and the Word was with God, and the Word was God. He was in the beginning with God. All things came into being through him, and without him not one thing came into being. What has come into being in him was life, and the life was the light of all people. The light shines in the darkness, and the darkness did not overcome it."

John 1:1–5

The opening words of the prologue of the Gospel of John mirror the opening words of Genesis. Just as light separated darkness in the old creation story, the Light will challenge and confront darkness in the new creation story. Both are the work of all three Persons in the Trinity.

The Greek word for *word* is "logos." To those first hearing these words, logos represented God's presence dwelling within all creation, as well as in the human soul. Therefore Jesus, represented as divine from his origin, continues to breathe God's life-giving presence into creation and into the human soul.

BReak open the Word

Themes in Scripture

Study the following scripture verses from the Gospel of John. What themes are depicted in each passage?

John 3:16–19, 35

John 5:26

John 6:33

John 7:37–39

John 8:12

John 9:5

John 10:17

John 11:9–10

John 12:31–36

John 14:6, 16–17, 26

John 15:9

John 16:7

John 17:20–26

John 19:30

When God speaks, the Word is eloquent—like the breath of life. In John the Word is the mirror image of who God is.

The author of John establishes Jesus as the pre-existent Son of God: "He (Jesus) was in the beginning with God. All things came into being through him . . ." (*John 1:2–3*). The Incarnation of Jesus and the glory of God the Father as revealed in Jesus are also central in the prologue: "And the Word became flesh and lived among us, and we have seen his glory, the glory as of a father's only son, full of grace and truth" (*John 1:14*).

The prologue concludes with "no one has ever seen God" (*John 1:18*). The Gospel of John sheds light on how people come to know and love our God, who is a mystery to us. Through Jesus—the Word made flesh—people come to recognize God the Father. Through the words and actions of Jesus, the glory of God the Father was revealed and the gift of God the Holy Spirit was given. The prologue, which lays the foundation for the entire Gospel, captures who Jesus is and what his mission was.

Symbols and Images in John

The images and the symbols in the Gospel according to John have special meaning to the author's audience. This Gospel illustrates these important aspects of Jesus' identity:

- Jesus is human and divine.

- Jesus is the Son of God, who reveals the identity of God the Father and who sends God the Holy Spirit.

- Jesus is the Word of God, who is superior to all prophets.

- Jesus is the Word Incarnate; he is the Word made flesh.

The author of John used images, symbols, metaphors, "I am" statements, irony, signs, and teachings to describe Jesus and his mission. The author also

Images of Jesus Read the following passages from the Gospel of John. What image of Jesus is depicted in each passage? What does each image reveal about who Jesus is, and what does Jesus reveal about God the Father?

John 5:19–29
John 6:35–40
John 8:12–20
John 10:7–18
John 11:25–27
John 14:6–14
John 15:5–17

states the Gospel's predominant themes in terms of opposing images: light and darkness, life and death, salvation and judgment, truth and falsehood, unity and division, love and hate, earthly world and heavenly world. These images illustrate the deeper meaning of the life of Jesus and the important events surrounding his mission. The opposing images allow the audience to understand that Jesus and his message stand in opposition to the culture and the values of the time.

These images allow us to understand, in similar fashion, the life and message of Jesus as it stands in opposition to today's worldly values and culture. The images help us express what is inexpressible in words alone—the divinity and mystery of God. The words and symbols in John are often poetic, universal, and mystical. We are drawn into the essence of the images, which reveal to us that Jesus is God the Father's Son. Through the Son's revelation, we are drawn into God's mystery, a mystery that remains beyond all the words we may use to describe it.

"I Am" Statements In the Gospel of John, Jesus speaks more in **allegories** than in parables. The author was more concerned with who Jesus is than with what the kingdom of God is. The "I am" statements in John use these symbols to describe who Jesus is.

The "I am" statements take four general forms. In the first form, Jesus identifies himself with something already known to his listeners: "I am the bread" and "I am the light." In the second form, three of the statements emphasize the relationship between Jesus and his followers: "I am the good shepherd," "I am the gate," and "I am the true vine." In the third form, two statements are straightforward declarations of Jesus as the life-giver: "I am the Resurrection and the life," and "I am the way, the truth, and the life." The final form of the "I am" statements is noted when Jesus responds to questions of self-identification. Jesus asks the soldiers coming to arrest him in the garden of Gethsemane, "Who are you looking for?" They answer, "Jesus of Nazareth." Jesus replies, "I am he."

Interpret the Art

"I am" Statements in Art Which "I am" statements are represented in this art? Illustrate on your own a statement that is not shown and share it with your classmates.

Like the symbols in the Gospel of John, the "I am" statements are meant to convey the divinity of Jesus. These pronouncements remind the audience of Moses' encounter with God in the burning bush, where God was revealed as "I AM WHO I AM" (*Exodus 3:14*). The name for God in the Old Testament is the Hebrew Yahweh, which literally means "I am who am." The Gospel of John features the "I am" statements as a way of saying that Jesus is, in fact, divine—the Son of God.

The "I am" Statements	
John 4:26	"I am he the [Messiah]."
John 6:35	"I am the bread of life. Whoever comes to me will never be hungry, and whoever believes in me will never be thirsty."
John 8:12	"I am the light of the world. Whoever follows me will never walk in darkness but will have the light of life."
John 8:28	"I am he [the Son of Man]."
John 8:58	"Very truly, I tell you, before Abraham was, I am."
John 10:9	"I am the gate. Whoever enters by me will be saved, and will come in and go out and find pasture."
John 10:11, 14	"I am the good shepherd. The good shepherd lays down his life for the sheep. . . . I know my own and my own know me . . ."
John 10:36	"I am God's Son."
John 11:25	"I am the Resurrection and the life. Those who believe in me, even though they die, will live."
John 14:6	"I am the way, and the truth, and the life."
John 15:5	"I am the vine, you are the branches. Those who abide in me and I in them bear much fruit, because apart from me you can do nothing."

Work with the Chart

Compare and Contrast In groups, discuss the "I am" statements, using the following questions:
1. *Which are definitive statements about Jesus' divine nature?*
2. *Which describe Jesus' role as mediator between his followers and the Father?*
3. *Which include references to life? How are these alike and how are they different?*
4. *Which statement best describes who Jesus is to you at this time in your life?*

The Ministry and Signs of Jesus

The images of Jesus give us clues into his identity, but the seven signs, or miracles, recorded in John give us a further glimpse into the mission and divine nature of Jesus. All the signs confirm the truth that Jesus is the Son of God. Miracles, therefore, are the work of God in Christ.

For the author of John, the Incarnation is the basis for all Jesus' miracles. For just as Christ's human flesh became the embodiment of divinity, so material substances like water and bread manifest divine life. The spiritual meaning of the signs, or miracles, is that they show new life in Christ. The fulfillment of the signs rests in Jesus' death and Resurrection.

The author of the Gospel according to John tells the readers that these signs are written so they may believe that Jesus is God's Son. The Gospel of John concludes, "But there are also many other things that Jesus did; if every one of them were written down, I suppose that the world itself could not contain the books that would be written" (*John 21:25*). Yet even with this abundant number of signs in Jesus' time, some still did not believe in him.

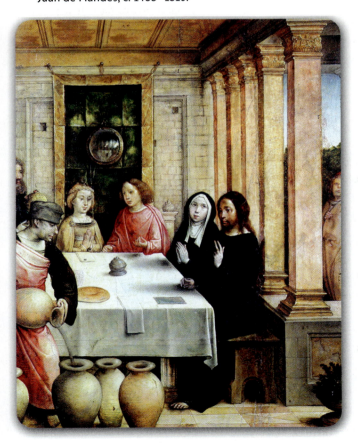

▼ The Marriage Feast at Cana by Juan de Flandes, c. 1465–1519.

The Seven Signs in John

First Sign Jesus changes water into wine. (See *John 2:1–11.*)

Mary and Jesus are guests at a wedding feast in Cana. While there, Mary informs Jesus that the wine has run out. Jesus says, "My hour has not yet come" (*John 2:4*). However, he reveals his glory and transforming power by changing the water in the stone jars into wine. This sign foreshadows a time when Mary, standing at the foot of the cross, will witness Jesus give the gift of his life, the blood (wine) of the New Covenant. As a result of this sign at Cana, Jesus' disciples believe in him.

Second Sign Jesus heals an official's son. (See *John 4:46–54.*)

In this narrative the centurion has faith in the power of Jesus' words to cure his son. Unlike others in the Gospel who need to see signs and wonders to believe, this man's faith is based on hearing the Word. Because of the centurion's faith, Jesus cures his son from a distance.

Third Sign Jesus heals a paralytic. (See *John 5:2–18*.)

In contrast to the centurion, the person who is lame initially does not have faith in Jesus—he does not even know who Jesus is. This person, paralyzed for thirty-eight years, is cured by Jesus on the Sabbath. The man reports the healing to the Jewish authorities. Some of those in power begin to plot to kill Jesus for curing on the Sabbath and for making himself equal to God.

Fourth Sign Jesus feeds the five thousand. (See *John 6:1–14*.)

Jesus satisfies the physical hunger of the multitude through the multiplication of the loaves. This sign alludes to the fact that Jesus, as the "Bread of Life," will satisfy spiritual hungers because only God can nourish our deepest hungers. This sign, which occurs shortly before Passover, symbolizes Jesus as the new bread, the manna from heaven. Jesus says, "I am the living bread that came down from heaven. Whoever eats of this bread will live forever; and the bread that I will give for the life of the world is my flesh" (*John 6:51*).

Fifth Sign Jesus walks on the water. (See *John 6:16–21*.)

As the signs continue to be revealed, Jesus' disciples become more aware of his divine powers. This sign demonstrates Jesus' control over nature, as well as the power he possesses to calm the fears of the disciples. Jesus' walking on water has been paralleled with the crossing of the Red Sea by the Jews during the Exodus.

Sixth Sign Jesus restores sight to a man born blind. (See *John 9:1–7*.)

The blind man comes to faith—"sees the light"—after Jesus cures him. He experiences the healing presence of Jesus. His physical cure symbolically parallels his spiritual insight that Jesus is the Son of Man. The story's conclusion emphasizes that blindness presents itself in those who choose not to believe in Jesus, such as the Jewish leaders.

Seventh Sign Jesus raises Lazarus to life. (See *John 11:38–44*.)

Jesus' human emotions surface when he weeps over the loss of his beloved friend Lazarus. The glory of God present in Jesus is again manifested as he gives new life to Lazarus. Human friendship and love motivate Jesus to restore life to his friend; human hatred and fear motivate Jesus' enemies to conspire to kill him. Through his death on the cross, Jesus reveals God's friendship and love to all humankind through the life he gives for the whole world. This sign prefigures the dying and rising of Jesus, God's greatest miracle.

Some consider a post-Resurrection story that tells about a miraculous fishing outing on the Sea of Tiberias to be an eighth sign. (See *John 21:1–6*.) The miracle symbolizes the commissioning of the Apostles to be missionaries to the world.

Each sign challenged the person(s) involved to respond in faith. Faith is the light that brings forth our spiritual birth—our new life in Christ. In the Gospel according to John, the light is faith. Those who accept Jesus live in the light. Those who reject the signs of Jesus remained in darkness, turning away from Jesus. For the author of John, the epitome of faith is seen in those who believe without hearing Jesus' words or witnessing his signs.

BREAK OPEN the Word

Jesus' Miracles Examine each of the miracle stories and state who had faith in Jesus' powers, who came to the light of faith as a result of the miracle, and who still rejected Jesus even after seeing the miracle.

Faith Activity

Jesus' Healing Imagine yourself as one of the people healed or restored to life by Jesus. What are the other people saying, doing, and feeling? How does Jesus respond?

In the Gospel of John, Jesus' signs are often opportunities for Jesus to dialogue with the person who was healed or with those who witnessed the event. Write a question you would like Jesus to answer. Exchange your question with another person. Answer the other person's question in the way you think Jesus would respond.

Choosing Light or Darkness

Throughout the Gospel the author continues to illuminate how Jesus repeatedly revealed his real nature and mission through his "I am" statements, miracles, and teachings or discourses. (See *John 13—17*.) Ultimately, who Jesus really was and why he came was not clearly understood by his Apostles and disciples until after his death and Resurrection.

Some choose to become one with the light that is faith; others do not. This was also true in Jesus' day. In many stories in this chapter, people's choices have been clear: either they choose to cooperate with the grace of God that brings faith or they choose not to do so.

Nicodemus One of the most interesting stories in the Gospel of John is that of Nicodemus, someone who underwent a gradual and slow process of conversion when he was enlightened by the light of faith. (See *John 3:1–21*.)

As a Pharisee and a member of the Sanhedrin, Nicodemus was a religious leader who observed Jewish laws and ceremonies. After seeing some of the "signs" Jesus performed, Nicodemus decided he wanted to know more about Jesus. He met with Jesus during the night so no one would see him. He was looking for truth. Jesus told him, "No one can enter the kingdom of God without being born of water and Spirit" (*John 3:5*). Jesus further instructed Nicodemus:

Faith Activity

Longing for God We live in a world that searches for answers and insight. Our friends, neighbors, and families long for appreciation, belonging, friendship, and attention. Like Nicodemus many people search for insight and a sense of direction. What are you longing to know about God, the world, and yourself?

scripture

"For God so loved the world that he gave his only Son, so that everyone who believes in him may not perish but may have eternal life. Indeed, God did not send the Son into the world to condemn the world, but in order that the world might be saved through him. Those who believe in him are not condemned; but those who do not believe are condemned already, because they have not believed in the name of the only Son of God. And this is the judgment, that the light has come into the world, and people loved darkness rather than light because their deeds were evil. For all who do evil hate the light and do not come to the light, so that their deeds may not be exposed. But those who do what is true come to the light, so that it may be clearly seen that their deeds have been done in God."

John 3:16–21

After Nicodemus spoke with Jesus, he was still unable to grasp who Jesus was or to understand his message. However, as time passed, Scripture tells us that Nicodemus found the courage to defend Jesus' legal rights before the Sanhedrin. Upon Jesus' death, Nicodemus assisted Joseph of Arimathea in claiming Jesus' body and burying him. Scripture states that he brought one hundred pounds of spices for burying Jesus, which implies that Jesus was given a royal burial.

Nicodemus stayed on the edge of the Light, wavering in indecision. Gradually through God's grace, he was more and more drawn toward the center of the Light until he accepted the gift of faith and Baptism that enlightened him. He discovered the truth that Jesus was the Light of the World and had the truthful answers to the questions that Nicodemus had been asking. Nicodemus then understood what it meant to be reborn in the Spirit. (See *John 7:51*; *19:39–40*.) The Gospel of John connects grace, faith, and Baptism. Baptism is a sign of new birth and the work of the Spirit among us. We attain relationship with Jesus, and thus salvation, through faith and Baptism.

Perhaps Nicodemus's journey of faith reflects our own. Our journey toward Jesus is a process. Each day we face many choices; some will lead us toward the Light; others will lead us away from the Light. We are free to choose, and therefore responsible for our choices and actions. We are responsible, but we are not alone. God's grace helps us to choose the Light, to choose to say *yes* to his offer to share in his life. God created us to be his daughters and sons, and grace helps us to respond to this calling. When we choose to believe in and follow Jesus, we become light for others.

Faith Sharing

Light of Jesus In your faith-sharing group, read John 8:12, the verse cited at the beginning of this chapter. How has Jesus been a light in the darkness for you? Where in your life do you need Jesus to enlighten you now? How will the Light of Jesus guide you in the future? How does the story of Nicodemus remind you of your journey of faith toward Jesus, the Light?

▼ The Deposition of Christ by Arcangelo di Cola di Vanni da Camerino, c. 1420–1430.

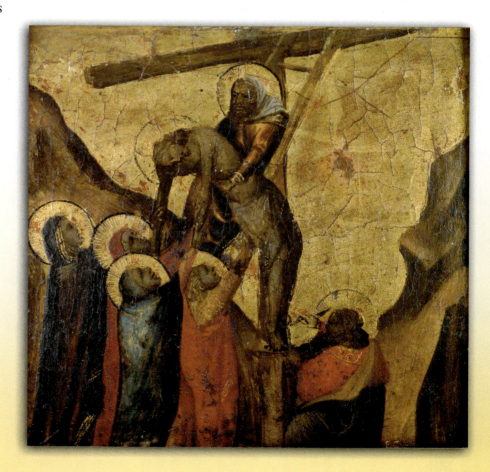

Break Open the Word

1. The Samaritan woman had to decide whether to risk giving a Jew a drink of water. Such an act would not be socially acceptable. Have you ever been faced with making a decision about the socially acceptable thing to do? Share the experience.

2. Some people judged the woman at the well because she was a Samaritan and a woman. Are women still treated unfairly in our society? In our homes? How about other nationalities?

The Samaritan Woman Unlike Nicodemus, the Samaritan woman was a Gentile, but like Nicodemus she was also converted into a believer through the life-giving Word of Jesus.

As John 4:1–27 opens, we imagine Jesus—very thirsty after walking, perhaps for many hours. Jesus stops at a well and tells a Samaritan woman to give him something to drink. She is surprised and probably suspicious because in Jesus' culture, speaking with Samaritans was not acceptable, nor could men speak with women they did not know. In his conversation with the Samaritan woman, Jesus broke those barriers to tell her where she could get the living water only he could give. In the story of the woman at the well, Jesus models a love that excludes no one.

The synoptic Gospels do not mention that Jesus ministered to the Samaritans. Yet in the Gospel according to John, the Samaritan woman is the first person to whom Jesus' reveals his identity. As the story ends, the woman tells other people of her encounter with Jesus. The Gospel states that because of the woman's testimony, many came to believe in Jesus. According to John, the Samaritan woman was the first to share the light of Jesus with others—the first evangelizer. The Samaritans then came to Jesus and invited him to stay with them. They learned for themselves that Jesus was truly the Savior of the World.

▼ Christ and the Samaritan Woman at the Well, early Christian fresco in the 4th Century Catacomb of Via Latina, Rome, Italy.

The Woman Caught in Adultery As with other stories, such as that of the Samaritan woman, the story reinforces the importance of not judging others.

In the story the scribes and Pharisees bring before Jesus a woman who had been caught in an act of adultery. (See *John 7:53—8:11*.)

According to Jewish law, the penalty for adultery was the death of both the woman and the man. (See *Leviticus 20:10*; *Deuteronomy 22:22*.) Stoning was the most common method at the time of Jesus. Jesus' adversaries were using the woman as a pawn in their attempt to draw him into a snare: if he stood up for the woman caught in the act of adultery, he would be in conflict with the Law of Moses and could himself be brought before the Jewish court.

Jesus calmly confronts the scribes and the Pharisees by saying, "Let anyone among you who is without sin be the first to throw a stone at her" (*John 8:7*). While the authorities ponder their reaction to Jesus, he simply writes in the sand. The lines between light and darkness are drawn as Jesus moves attention away from the sins of the woman to the sinfulness of her accusers.

scripture

"And once again he (Jesus) bent down and wrote on the ground. When they heard it, they went away, one by one, beginning with the elders; and Jesus was left alone with the woman standing before him. Jesus straightened up and said to her, 'Woman, where are they? Has no one condemned you?' She said, 'No one, sir.' And Jesus said, 'Neither do I condemn you. Go your way, and from now on do not sin again.'"

John 8:8–11

The woman is freed from her accusers and from the weight of the sin she has committed. Jesus does not condemn her but instructs her not to sin again.

Jesus' Teachings and Example

The Book of Glory, the second major part of the Gospel of John, includes the discourses of Jesus, the Last Supper, and the narrative of Jesus' suffering, death, and Resurrection. This section of the Gospel continues to reveal Jesus as the Son of God, the one who has been sent by God the Father. The author used symbolism and irony to help us understand that we, too, belong to God and must choose to follow the light rather than darkness.

The Last Supper and Service

The Book of Glory opens with the Last Supper, giving a different portrayal from that of the synoptic Gospels. The author of John focused not only on the meal, but also on Jesus as servant. The Gospel of John demonstrates Jesus' teaching about serving others and taking care of others. To illustrate this fact, the Last Supper begins with Jesus' washing the feet of his disciples.

The author depicts Jesus washing and drying the feet of his disciples like a slave. In this great expression of humility, Jesus models how we are to treat one another. When he finishes, Jesus says to his disciples, "You call me Teacher and Lord—and you are right, for that is what I am. So if I, your Lord and Teacher, have washed your feet, you also ought to wash one another's feet. For I have set you an example, that you also should do as I have done for you" (*John 13:13–15*). Remarkably, Jesus eats with and even washes the feet of Judas, his betrayer, whose intent and plan Jesus knows.

Faith Activity

Serving Others Do you know someone who has been a good role model for serving others? Write a short essay describing this person and the service she or he does or has done that models love, service, and examples of Jesus' command to love and serve others.

▼ Pope John Paul II kisses the foot of a priest during the washing of feet at the Holy Thursday Mass.

New Commandment Following the washing of the disciples' feet, Jesus teaches the disciples the central principle of all of his teaching: "I give you a new commandment, that you love one another. Just as I have loved you, you also should love one another. By this everyone will know that you are my disciples, if you have love for one another" (*John 13:34–35*).

Jesus taught that love is the heart of Christian service. Jesus' lesson in the washing of his disciples' feet illustrates that loving one another means being willing to serve one another. To love as Jesus loves means to love others without expecting anything in return.

The Last Supper Discourses

The Last Supper in the Gospel of John continues with a series of speeches or discourses that Jesus gives to his disciples. In this way Jesus teaches his disciples the importance of the Holy Spirit, the unity that exists among the Trinity, and the necessity for the followers of Jesus to be united to the Trinity and to one another.

The Spirit of Truth At the Last Supper Jesus offers his disciples reassurance, especially in the face of what is about to occur—his Passion and death. Jesus tells them, "If you love me, you will keep my commandments. And I will ask the Father, and he will give you another Advocate, to be with you forever. This is the Spirit of truth, whom the world cannot receive, because it neither sees him nor knows him. You know him, because he abides with you, and he will be in you" (*John 14:15–17*).

The Holy Spirit, the Advocate, would continue to lead the disciples. Jesus tells his disciples, "I have said these things to you while I am still with you. But the Advocate, the Holy Spirit, whom the Father will send in my name, will teach you everything, and remind you of all that I have said to you" (*John 14:25–26*). On the night before he dies, Jesus promises his followers that he will not leave them orphans.

This communion of the Father, the Son, and the Holy Spirit brings the Church into being. Our awareness of our unity with God makes it possible for us to recognize our oneness with all of those who believe in and follow Jesus.

Faith
Activity

Community Outreach
Discuss some activities of service performed in your parish and in the community. How does your parish reach out to help others? Does your parish have a Society of Saint Vincent de Paul conference that helps the poor? How can your school reach out in service to the wider community?

SYMBOLS OF THE HOLY SPIRIT

Because we cannot see the Holy Spirit, the Church often uses symbols or images to describe the Holy Spirit's action in our Church, in our lives, and in the world. Many images come from Scripture, and throughout history artisans have crafted those images in stained-glass windows, in fine art, and in sculptures.

Water Throughout history, people have used water for cleansing and for drinking; water is a symbol for the action of the Holy Spirit in Baptism. The Holy Spirit is living water that enables us to share in God's own eternal life. (See *1 Corinthians 12:13*.)

Anointing with oil Oil is used as food, for healing, and to produce light. To anoint a person is to make him or her sacred, or set apart for God. (See *1 Samuel 16:13*.) Anointing with oil symbolizes the action of the Holy Spirit in Baptism, in Confirmation, and in Holy Orders. (See *2 Corinthians 1:21*.)

Fire Fire was used in traditional religious sacrifice to God. Throughout the centuries, fire has also been a source of warmth and light. (See *Exodus 3:2*.) Fire has a transforming effect; it changes metal into usable tools and weapons. At Pentecost the Holy Spirit appeared to the Apostles as tongues of fire.

Clouds and light Clouds and light are symbols of God's guidance and protection. They often occur together in biblical manifestations of the Holy Spirit. (See *Exodus 13:21*; *24:15–18*; *33:9–10*.) Clouds and light also appear together at the Transfiguration of Jesus as a symbol of the Spirit's presence. (See *Luke 9:28–36*.)

Seal In ancient times a seal was a stamp, a legal sign of identity, that took the place of a person's signature. A seal was also a sign of covenant between two people. (See *John 6:27*.) The seal is a symbol of the Holy Spirit's indelible effect on those anointed.

Hand Hands are signs of power, strength, and action. When the Apostles laid hands on new converts, their action was a sign of the giving of the Holy Spirit. (See *Acts 8:17*.)

Finger In the Bible the finger of God is used to mean his power and action. (See *Luke 11:20*.) The finger of God is also a symbol of the Holy Spirit, who wrote God's Law on tablets of stone. (See *Exodus 31:18*.)

Dove The dove is a traditional biblical symbol of God's presence and faithful love. (See *Matthew 3:16*.)

Connect to the Past

Holy Spirit Artisans have incorporated images of the Holy Spirit into their work for centuries. *What do these images tell you about the Holy Spirit's action in your life and in the lives of your family and friends?*

The Vine and the Branches

The image of the vine and the branches further emphasizes the unity of God and his people. We are united to God and to one another through the Church. And the Church is called to become one in God, to bear fruit in his name, and to be a sign of that oneness and the new everlasting life that comes through it.

In John 15:1–8 Jesus describes himself as the vine, his Father as the vine-grower, and his disciples as the branches. The good works of the disciples who follow Jesus' commands give glory to the Father. Jesus tells them: "Just as the branch cannot bear fruit by itself unless it abides in the vine, neither can you unless you abide in me. I am the vine, you are the branches. Those who abide in me and I in them bear much fruit, because apart from me you can do nothing" (*John 15:4–5*).

The Prayer of Jesus

The Last Supper discourses end with Jesus' offering of a prayer to God the Father. (See *John 17:1–25*.) Jesus begins the prayer by giving glory to the Father and by asking for the Father to glorify him. Jesus continues his prayer by relating to the Father what he has done and how his followers belong to the Father. Finally, Jesus asks the Father to bless his disciples with the truth and to make them all be one.

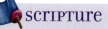 scripture

"I have given them your word, and the world has hated them because they do not belong to the world, just as I do not belong to the world. I am not asking you to take them out of the world, but I ask you to protect them from the evil one. . . . Sanctify them in the truth; your word is truth. . . . I ask not only on behalf of these, but also on behalf of those who will believe in me through their word, that they may all be one."

John 17:14–15, 17, 20–21

As Jesus concludes his prayer to his heavenly Father, guards arrest him, and his hour to glorify God the Father begins. Long before the Passion of Jesus begins, his impending death at the hands of his enemies becomes evident. The reader grows in understanding that the death of Jesus will be a triumphant expression of God's love for the world. Even the prologue carries a hint of Jesus' fate. God's love is given through Jesus so that all who believe in him will not perish but have eternal life. (See *John 3:16*.)

 **Faith Activity**

Jesus' Values Watch the evening news or read the local news online. Summarize two stories and make a judgment about whether the story reflects Jesus' teachings of love, service, and unity. How are the values shown in the news stories like or unlike Jesus' values? Have the people in the stories chosen light or darkness?

WEEK OF PRAYER
FOR CHRISTIAN UNITY

During his final hours, Jesus expressed his concern for unity among his followers. He lifted up to his Father in prayer the hope that his disciples might be one. The Catholic Church remains committed to Jesus' wish for unity. **Ecumenism** is the effort to strive toward unity among all Christians. Just as Jesus prayed, the Christian Church prays for unity among Christians of all faiths, particularly during the Week of Prayer for Christian Unity.

In 1908 the Episcopal Church in New York began observing this week. In 1935 a French Catholic priest advocated for such a week, and this week of prayer for unity continued to spread across the world. During the Second Vatican Council in the 1960s, the Vatican encouraged Catholic Church members to participate in this observance.

In 1966 the World Council of Churches and the Vatican's Pontifical Council for Promoting Christian Unity started working together on prayer texts for use worldwide. The collaboration continues today.

The annual Week of Prayer for Christian Unity takes place in January. Each year's observance has a different theme. Different prayer texts are developed around the theme, and then Christians all over the world pray using the same prayers.

It is important to remember that all Christians follow and believe in Jesus Christ as the Son of God, Messiah, and Anointed One. Productive dialogue can take place when everyone remembers that they share and are united by such a core belief. Jesus willed his Church to be one, and God the Father wants all people to know the truth of his love and his plan of redemption in Christ. All salvation comes from Christ though the Church.

Faith Activity

Prayer and Unity In recent years the themes for the Week of Prayer for Christian Unity have been: the gift of Jesus' peace; Jesus as the fountain of life; Jesus as the way, the truth, and the life; and the Spirit that helps us in our weakness. Research this year's theme, and find out how your parish and diocese celebrated. What can your class do now to pray for and to work toward Christian unity?

The Glory of the Cross of Jesus

The climax of the Gospel according to John is the story of God the Father's self-giving act of friendship and love in allowing his Son, Jesus, to willingly lay down his life for others. Judas, the betrayer, comes at night, a time that symbolizes the influence of the power of darkness. Jesus, the power of the light, takes control of the situation from the beginning in the Gospel of John.

Jesus' Passion and Death

Those who have come to arrest Jesus step back and fall to the ground. They then take Jesus for separate interrogations before Annas, Caiphas, and Pilate. Even though Jesus is a prisoner, the religious and political authorities do not have true power over him. The power and authority Jesus possesses come not from this world, but from above—it is divine. The Gospel of John illustrates the divine nature of Jesus' power and authority when Pilate asks Jesus: "'Do you refuse to speak to me? Do you not know that I have power to release you, and power to crucify you?' Jesus answered him, 'You would have no power over me unless it had been given you from above'" (*John 19:10–11*).

Pilate seats Jesus on the judge's bench, a detail found only in the Gospel of John. The author intended to show Jesus as the judge of the world, as the one in control of his fate. Pilate then hands Jesus over to be crucified. As Jesus journeys toward the completion of his mission, he carries his cross alone, for he has command over life and death.

The Seamless Tunic When Jesus is stripped of his clothes, the soldiers divide his garments among themselves. All four Gospels record the removal of Jesus' clothes, but only the Gospel according to John mentions that the soldiers also took Jesus' tunic.

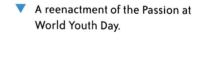

▼ A reenactment of the Passion at World Youth Day.

scripture

"When the soldiers had crucified Jesus, they took his clothes and divided them into four parts, one for each soldier. They also took his tunic; now the tunic was seamless, woven in one piece from the top. So they said to one another, 'Let us not tear it, but cast lots for it to see who will get it.' This was to fulfill what the scripture says,
   'They divided my clothes among themselves,
   and for my clothing they cast lots.'
   And that is what the soldiers did."

John 19:23–24

Faith Activity

Jesus' Sacrifice

Re-examine the list of what the Gospels present about Jesus' suffering and death. Reflect on these questions:

1. What kind of sacrifices can you make for your family, your school, your parish, and your friends that express your obedience to God the Father?

2. What struggles occur between the power of life and the power of death in the world that affect the way you live your life? What can you do to bring the power of life to your parish, your school, your family, and your friends?

This story of the seamless tunic in the Gospel of John symbolizes the unity of the Church, thus established through Jesus and his saving death and Resurrection. Like Jesus' seamless tunic, the Church centered on Christ must be united to God, united to one another, and united in its mission to the world.

His Death Jesus' death will be the final sign of who he is. As he dies on the cross, Jesus does not cry out as he did in the synoptic Gospels. Instead, he says, "It is finished" (*John 19:30*). His hour has come. His death is the hour of glory because God's love has been revealed to the whole world. His mission is complete. A sense of victory and triumph prevails.

As Jesus dies on the cross, according to the Gospel of John, he bows his head and hands over his spirit. Now Jesus' mission is complete. He has glorified the Father, and with the sending of the Spirit, the work of the Church begins. Following the orders of Pilate, the soldiers begin breaking the legs of those crucified with Jesus.

scripture

"Since it was the day of Preparation, the Jews did not want the bodies left on the cross during the sabbath, especially because that sabbath was a day of great solemnity. So they asked Pilate to have the legs of the crucified men broken and the bodies removed. Then the soldiers came and broke the legs of the first and of the other who had been crucified with him. But when they came to Jesus and saw that he was already dead, they did not break his legs. Instead, one of the soldiers pierced his side with a spear, and at once blood and water came out."

John 19:31–34

The flowing of blood and water from the side of Jesus was another sign of the life-giving presence of Christ and the salvation he won for us by his death and Resurrection. Scholars attach great importance to the blood and water that flowed from Jesus' side. They regard the blood and water as a reference to the sacraments of Eucharist and Baptism, respectively. In his death Jesus poured out upon his followers his Spirit and these symbolic signs of salvation.

Central Message While the four Gospels differ in what they highlight, each presents Jesus' suffering and death as:

- a sacrifice that expresses Jesus' obedience to God the Father, Jesus' virtue, and Jesus' mission of redemption
- the result of commitments Jesus made as part of his mission
- the struggle between the power of life and the power of death
- the pattern for, and example of, true discipleship

In the Gospel of John, some of those Jesus loved remained with him and stood at the foot of his cross—his mother; his mother's sister, Mary the wife of Clopas; Mary Magdalene; and the disciple Jesus loved. In the synoptic Gospels, no one stands at the foot of Jesus' cross; instead, we read that only the women and all Jesus' acquaintances, who had followed him from Galilee, watched from a distance. Finally, Jesus is buried in a tomb borrowed from Joseph of Arimathea. The Passion narrative from the Gospel of John is proclaimed every Good Friday.

The message of Jesus' ultimate return of love to God the Father is his pure self-sacrifice, as illustrated in the glory of the cross in the Gospel of John. The glory of Christ crucified is the hour when humanity is saved and God the Father is glorified in Jesus' sacrifice. This message was the one the author's community needed to hear. It is a message we need to hear as well. Like Jesus, we must be willing to lay down our lives for one another out of pure self-sacrificing love.

The Gospel of John shows that death is not the end. Jesus, lifted high on the cross toward heaven, is lifted back to God the Father, for he is going home. The Word came into the world and, through his death and Resurrection, returned to the Father with all humanity—the final purpose of Jesus' mission to the world. At the end of our earthly lives, we also will be welcomed home by the God of Light and Love.

▼ Pious Women at the Tomb by Fra Angelico.

Group Discussion Read the Resurrection accounts in all four Gospels: Matthew 28:1–10; Mark 16:1–8; Luke 24:1–12; and John 20:1–10. In groups, discuss the following questions:

1. In what ways do the accounts agree? Differ?

2. What common elements are found in all four Gospels?

3. How would you describe the reaction of those at the tomb?

4. How would you have reacted if you had been the first to discover the empty tomb?

The Resurrection of Jesus

All four Gospels address the historical event of the Resurrection. Each Evangelist addressed the particular need and the background of his audience. However, all the Gospels profess the following beliefs:

- Jesus was crucified and was raised from the dead.

- Jesus appeared to some women and other disciples.

- Jesus' disciples were to share the Good News of Jesus with others.

Scholars believe the accounts of Jesus' Passion, death, and Resurrection were the first sections of the Gospels to be written. However, even before the Gospels, Saint Paul recounted the events in his first Letter to the Corinthians approximately twenty-five years after the death of Jesus. (See *1 Corinthians 15:3–8.*) Paul taught his audience about the reality of Jesus' death and Resurrection. Similar passages are documented in the Acts of the Apostles and proclaimed from the beginning of the apostolic tradition.

Heart of Our Faith The Resurrection is a central truth of the Christian faith. It is an unparalleled intervention of God into human history. The entire New Testament witnesses to the Resurrection of Jesus. Both the Gospels and the Church maintain that Baptism unites Catholics not only with the death of Jesus, but also with his Resurrection. The Resurrection of Jesus frees us from sin and gives us the hope of new life in Baptism. The Catholic Church celebrates the Resurrection of Jesus at every Mass, especially on Easter Sunday.

The Appearances Each Gospel records different appearances of the Risen Christ. In Matthew Jesus appears suddenly as the women go to report the empty tomb, and he appears again to the eleven disciples when he commissions them to baptize and teach all nations. In Mark Jesus appears to several of his disciples and also commissions the eleven. In Luke the disciples encounter the Risen Christ on the road to Emmaus and recognize him in the breaking of the bread. However, most post-Resurrection appearances of Jesus occur in John.

The Gospel of John is about light encountering darkness. Throughout this Gospel, many people respond to the Light—either positively or negatively. As the Gospel closes, the same theme

◀ Noli me tangere by Maurice Denis, 1895.

continues as people discover that Jesus is no longer in the tomb. The choice is still there for them to make: Will they believe in the Resurrection of Jesus, or will they live in the shadow of uncertainty? Do they have faith? Darkness remains in the Resurrection story until someone comes to believe in the Risen Jesus.

Who Believes?
Simon Peter—enters the empty tomb; does not see Jesus but believes he is risen (John 20:1–10)
Beloved disciple—enters the empty tomb; does not see Jesus but believes he is risen (John 20:1–10)
Mary Magdalene—does not enter the tomb but looks inside; does not believe Jesus has risen until she recognizes him in the garden (John 20:11–18)
Disciples—believe when they see Jesus (John 20:19–23)
Thomas—does not believe until he sees and touches the wounds of Jesus. (John 20:24–29)

Like the other disciples, Thomas does not believe in the Risen Christ until he sees him and touches Christ's wounds. Jesus then directs future believers by saying, "Have you believed because you have seen me? Blessed are those who have not seen and yet have come to believe" (*John 20:29*).

Breakfast on the Beach The Gospel according to John includes another unique appearance of the Risen Jesus. Jesus appears to seven of his disciples at the Sea of Tiberias. After a long night of fishing and catching nothing, the disciples return to shore. Jesus is standing on the shore when they return, but the disciples do not recognize him. When Peter realizes that he was once again in Christ's presence, he jumps into the water and swims to shore. It is in this appearance that Jesus asks Peter to "Feed my lambs" and "Tend my sheep" (*John 21:15–17*). We see in this Peter's unique role as the new shepherd of Jesus' flock and leader of his church.

Break open the Word

Gathering Followers
Some consider the disciples' amazing catch of fish and the record of the exact number "a hundred fifty-three of them" as symbolic and relating to the mission of the Apostles to gather followers to Christ. Read the story of the appearance to the seven disciples in John 21:1–14 to learn more.

▼ The First Miraculous Draught of Fish by James Jacques Joseph Tissot, c. 1886–1896.

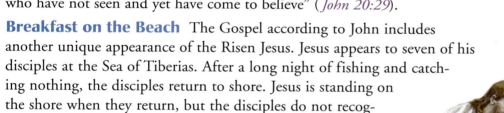

Dom Helder Camara (1909–1999)

Dom Helder was born in Fortaleza, Brazil, on February 7, 1909. He was ordained a priest in 1931. As a priest, he devoted himself to ministering to the millions of people who were poor in his country. He labored to obtain human rights and to involve the church in that struggle.

In 1952, he became auxiliary bishop of Rio de Janeiro. When he was given the title of archbishop in 1964, he refused to live in the archbishop's palace, choosing instead to live in a simple room in the church. He also wore a plain wooden cross, abandoning the large silver or gold cross worn by most bishops. At Vatican II, he urged other bishops to do the same. He requested that his seminarians live for a while in the slums with people who were poor, to learn the reality of their plight.

As the voice of the poor, he confronted the evil of injustice and became known throughout the world as a defender of human rights. He was nominated for the Nobel Peace Prize four times. Within his country, from 1964 through 1985, however, his words and actions were met with anger by those in authority. He was harassed, his phones were tapped and he received numerous death threats and many attempts on his life were made.

This did not silence him. The statement he is probably best known for is, "When I feed the poor, I'm called a saint. When I ask why the poor have no food, I'm called a communist." Dom Helder was not a communist; he was a witness for the justice and love taught by Jesus in the Gospels. His commitment to nonviolence extended into his relationships with those who persecuted him. He chose to love his enemies—not hate them.

A book about Dom Helder entitled *The Violence of a Peacemaker* states that he spent his life challenged with some of the most excruciating problems of our time. The author wrote, "Dom Helder combines, in a unique way, intense suffering and a spirit of joyous abandon."

He died at the age of ninety on August 27, 1999. The President of Brazil, Fernando Henrique Cardose, declared three days of national mourning.

A Poem of Dom Helder Camara

In the heavy hours
when solutions do not come,
go spin a top,
it counterfeits a game,
it is a prayer:
the discovery that not so very different
is the merry-go-round of life
and we know not when
it will run down and stop.
Often
a confident and childlike attitude—
mixture of play and prayer—
brings God's enlightenment.

Prayer

Begin by praying the Sign of the Cross.

Leader: God of Wonder, our words fail to capture your mystery, but we desire to honor you with images and titles that describe your power active in our lives.

Slowly pray each image aloud, pausing to reflect on God's presence in our lives.

Gentle One . . .
God of Power . . .
Eternal One . . .
Seeker of Silence . . .
Graced One . . .
Giver of Hope . . .
Eternal God . . .
Compassionate One . . .
Spirit Within . . .
Father of the Poor . . .
Provident God . . .
God of Miracles . . .
Forgiving One . . .
Giver of Gifts . . .
Precious One . . .
Healer . . .
God of all Hope . . .
Breath of Life . . .
Creator . . .
Holy Light . . .

Leader: Let us close our prayer with the prayer Jesus taught us.

All: Our Father . . .

End by praying the Sign of the Cross.

Review

1. Explain how the prologue of the Gospel of John relates to the Book of Genesis.

2. How is the divinity of Jesus handled in the Gospel of John? How does this compare to the image of Jesus and his divinity as recorded in the synoptic Gospels?

3. What do the images and the "I am" statements in the Gospel of John convey about Jesus?

4. What do the signs in the Gospel of John reveal about Jesus and who he is? How is faith part of each of the signs?

5. According to the Gospel of John, what is the basis for all of Jesus' miracles?

6. How does the faith journey of Nicodemus reflect our faith journey?

7. What does the forgiveness shown the woman caught in adultery demand of us?

8. What is the heart of Christian service? What important directive does Jesus give his disciples after he washes their feet?

9. What importance is placed on unity in the Gospel of John? How is the unity of the Father, Son, and Holy Spirit shown? What is the role of the unity of the Trinity in the Church?

10. How does Jesus' prayer to the Father show his love for God the Father and his love for his followers?

11. How is Jesus' death the hour of his glory? What is symbolic about the seamless tunic and the blood and water that flows from Jesus' side?

12. How do the post-Resurrection appearances of Jesus in the Gospel of John illustrate the interplay between light and darkness? What important role does Peter play?

Key Words

allegories (p. 156)—Expressions of truths or generalizations of human experiences through the use of symbolic fictional figures or actions.

ecumenism (p. 168)—The effort to strive toward unity among all Christians.

Teen to Teen

Jesus tells us that we are the light of the world, and we must shine forth our good deeds through all the earth. Jesus also tells us that he is the Light of the World, and if we follow him we will have the light of life. Who is the light in your world? Who shines for you in your life? Who reminds you—through their good deeds—that Jesus is at work within them?

"My older brother has always been an inspiration to me. I remember his standing up for some kids at the bus stop who were getting bullied almost every day when I was in middle school. My brother wasn't the most popular kid in school; he wasn't the biggest; and he wasn't the strongest. But he always stood up for the other kids. Jesus did the same. He always took the side of the underdog—those who were poor, sick, and weak."

Mike R.

"I had a teacher my first semester in high school who wanted us to do three volunteer projects by the end of the semester. He put up a list of different volunteer opportunities for each upcoming weekend, usually one each on Saturday and Sunday. My friends and I signed up for a meals-for-the-elderly program, where we would be doing basic prep work in a kitchen. When we arrived, we saw our teacher there already hard at work. I later came to find out that he not only researched all of these opportunities for us, he was giving his own time, helping alongside his students."

Michelle T.

Personal Challenge

When we follow Jesus, we are following his light. When we reflect the life of Jesus, our own light is what shines. Let your light shine this week, and find a way you can shine for your friends, family, and loved ones. Don't stop there, though; shine your light to all people, to all your neighbors in your community.

Break Open the Word

Jesus' Light Read John 8:12. Then compare John 8:12 to Matthew 5:14–16. What similarities do you see? How are the verses different? What conclusions can you draw about the use of the word *light* and its many meanings?

A.D. 14–37
Tiberius ruler
over Roman Empire

A.D. 28–29
John the Baptist's
active ministry

A.D. 33
Crucifixion, death, and
Resurrection of Jesus

A.D. 49–52
Paul's second
missionary journey

A.D. 14–37

A.D. 47

A.D. 26–36 Pontius Pilate
the Roman procurator
over Judea and Samaria

A.D. 29
Jesus' baptism; beginning
of his public ministry

C. A.D. 45–49
Paul's first
missionary journey

Called to Share the Good News

"... you will be my witnesses in Jerusalem ... and to the ends of the earth."

Acts of the Apostles 1:8

Chapter Goals

In this chapter, you will:

- study about the author of and key themes in Acts.

- learn about Pentecost and the beginnings of the Church after Pentecost.

- consider the Church's outreach to the Gentiles, which resulted in its growth, persecution, and the conversion of Paul.

- explore the missionary journeys of Paul and the establishment of Church communities.

- learn about Saint Catherine of Siena, Saint Teresa of Ávila, and Saint John of the Cross.

A.D. 64
Rome ravaged by fire; martyrdom of Peter and Paul

A.D. 68
Nero deposed; commits suicide shortly thereafter

A.D. 70
Second Temple destroyed

C. A.D. 95
Revelation written

A.D. 69

A.D. 102

C. A.D. 53–58
Paul's third missionary journey

A.D. 66–70
Dead Sea Scrolls hidden in Qumran region

A.D. 90–100
Acts of the Apostles written

The Acts of the Apostles

For the first disciples, the decision to follow Jesus was not always an easy one. Saying "yes" could result in **persecution** and even death. In this chapter we follow the journey of the early Christians, through their joys and persecutions, as they strove to follow Jesus' command to preach the Gospel to the world.

Overview of Acts

The Acts of the Apostles, also called the Book of Acts, is a sequel to the Gospel according to Luke. Some see them as part one and part two of Luke's work. When we look at the themes presented in the Acts of the Apostles, we find that they compare to those found in the Gospel according to Luke.

Similar Themes in Luke and Acts
Jesus' words and deeds
Centrality of the Christian community
Importance of prayer
Holy Spirit as a life giver
Role of God the Father in our lives
Mary as the model for discipleship
Sacramental life of the Church
Opposition to sin and the place of forgiveness
A simple lifestyle
Justice
Acceptance of all people as children of God

Whereas the Gospel according to Luke portrayed Jesus' birth and his growth into maturity, the Book of Acts shows the birth and growth of the early Christian Church. Both books begin with a greeting to Theophilus, which means "friend of God." Whether Theophilus was a real person or the greeting was meant in general for all who loved God is unknown.

Both books describe times of prayer and waiting (Zechariah in the Gospel, the disciples in Acts); both have a descent of the Holy Spirit (on Jesus in Luke 3:21–22, on the disciples in Acts 2:1–4); both indicate a ministry of preaching and healing; both have journeys; and both include opposition from political and religious authorities. The Gospel of Luke teaches that an important goal of the Christian life is to imitate Christ's life, and Acts tells Christians they should expect to experience opposition as Jesus did.

The progressive movement in the Gospel according to Luke is toward Jerusalem. In Acts the movement is away from Jerusalem. The mission of the Apostles began in Jerusalem; extended to Judea, Samaria, Asia Minor, and Europe; and ended in Rome.

Author, Date, Structure, and Themes of Acts The author of Acts is unknown. When the canon of Scripture was developed, these books were attributed to Luke. Some scholars believe that Luke, a Gentile physician and companion of Paul, wrote Luke and Acts. Other scholars believe that the author was a companion of Paul who came to be known as Luke. Some think that the books were written by an anonymous author. Most scholars agree that Acts was written somewhere between the sixties and the nineties.

Explore the Land

Early Journeys Peter, Paul, and Philip journeyed throughout Palestine and the Mediterranean basin spreading the Good News of Christ.
Why do you think Paul was an ideal preacher? Why did Paul return to Antioch so many times?

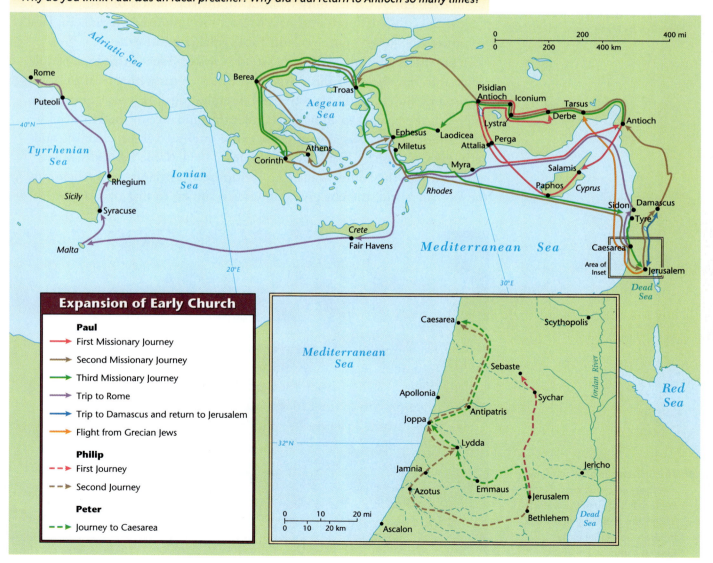

Expansion of Early Church

Paul
- → First Missionary Journey
- → Second Missionary Journey
- → Third Missionary Journey
- → Trip to Rome
- → Trip to Damascus and return to Jerusalem
- → Flight from Grecian Jews

Philip
- --→ First Journey
- --→ Second Journey

Peter
- --→ Journey to Caesarea

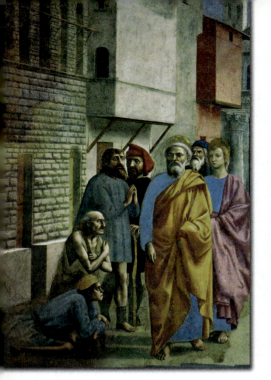

▲ Saint Peter Healing with His Shadow by Masaccio, c. 1425–1426.

Acts has been structured or divided in various ways. The book revolves around two key figures, Peter and Paul. The early chapters stress Peter's ministry, while the latter chapters present the ministry of Paul, largely in the form of missionary journeys.

Acts can be divided into these five main sections:

Structure of Acts
The Preparation for the Christian Mission (Acts 1:1–2, 13)
The Mission in Jerusalem (Acts 2:14–8; 3)
The Mission in Judea and Samaria (Acts 8:4–9, 43)
The Inauguration of the Gentile Mission (Acts 10:1–15, 35)
The Mission of Paul to the Ends of the Earth (Acts 15:36–28, 31)

Key events in Acts include Pentecost; Peter's speech in Acts 2:14–36; his preaching and ministry; the miracles of the Apostles; the spread of Christianity in Judea, Samaria, and beyond; the death of Stephen; the movement of Christianity to Antioch; the conversion of Paul; the spread of the Church into Asia Minor; the Council of Jerusalem; Paul's three missionary journeys; and Paul's final trip to Rome.

Acts centers around sharing the Good News of Jesus Christ by a people called into the world for this purpose. It offers an early history of the Christian Church, as the Apostles and disciples fulfilled Jesus' commission to preach the Gospel to all nations under the guidance of the Holy Spirit. The author of Acts was an evangelist, more interested in proclaiming and verifying the truth of Jesus than in historical data. Some biblical scholars indicated that the author wanted to legitimize Christianity as a religion in the Roman world, thereby giving it a status similar to that of Judaism.

▶ The Church has baptized new members since the day of Pentecost. Through the waters of Baptism and the guidance of the Holy Spirit, the early Church continued to grow.

Pentecost and the Early Christian Community

The last time Jesus was with his disciples, he promised to send them the Holy Spirit. Then he was lifted up in a cloud and disappeared from their sight. From the Mount of Olives, where Jesus' Ascension occurred, the disciples went back to Jerusalem and soon gathered in the upper room of the house where they were staying. There, "all these were constantly devoting themselves to prayer, together with certain women, including Mary the mother of Jesus, as well as his brothers" (*Acts 1:14*). This is the final time that Scripture mentions Mary, who was a continuing witness to Christian discipleship. She not only gave birth to Jesus, but also helped give birth to the Church. Because of this, Mary is called the Mother of the Church.

A few days later, after the disciples returned to Jerusalem, Peter indicated that the community needed to replace Judas. After nominating Joseph, called Barsabbas, and Matthias, those who were assembled prayed and drew lots. They selected Matthias, who took his place with the other eleven Apostles. This nomination was important to the early followers of Jesus because the twelve Apostles represented the twelve tribes of Israel.

Pentecost Acts describes the Pentecost event, with the Apostles and disciples assembled for this feast in the upper room. They were celebrating the Jewish Feast of Weeks. In Hebrew, Pentecost is called *Shavu'ot* which means "weeks." It comes fifty days after the waving of a barley sheaf during Passover and indicates the start of the Jewish offering to God of the first fruits of their labors. (See *Leviticus 23:9–11*.) In the New Testament the Holy Spirit came to serve as a guide to Christians, similar to the way the law served the Jews in the Old Testament.

After the disciples assembled for Pentecost, something like a rush of wind entered the room, and tongues of fire rested on everyone gathered. The Holy Spirit came upon them. The same Spirit who was present in Jesus now entered his followers. "All of them were filled with the Holy Spirit and began to speak in other languages, as the Spirit gave them ability" (*Acts 2:4*). Witnesses to this sacred event from different nations understood what was said in their own language. This event marked the beginning of the manifestation of the gifts and fruits of the Spirit.

Faith Activity

Mother Mary In small groups, discuss various titles given to Mary and what they mean. Bring in statues or pictures of Mary from home, or illustrate your own image of Mary using one of the titles mentioned in the discussion. Share with your group the special meaning the pictures or statues of Mary have for you.

▼ The Coming of the Holy Spirit by Soichi Watanabe.

Faith Activity

Prayer and Community

Before the Spirit came at Pentecost, those in the upper room lived in fear. Yet the gifts of prayer and community supported them. Write about a time in your life when fear was very real to you. How did your faith and important people in your life help you?

scripture

"But Peter, standing with the eleven, raised his voice and addressed them, 'Men of Judea and all who live in Jerusalem, let this be known to you, and listen to what I say. . . . Let the entire house of Israel know with certainty that God has made him both Lord and Messiah, this Jesus whom you crucified.'

Now when they heard this, they were cut to the heart and said to Peter and to the other Apostles, 'Brothers, what should we do?' Peter said to them, 'Repent, and be baptized every one of you in the name of Jesus Christ so that your sins may be forgiven; and you will receive the gift of the Holy Spirit. For the promise is for you, for your children, and for all who are far away, everyone whom the Lord our God calls to him.' . . .

So those who welcomed his message were baptized, and that day three thousand persons were added."

Acts 2:14, 36–39, 41

The Church in Jerusalem

"*. . . You will be my witnesses in Jerusalem . . .* "

After Pentecost, the Christians boldly proclaimed Jesus' message of salvation. Peter's address to the crowd gives us an early testimony to the spirit of Christian evangelization, which concentrates on Jesus the Messiah. Jesus fulfilled the biblical prophecies of a savior and accomplished our redemption through his death on the cross. But his Father raised him up to glory.

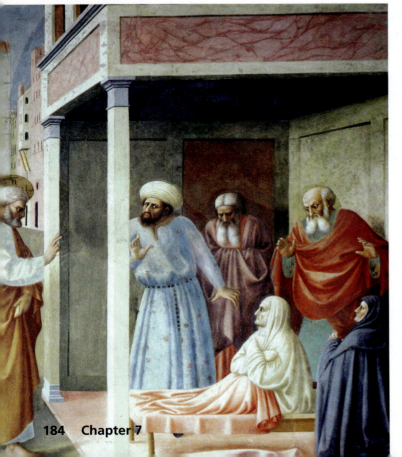

▼ The Healings of Saint Peter
Saint Peter healing a cripple, and the raising of Tabitha by Tomasso Masolino da Panicale, c. 1427.

Through the testimony of Peter and the other apostles, many repented, believed, and were baptized. The early followers of Jesus were faithful to his words, to prayer, and to the Eucharist— referred to as breaking the bread. (See *Acts 2:42.*) The community was centered around the leadership of the Apostles, who witnessed to Christ by words and miracles. The Apostle Peter healed a crippled beggar, spoke before a large crowd, and thousands believed. (See *Acts 3—4.*)

The communal life of the Church was central to these new communities. The community members were generous, kind, and loving, and God protected them. An example of God's protection is the story of Peter's and John's preaching. They boldly professed their faith before the Sanhedrin. They defied the Sanhedrin's order to stop preaching about Jesus. As Peter and John stated, "Whether it is right in God's sight to listen to you rather than to God, you must judge; for we cannot keep from speaking about what we have seen and heard" (*Acts 4:19–20*).

BREAK OPEN *the Word*

Christian Communities Read Acts 2:42–47 and 4:32–37, and summarize the way the early Christians lived justly and cared for all members of their community. Are there any similarities between early Christian customs and what your parish community does?

In Acts 5:29 Peter and the Apostles said, "We must obey God rather than any human authority." Modern-day prophets who advocate **civil disobedience**, such as Martin Luther King Jr., have often used these quotes when disobeying an unjust law.

After Peter and John were arrested, a series of miraculous events occurred. An example was when Gamaliel, a wise Pharisee who was member of the Sanhedrin and a teacher of the law, advocated that the Apostles be left alone. He contended that if the Apostles were not doing God's work, they would fail. If, however, they were doing God's work, no one would be able to stop them. If this were the case, the Sanhedrin would be fighting against God. (See *Acts 5:38–39*.)

As the number of disciples increased, the Twelve decided that seven men had to be selected to help serve the needs of the community and to handle conflicts that arose between the Hebrews and the Greek-speaking Jews. The community approved, and the first seven deacons were appointed. One of the deacons was Saint Stephen, who became one of the first Christian martyrs. **Martyr** in Greek means "witness." The martyrs gave the ultimate witness by suffering persecution and death for their beliefs. (See *Acts 6—7*.)

The love and good deeds of the early followers of Jesus, inspired by the Holy Spirit, captured the attention of those living in Jerusalem. Many became believers. Others, however, did not accept what was happening as the work of the Spirit. Conflicts and tensions arose between Jesus' followers and Jewish and Roman authorities. These conflicts eventually led to persecution and martyrdom.

Interpret the Art

St. Stephen The Arrest and Stoning of St. Stephen. Like Jesus, Saint Stephen was also accused by false witnesses. *What other parallels does the author make between Jesus' trial and crucifixion and Stephen's martyrdom?*

Persecution of the Church Saul, a zealous Jew from Tarsus, opposed and persecuted the new movement. In Acts we read Stephen's speech testifying to Jesus as the Messiah. His testimony led to his being stoned to death. During the stoning, Saul stood nearby and approved. On the day of Stephen's martyrdom, "a severe persecution began against the church in Jerusalem, and all except the apostles were scattered throughout the countryside of Judea and Samaria. . . . Saul was ravaging the church by entering house after house; dragging off both men and women, he committed them to prison" (*Acts 8:1–3*).

As in the Gospel according to Luke, Acts identifies certain people with the events that occurred within the Christian Church. (See *Acts 18:12.*) The author tells of conflicts and the people who governed Palestine, Asia Minor, and Europe. (See *Acts 12:20–22*; *19:29–31*; and *18:12–17.*) For the most part, Acts shows that the Christian movement was politically harmless and did not need the intervention of government officials to function. In Acts 18:14–15 the author uses the action of Gallio, the proconsul of Achaia, as an example of how officials should remove themselves from the affairs of Christians.

The beginning of the Acts of the Apostles demonstrates that the Church did not start on its own initiative. The Holy Spirit empowered the early Christians to proclaim the Good News of Jesus. As this first section of Acts ends, the consequences of following Jesus are highlighted. Persecution of early Christians, nonetheless, did not stop the Gospel message from spreading. Instead, as Acts continues, it becomes clear that persecution was a means for the Church to grow.

Outreach to Gentiles

". . . You will be my witnesses in all Judea and Samaria . . ."

With the stoning death of Stephen, the Jerusalem community scattered. Many found safety in neighboring communities. The Hellenists were especially threatened and sought refuge in Judea and Samaria. Philip, a Hellenist and one of the seven deacons, began to preach the good news to the Samaritans. He was the first to bring Christianity outside of Judea.

Acts tells us that "the crowds with one accord listened eagerly to what was said by Philip, hearing and seeing the signs that he did, for unclean spirits, crying with loud shrieks, came out of many who were possessed; and many others who were paralyzed or lame were cured. So there was great joy in that city" (*Acts 8:6–8*). When the Apostles in Jerusalem heard about the conversion of the Samaritans, Peter and John went to Samaria. Although the Samaritans had been baptized in the name of Jesus, they had not received the Holy Spirit. Peter and John laid their hands on them, and the Samaritans received the Holy Spirit.

In this section of Acts (*Acts 8:25*), Philip made another interesting convert. At the command of an angel, Philip traveled a wilderness road from Jerusalem to Gaza. There he encountered an Ethiopian eunuch, a court official for the queen of Ethiopia. The Ethiopian was returning home after going to Jerusalem to worship.

The Spirit prompted Philip to approach the Ethiopian's chariot. Philip heard the Ethiopian read the following passage from the book of the prophet Isaiah: "Like a sheep he was led to the slaughter, and like a lamb silent before its shearer, so he does not open his mouth. In his humiliation justice was denied him. Who can describe his generation? For his life is taken away from the earth" (*Acts 8:32–33*; see *Isaiah 53:7–8*).

The eunuch asked Philip to explain the passage. Philip not only complied with the request, but also proclaimed the Good News about Jesus. After hearing Philip, the eunuch asked Philip to baptize him. Then, Acts concludes with a surprising ending—after Philip and the eunuch came out of the water of Baptism, the Spirit "snatched Philip away" (*Acts 8:39*). The eunuch did not see Philip again and went away rejoicing in his Baptism.

Faith Activity

Philip The story of Philip is a powerful one. The early disciples, who were concerned with their safety after the stoning of Stephen, retreated to Judea. Philip boldly preached and converted many Gentiles in Samaria. Discuss in a small group how Philip might have felt preaching in a land unfamiliar to him and without allies.

Paul's Conversion

Saul, the relentless persecutor of the followers of Jesus, experienced a life-changing event while on the road to Damascus. This conversion experience transformed him so completely that he became a zealous Christian. The experience is described in Acts 9:

scripture

"Meanwhile Saul, still breathing threats and murder against the disciples of the Lord, went to the high priest and asked him for letters to the synagogues at Damascus, so that if he found any who belonged to the Way, men or women, he might bring them bound to Jerusalem.

Now as he was going along and approaching Damascus, suddenly a light from heaven flashed around him. He fell to the ground and heard a voice saying to him, Jesus: 'Saul, Saul, why do you persecute me?' He asked, 'Who are you, Lord?' The reply came, 'I am Jesus, whom you are persecuting. But get up and enter the city, and you will be told what you are to do.' The men who were traveling with him stood speechless because they heard the voice but saw no one. Saul got up from the ground, and though his eyes were open, he could see nothing; so they led him by hand and brought him into Damascus. For three days he was without sight, and neither ate nor drank.

Now there was a disciple in Damascus named Ananias. The Lord said to him in a vision, 'Ananias.' He answered, 'Here I am, Lord.' The Lord said to him, 'Get up and go to the street called Straight, and at the house of Judas look for a man of Tarsus named Saul. At this moment he is praying, and he has seen in a vision a man named Ananias come in and lay his hands on him so he might regain his sight.'

But Ananias answered, 'Lord, I have heard from many about this man, how much evil he has done to your saints in Jerusalem; and here he has authority from the chief priests to bind all who invoke your name.' But the Lord said to him, 'Go, for he is an instrument whom I have chosen to bring my name before Gentiles and kings and before the people of Israel; I myself will show him how much he must suffer for the sake of my name.' So Ananias went and entered the house. He laid his hands on Saul and said, 'Brother Saul, the Lord Jesus, who appeared to you on your way here, has sent me so that you may regain your sight and be filled with the Holy Spirit.' And immediately something like scales fell from his eyes, and his sight was restored. Then he got up and was baptized, and after taking some food, he regained his strength."

Acts 9:1–22

◀ The Conversion of Saint Paul by Aelbert Cuyp.

Faith Activity

Blindness Have there been times when you were blinded by the truth of God's forgiveness and love for you? Are there times when you are blind to your gifts? To your faults?

This incident was so important to the early Church that it was recorded three times in the Acts of the Apostles: Acts 9:1–22, 22:3–16, and 26:12–18. Paul himself describes the experience in Galatians 1:12–17. This event was significant for several reasons. It revealed that the expansion of Christianity would include Gentiles, foretold Paul's role in their conversion, and implied that anyone can be transformed and become an instrument of God.

Unlike Peter and the Apostles, Paul was not a Palestinian Jew. He was raised in a community in Tarsus, the capital of the Roman province of Cilicia in Asia Minor. At that time Tarsus was a center of Hellenistic education and culture. Paul received an excellent education, which included knowledge of Greek language and philosophy. He was also a Roman citizen. Because of his urban background, he used language meaningful to an urban audience in his preaching. This language included legal imagery and games in the stadium, rather than the agricultural imagery that Jesus used.

Paul, like other Jews, probably received his religious training at home and at his local synagogue. He was proud of his Jewish heritage and the fact that he belonged to the tribe of Benjamin. Raised as a Pharisaic Jew, Paul was deeply committed to his Jewish beliefs and traditions. As a Pharisee, he was trained to fulfill the letter of Jewish law. Paul's life centered on strict observance of all the laws.

Paul's religious training continued in Jerusalem, where he studied under Gamaliel. There he came into contact with the Apostles and followers of Jesus. He persecuted them because he believed they blasphemed God. Yet God chose Saul to bring the Good News to the Gentiles. His vocation was to be a missionary to the Gentiles. His conversion made him a passionate and energetic follower of Jesus, who preached the law of love over practicing the letter of the law.

Saul did not change his name to Paul after his conversion. He had both an Aramaic and a Latin name, which was not uncommon for Jews who were also Roman citizens. Acts never mentions a name change and refers to him as Saul after his conversion. (See *Acts 9:22–25*; *12:25*; and *13:1–2*.) After Acts 13:9, Saul is referred to as Paul. The use of two different names might have been the result of the author's use of different sources.

Faith Activity

What's in a Name? We see that Paul had both an Aramaic name and a Latin name. Is there anyone you know who has two names in two different languages? Perhaps you know someone who prefers to go by a nickname or by a Confirmation name instead of her or his given name. Why do you think a person might change her or his name? Was the change from one name to the other sudden or gradual?

The Christian Symbol of the Fish

Along with the cross and the crucifix, the symbol of the fish is among the most recognizable symbols of Christianity. The fish represents life and all people. The first Apostles were fishermen to whom Jesus said, "I shall make you fishers of men" (*Mark 1:17*). The New Testament has many other references to fish and fishermen. In Matthew 14:17 the Apostles cast their nets over one side of their boat, but caught no fish. They then cast their nets over the other side and caught more fish than they believed their nets could hold. The image of fish appears again in smaller numbers, and later, in the feeding of the 5,000.

Some scholars believe that the Greek word for fish, *ichthys*, is actually an acrostic—an arrangement of words in which the first letters spell out another word—in this case, "Jesus Christ, Son of God, Savior." Thus the symbol of the fish as drawn by the early Christians would have been a reminder of faith. The symbol might also have been a password, allowing the person who drew it to signify to others that he or she was Christian. The need for secrecy and passwords was largely a result of Nero's violence against Christians. The symbol persists today as a symbol of Christian pride.

Faith Activity

Greek Letters This chart shows the Greek letters for the acrostic *ichthys*. Each letter stands for the Greek word on the right. Research the meanings of these Greek words. How does the meaning of the symbol change for you when you know the meaning of the words in Greek?

Connect to the Past

Jesus in Egypt This fish with a cross is from a fourth century Coptic cemetery in Egypt. Egypt holds the special significance of providing refuge for the Holy Family for nearly four years during Herod's reign. In recent years Egyptians have attempted to re-pave the roads of the Holy Family's travel. Read Matthew 2:13–23, and then research the Christian landmarks that are being preserved in Egypt today. *What landmark of Jesus' life would you like to visit and why?*

Greek Letters	
I Iota	the first letter in the Greek word Iesous
X Chi	the first letter in the Greek word Christos
Θ Theta	the first letter in the Greek word Theos
Υ Upsilon	the first letter in the Greek word Yios (Huois)
Σ Sigma	the first letter in the Greek word Soter

The Early Evangelism of Paul

Not long after his conversion, Paul started preaching in the synagogues in Damascus. The majority of Christ's followers who lived in Jerusalem and Damascus did not initially accept Paul's conversion experience. After all, he was partially responsible for the suffering, persecution, and death of many in these communities. (See *Acts 9:20–22*.) After he arrived at Jerusalem, the disciples feared him for they knew of his prior reputation.

Barnabas, however, supported him, and soon Paul accompanied the Apostles as they preached. The Apostles soon believed that the Holy Spirit was at work within Paul and they sent him to Tarsus for safety. While there, he might have begun new communities. He spent time in prayer, preparing for the work of the Lord.

Peter's Vision When Peter was in Jaffa, an angel of God came to Cornelius, a God-fearing person. The angel instructed him to send for Peter. In the meantime, Peter had a vision of a sheet containing all sorts of animals. Peter was told to eat, but he hesitated, for he had never before eaten any unclean animal. The second time, a voice told him, "What God has made clean, you must not call profane" (*Acts 10:15*). After this happened three times, the vision ended. Peter wondered what it meant. Then the Spirit told Peter that three men were looking for him, and that he should go with them without hesitation.

After the men who had been sent by Cornelius arrived, Peter went with them. Because he had seen the vision, Peter visited Cornelius and those who were assembled. Peter's visit was a radical move because Jews were forbidden to mix with those of another race. Peter learned from the vision that no one is profane or unclean. Cornelius was told in his vision that Peter, his visitor, would give them a message from God. Peter then announced to those gathered that anyone who fears God, whatever one's race, is acceptable to God. He went on to tell Cornelius and his family about Jesus, whom the Father anointed with the Holy Spirit. As Peter spoke to them, the Holy Spirit descended on the gathering, and they began to speak in foreign languages and praise God. After that, Peter baptized them in Jesus' name. (See *Acts 10:44–48*.) Cornelius, his household, and his friends were the first Gentiles to be baptized in the name of the Lord.

After Stephen's stoning, some disciples traveled as far as Cyprus and Antioch. Usually they preached to Jews. Other disciples from Cyrene and Cyprus made their way to Antioch and began proclaiming Jesus' message to the Greeks. Many of those living in Antioch became followers of Christ.

Becca's BFv.

▲ Saint Paul by Etienne Parrocel il Romain, c. 1740.

Jews and Gentiles in the Church After the Church in Jerusalem found out what was happening in Antioch, they sent Barnabas there. When Barnabas saw the interest in Jesus in Antioch, he went to Tarsus and found Saul. Together they returned to Antioch to serve a new community of Christ's followers. This community, originally founded by those escaping persecution in Jerusalem, eventually became the second-largest Christian community. Only the apostolic community in Jerusalem was greater in number.

Antioch was the first Church that welcomed both Jewish and Gentile converts. Here, for the first time, the followers of Jesus were referred to as Christians. Antioch was a Christian community in both name and action. When this Church learned that Christians in Jerusalem were suffering from famine, they contributed money to help those in need.

Just as Jesus' disciples continued to share the Good News of Jesus, we are called to share our faith with others, in words and in actions. The disciples often suffered for their choice to follow Jesus, but they were dedicated to his mission. They knew that there was more to life than the world in which they were living. We also have a duty to proclaim the kingdom of God and to work toward its fulfillment. When we continue the work of Christ in today's world, we help further his kingdom.

Faith Activity

Almsgiving The Church at Antioch was among the first to provide financial assistance to a sister Church in need. Donation and almsgiving were essential in keeping early Churches operational. Find out about local charities, sister parishes, and missions that your church supports so you can see for yourself how much help your church community gives to others.

Paul's Missionary Journeys

Paul is called the Apostle to the Gentiles because of his missionary efforts in evangelizing the Gentile world. After his time in Antioch, he spent his life traveling through Asia Minor and Europe proclaiming that Jesus is Lord. (See *Acts 13:1—28:31*.)

Paul's First Missionary Journey (A.D. 46–48)

The Holy Spirit blessed the Church at Antioch, and prophets and teachers began to emerge. "While they were worshiping the Lord and fasting, the Holy Spirit said, 'Set apart for me Barnabas and Saul for the work to which I have called them.' Then after fasting and praying they laid their hands on them and sent them off" (*Acts 13:2–3*).

With the prayers and the support of the Antioch community, Paul, Barnabas, and Barnabas' cousin, John Mark, set sail for Cyprus to share the message of Jesus the Messiah. Aided by safe sea routes, good roads, and knowledge of the Greek language, these missionaries met with varying degrees of success. They preached first to Jews in the synagogues. Some listeners accepted the message, while others were openly hostile to it.

As the journey continued, John Mark decided to return to Jerusalem. Paul and Barnabas kept moving through Asia Minor. Again, they met with some success among the Jews. Some resisted their message—at times responding to the message with violence. Believing that salvation was intended for both Jews and Gentiles, Paul and Barnabas preached the Good News first in synagogues and then in Gentile communities. After establishing mixed communities of Jews and Gentiles apart from the synagogues, Paul and Barnabas would move to another place.

When returning to Antioch after the first missionary journey, Paul and Barnabas discovered that controversy had been growing in their absence. The community was divided between those who thought becoming a follower of Jesus was a one-step process and those who thought it should be a two-step process.

Faith Activity

Decisions Often the road to making decisions includes doubts, challenges, distractions, denials, acceptance, and ultimately, persistence toward truth. With a small group, discuss difficult decisions you have made, and what growth occurred because of them. How can sharing your experiences help others in need?

The Council of Jerusalem

Did Gentiles have to accept and follow Jewish law to follow Jesus? Did male Gentile Christians, for example, have to be circumcised as Jews were? Circumcision was performed on male Jews when they were eight days old as a sign of the Jewish covenant with God. Circumcision identified them as members of the Jewish community.

Many Gentiles converting to Christianity were adult men. Some of them preferred not to be circumcised. They questioned whether circumcision was a necessary part of their initiation into the Church. Paul's argument that Gentiles did not need to be circumcised was not based on practical concerns. It was based on his theological conviction that this was not God's intention for Gentiles. Paul believed that in the new covenant, which was sealed with Jesus' blood, following Jesus did not require Gentiles to be circumcised.

Following the Jewish dietary laws carried other concerns: Did Gentile converts have to observe the many dietary customs prescribed by Jewish law? Jewish law forbade Jews to eat with non-Jews. How could Jewish and Gentile Christians be united if they were not allowed to share a meal together? Was following Jewish law more important than faith in Jesus?

The Antioch community sent Paul and Barnabas to Jerusalem to discuss these issues. This meeting in Jerusalem is often called the *Council of Jerusalem* because of its similarity to the later councils of the Church. It was called to resolve the growing controversy over whether Gentile Christians had to observe Jewish law.

Some followers of Jesus believed that it was necessary to keep these laws. After debating the issue, Peter stood up and reminded the others that he had been chosen to bring the Good News to the Gentiles:

scripture

"And God, who knows the human heart, testified to them by giving them the Holy Spirit, just as he did to us; and in cleansing their hearts by faith he has made no distinction between them and us. Now therefore why are you putting God to the test by placing on the neck of the disciples a yoke that neither our ancestors nor we have been able to bear? On the contrary, we believe that we will be saved through the grace of the Lord Jesus, just as they will."

Acts 15:8–11

Peter's words reflected his authority in the early Church. He held the place of authority over the other Apostles because Jesus had selected him to head his Church. Peter was the first pope, because he was the starting point of the papacy we know today.

Paul and Barnabas told the Apostles and the elders who were gathered of the deeds and wonders God had worked with the Gentiles. James, the head of the church of Jerusalem, then issued a letter stating that in accordance with the Holy Spirit, they would "impose on you no further burdens upon them than these essentials: that you abstain from what has been sacrificed to idols and from blood and from what is strangled and from fornication. If you keep yourselves from these, you will do well. Farewell" (*Acts 15:29*).

The Council of Jerusalem, under the leadership of the Apostles and the elders, and guided by the Holy Spirit, lifted barriers that could have kept the Church from spreading. Within a short time, Gentile Christians outnumbered Jewish Christians. However, the conflict over the decision to not impose Jewish law on Gentiles continued. For many years a tension persisted, as some Jewish Christians believed that following the Jewish law was essential to the Christian faith. At this time, Jesus' followers who were Jewish still professed their Jewish faith.

Faith Activity

Strengths and Weaknesses Throughout the Gospels, we see examples of Peter's weaknesses. However, in Acts Peter's strengths are highlighted. Peter is an example of how a person's weaknesses and strengths can both be used as God's instruments. Think of examples from your life of how a weakness or a strength can have both a positive and a negative side.

▶ Saint Peter's statue in the Piazza San Pietro by Giuseppe de Fabris.

Paul's Second Missionary Journey (A.D. 49–52)

After the Council of Jerusalem, Paul and Barnabas went separate ways. (See *Acts 15:36–39*.) Paul chose Silas to accompany him on his next journey. Together, they left Antioch and traveled to Syria, Cilicia, Derbe, and Lystra. Timothy, who became a trusted companion of Paul, joined them in Lystra. After traveling through Phyrygia and Galatia, they journeyed to Mysia and Troas, where Luke is believed to have possibly joined them in their work. After receiving a vision, Paul moved on to Philippi, an important city in Macedonia—the first place in Europe where the Gospel was preached.

There they met Lydia, a dealer in purple cloth. She listened to Paul, and the Lord opened her heart to accept the Gospel. After she and her household were baptized, Paul and his companions stayed at her home.

However, some in Philippi were not hospitable to Paul and his companions. In one instance, Paul and Silas were severely flogged and imprisoned for expelling a demon from a slave-girl. The girl's owners, who could no longer earn money from the girl's fortune-telling, brought Paul and Silas before the authorities.

After their release from jail, Paul and Silas stopped in Thessalonica, where reaction to their message was mixed among the Jews but accepted by many devout Greeks. Later Paul was forced to leave Thessalonica for reasons of personal safety. He fled to Beroea. From there he moved on to Athens, where he preached but did not start a community.

Finally, Paul arrived in Corinth where he met Aquila and Priscilla, a married couple who were tentmakers like Paul. Paul stayed with them for a year and a half. They worked together and also established a large Christian community—mostly Gentile—who met for worship at Priscilla and Aquila's home. Eventually Priscilla and Aquila became missionaries.

Paul's Third Missionary Journey (A.D. 53–57)

After returning to Antioch, Paul traveled to Ephesus, the capital of Asia. Paul proclaimed the Good News until those living in that part of Asia—Gentiles and Jews alike—heard the word of the Lord. He remained in this area for almost three years during which time, "God did extraordinary miracles through Paul, so that when the handkerchiefs or aprons that had touched his skin were brought to the sick, their diseases left them, and the evil spirits came out of them" (*Acts 19:11–12*). Paul's words and deeds attracted many followers to Christianity.

As Paul journeyed to Jerusalem, he stopped along the way to visit the communities he had started. He advised them and offered final farewells because he realized their paths would not cross again. When he reached Caesarea, he met the prophet Agabus, who warned Paul that he would be imprisoned soon.

Living Out
The Good News

CRS workers measure out corn soya blend for displaced children in war-torn Uganda.

The bishops of the United States founded Catholic Relief Services (CRS) about sixty years ago. Their goal was to help those who are poor and suffering, while promoting development in third-world countries. CRS operates in more than ninety countries around the world. One focal point in CRS' campaign to alleviate suffering is the Sudan, particularly the Darfur region, where a violent civil war has killed thousands. The resulting lack of food and water has killed thousands more.

The Catholic Campaign for Human Development (CCHD) is an organization similar to CRS, though it focuses on the domestic front. Since CCHD's founding about thirty years ago, eliminating poverty and achieving social justice in communities around the United States have

been its main goals. The organization has compiled statistics that identify the states that have the highest and lowest percentages of poverty. Mississippi has the highest percentage of people living below the poverty line, and New Hampshire has the lowest.

CRS and CCHD both show great care for our neighbors—inside the country and outside of it. These two groups and the care they show to all people—particularly the least of our brethren—are examples of how groups can live out the Good News. Both groups offer many options for people to join in their missions to end poverty and social injustice. In fact, chances are good that CCHD is active somewhere near your community.

BREAK OPEN *the Word*

Paul's Journey Acts 27 and 28 describe Paul's hazardous journey to Rome. Illustrate, write a short story or a poem, or write a song about the journey, including as much detail as possible.

Paul's Trip to Rome (A.D. 59–60)

Upon Paul's return to Jerusalem, he informed James and the elders of the success he experienced among the Gentiles. The Jerusalem community, in turn, shared with Paul their successes with the Jews. Although all did the work of the Lord, tension existed between Paul and those in Jerusalem. The tension escalated into a riot. Roman soldiers took Paul into custody and brought him to Caesarea, the Roman capital of Palestine. There he lived under house arrest for two years until he was transferred to Rome.

Paul's eventful journey to Rome, sometimes referred to as his fourth missionary journey, brought him to the capital of the empire. In Rome Paul was placed under house arrest but allowed to proclaim the Word. Again Paul met with resistance from some members of the Jewish community. As a result, he told them, "Let it be known to you then that this salvation of God has been sent to the Gentiles; they will listen" (*Acts 28:29*). Paul remained in Rome. At the conclusion of Acts, Paul "welcomed all who came to him, proclaiming the kingdom of God and teaching the Lord Jesus Christ with all boldness and without hindrance" (*Acts 28:30–31*).

Acts is a reflection of the first thirty years of the experiences of the early Church. The story of Acts connects the life of Jesus with the life of the Church. It describes how Jesus' way of life became the Way of life for his followers. Sometimes called the Gospel of the Holy Spirit, Acts shows how the Holy Spirit strengthened the community of disciples to encounter problems and challenges with courage and trust in the Lord. The Acts of the Apostles offers us deeper insight into our present time, when we respond in faith to our challenges, as did the early followers of Jesus.

Connect to the Past

Ephesian Ruins The ruins pictured are of the Temple of Artemis (Diana) in Ephesus, one of the seven wonders of the ancient world. This temple shows the Ephesians' dedication to the Cult of Diana.
How do you think Paul felt when preaching the Gospel to these people?

The Martyrdom of the Disciples

Although the original Greek word *martyr* meant a witness who testified to a belief or fact, the word almost immediately began to take on shades of another meaning. More than mere witnesses, the witnesses who openly proclaimed their faith were often in danger of severe punishment or death. A martyr became someone who could be called upon at any time either to deny his or her beliefs or to suffer punishment and death.

Witnessing to the message and values of Jesus exacted a high price. Saint Paul summed up his hardships in his letter for the people of Corinth:

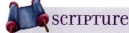

scripture

"Five times I have received from the Jews the forty lashes minus one. Three times I was beaten with rods. Once I received a stoning. Three times I was shipwrecked; for a night and a day I was adrift at sea; on frequent journeys, in danger from rivers, danger from bandits, danger from my own people, danger from Gentiles, danger in the city, danger in the wilderness, danger at sea, danger from false brothers and sisters; in toil and hardship, through many a sleepless night, hungry and thirsty, often without food, cold and naked."

2 Corinthians 11:24–27

Faith Activity

Times of Trouble
Compare your life to Paul's life. How do your difficulties compare? How do your times of trouble compare to Paul's times of trouble? Would you choose this life if you knew it would change the world for the better?

This doesn't sound like the way anyone would choose to live, at least not unless you were clear about why you were enduring these things. Saint Paul was very clear. He wanted to share the Good News with others, regardless of the personal costs, and to praise the Lord until the day that he died. Many since Saint Paul have chosen this same purpose for their lives and as a result, have died with the name of Jesus on their lips.

Discipleship begins as we are called and challenged to emulate the life of Jesus. When we accept this invitation, as members of the Church, we become part of the never-ending story of Jesus. Faith and hope were alive in Jesus' followers. Their faith, hope, and trust in the Risen Jesus were the final word.

Jesus' first disciples experienced severe persecution—almost all suffered and died in service of the faith. This persecution strengthened the disciples; martyrdom brought more to Christianity than it took away. The gifts of the Holy Spirit enabled new disciples to pick up where others had left off.

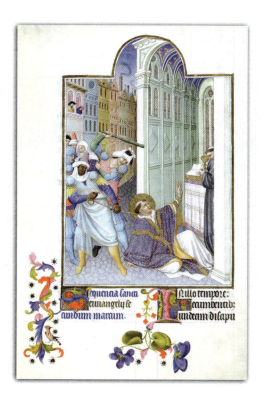

▶ The Martyrdom of St. Mark by Pol de Limbourg c. 15th century.

Called to Share the Good News   199

Faith Activity

Strength of Character
Research other people who were martyred in the twentieth century. Consider Jean Donovan and her fellow lay missionaries in El Salvador, or Sister Barbara Ann Ford in Guatemala—among many others—when you do your research. What defines the people you have researched? What similarities do you see in their character?

At Pentecost Jesus' Apostles found the strength they needed to spread the Gospel. Filled with the Holy Spirit, they were no longer afraid to suffer and serve as Jesus had. They became living witnesses to God's love and to the power that comes from believing, loving, and trusting Jesus.

Work with the Chart

Distance from Jerusalem Look at the chart below, and make a list of the different places where the Apostles were martyred or died. Using a map, estimate the distance from Jerusalem to those places. Most of the Apostles established communities of faith in places where they eventually were martyred or died.
What effect do you think their deaths had on the communities?

How the Apostles Died	
Andrew	He was crucified on an X-shaped cross in Greece.
Bartholomew	He was tortured and killed with knives near modern-day Armenia.
James (the Elder)	He was killed by a sword about A.D. 44 in Jerusalem; he was the first martyred apostle.
James (the Less)	He was stoned in Jerusalem.
Jude	He was executed with an ax.
Matthew	He suffered a sword wound and died in Ethiopia.
Peter	He was crucified upside down in A.D. 67 in Rome.
Philip	He was hanged near modern-day Turkey.
Thomas	He was martyred in India.
Simon the Zealot	He was beaten and then cut into pieces.
John	He was imprisoned for a while on the island of Patmos near Greece; he died of natural causes.

Communion of Saints

The Apostles and first disciples encouraged others to proclaim the Good News and to live a holy and just life. The Church grew as communities of believers accepted and believed. As the first Christians died, they continued the Church in heaven. The Church consists of those living on earth and still striving to follow the Gospel; those who have already died and are in heaven; and those who have died and are in purgatory, being purified in preparation for entering heaven. We call the entire assembly of Church members the **communion of saints**.

All faithful members of the Church are called saints because Jesus has called us to be the holy people of God. In another sense the term saint refers to a person who has gone through the process of **canonization**—an official Church statement by which a person is declared a saint for having lived a holy life of heroic virtue, and is recognized in heaven.

Modern Martyrs Martyrdom did not end in the early Church but continued throughout the centuries. Thousands of followers have witnessed the mission of Jesus, regardless of governmental or societal circumstances at the time.

In the late 1700s, a fledgling Korean Church founded by laypeople endured intense persecution. As one of the martyrs, Saint Andrew Kim, wrote, "The Church in Korea was founded on the strong faith of these martyrs who endured persecutions for over a hundred years. Much of the Korean Church history had been written in their blood." For the next century members of this Church were persecuted, murdered, and driven into the mountains of Korea. There, the Church took hold and began to grow. In small mountain villages, the followers of Christ spread the Good News, despite wave after wave of persecution in which thousands were martyred. On May 6, 1984, the Church canonized 103 Korean people, ranging in age from thirteen-year-old Peter Yu Tae-chol to seventy-two-year-old Mark Chong.

In 1980 Archbishop Oscar Romero, like Saint Paul, spoke out against the tyranny and the killing carried out by the corrupt military leadership in El Salvador. In a country of only five million people, three thousand Salvadorans a day disappeared or were murdered. Many victims were poor farmers and other catechists. Amid constant death threats, Archbishop Romero refused to be silenced. Instead, he preached, "Any human law to kill must be subordinate to the law of God, which says, 'Thou shalt not kill.'" Romero was murdered the day after he spoke these words. His legacy lives on in the Salvadoran people. As he said days before his death, "You can tell the people that if they succeed in killing me, that I forgive and bless those who do it. Hopefully, they will realize they are wasting their time. A bishop will die, but the Church of God, which is the people, will never perish."

▼ A meeting of Pope John XXIII's ecumenical council in St. Peter's Basilica, Vatican City. This meeting of worldwide Catholic clergy was popularly known as the Second Vatican Council.

Communal Life of the Church

The Acts of the Apostles records the life of the early Church and provides an example of how a communal Church, centered in Christ, should exist. "All who believed were together and had all things in common; they would sell their possessions and goods and distribute the proceeds to all, as any had need" (*Acts 2:44–45*). The communal life of the Church also included praying together, fidelity to the teachings of the Apostles, fellowship, breaking of the bread, and being of one heart and soul. (See *Acts 2:46–47, 4:32–35*.)

The internal dynamics in Acts reveal key unspoken themes which are a monitor for the growth and the faithfulness of the Church through the ages.

- Living the message of the kingdom of God by the community as a whole and by individual Christians

- Carrying out the mission of Christ, entrusted to his Church, under the guidance of the Holy Spirit

- Engaging in works of ministry to those who are poor and disenfranchised, as well as serving the needs of the entire community of faith in the ministries of the Word, worship, and service

- Looking to the Church community for understanding of faith, consistent with the teachings of Jesus

In this context Church leaders, especially Peter and the other Apostles, grounded the Church's hierarchy, called by Christ to preach, minister, and govern the Church under the leadership of the pope.

The early Church also valued the presence, participation, and witness of women in the early Church. Women, filled with holy boldness, risked standing at the foot of the cross to witness to the death of Jesus. Women, filled with holy love, went to the tomb and were the first to witness to the Resurrection of Jesus. Women, filled with holy wisdom and strength, witnessed to and contributed to the formation of the early Church.

The communities of the early Church modeled interdependence between men and women as they served alongside each other. Their own examples of unity broke the customs of this time. Today women continue to persevere as they use their creative powers and energy to spread the message of Christianity.

Christians have always been sacramental people. This expression means that the sacraments are a vital part of our lives. The sacraments help us grow in our spiritual life, our relationship with the Trinity. The term sacramental people also means that the whole community of the Church, united with Jesus, celebrates the liturgy.

The Sacraments of the Catholic Church

We learn from the Acts of the Apostles that the first Church members followed Jesus' command to break bread in his name. The communities gathered to proclaim the Scriptures, to share in Christ's Body and Blood, and to care for the needs of others. Since then, the Church has continued to gather to worship in Jesus' name. The Church celebrates seven sacraments: Baptism, Confirmation, Eucharist, Reconciliation, Anointing of the Sick, Holy Orders, and Matrimony.

Baptism In Baptism, the Church continues the Apostles' mission to baptize and teach all nations. Baptism is the first of three Sacraments of Christian Initiation. Through the waters of Baptism, there is a new birth. The Holy Spirit received at Baptism makes those baptized into brothers and sisters of Jesus as they are incorporated into the Body of Christ and made members of his Church.

Confirmation The Sacrament of Confirmation is the second of the three Sacraments of Christian Initiation. At Confirmation, the confirmand receives a special outpouring of the Holy Spirit. Baptismal graces are increased and deepened. Recalling Jesus' giving of the Holy Spirit to his followers and the coming of the Holy Spirit at Pentecost is the scriptural basis for the sacrament.

Eucharist The Eucharist is the third of the three Sacraments of Christian Initiation. The Eucharist is the Body and Blood of Christ, which nourishes his followers and builds the Church. There can be no Church if there is no Eucharist. We cannot strive to build community with others unless we are continually nourished by the Eucharist. Given by Jesus to the disciples at the Last Supper, the Eucharist remains the central action of the Church at liturgy and prayer.

Penance and Reconciliation The Church celebrates God's forgiveness in the Sacrament of Reconciliation. The person who receives the sacrament is reconciled with God and the Church. Jesus forgave sinners throughout his ministry. He continues to forgive sinners through the power of the Holy Spirit poured out in this sacrament. The bishop or priest, who acts in Christ's name, forgives sins in the name of the Father, and of the Son, and of the Holy Spirit.

Anointing of the Sick God initiates spiritual and sometimes physical healing in the Sacrament of the Anointing of the Sick. Jesus ministered to those who were sick in body, mind, and spirit. He forgave their sins and healed them of various illnesses. The Church continues the forgiving and healing presence of Christ by anointing members who are seriously sick or are suffering from illness caused by advanced age. In turn, the sick person is united to the sufferings of Christ, strengthened to endure suffering in a Christ-like manner, and forgiven for his or her sins, and may have physical health restored if that is God's will.

Holy Orders The Sacrament of Holy Orders pours out the Holy Spirit and his gifts upon the newly ordained. The recipient is configured to Christ to act as his representative as an ordained leader in the Church. As Jesus selected the Apostles to be his followers and to lead others to him, those ordained in the Church are selected for the special ministry of leading, teaching, and caring for God's people.

Matrimony This sacrament celebrates the commitment of a man and a woman, both being baptized Christians, to love each other in imitation of the faithfulness that God has shown to humanity throughout history. Through marriage, the couple embarks upon a life of commitment to each other and to God, to love each another with self-giving love and faithfulness. The grace of the Sacrament of Matrimony strengthens the couple to be true and to love each other as Christ loves the Church. The Catholic Church supports them in their promise of fidelity.

The sacraments are intimately related to Jesus' Paschal mystery. The graces won through Jesus' Passion, death, and Resurrection flow through each sacrament. Christ continues to work in each sacrament, thereby continuing the saving activity effected through his death and Resurrection.

Saint Catherine of Siena

Saint Catherine of Siena
(1347–1380)

Saint Teresa of Ávila
(1515–1582)

Saint John of the Cross
(1542–1591)

These three saints, as well as thirty-three other saints and venerables constitute the doctors of the Church. The doctors of the Church are people who have contributed great writings to the Church and have advanced the knowledge of all Christians through their interpretations of doctrine. Of those named doctors of the Church in the twentieth century, Saints Catherine of Siena, Teresa of Ávila, and John of the Cross are the most recent additions.

Catherine of Siena was blessed from an early age with the gift of seeing guardian angels while they protected people. She became a Dominican nun and lived during the Western Schism—a time when the Papacy attempted to return to Rome from Avignon, France. Catherine stayed true to the Roman Pope Urban VI, and moved to Rome at his request. From Rome, she wrote nearly 400 letters and the "Dialogue" or the "Treatise on Divine Providence." The latter piece can be seen as a discussion between the Lord and the soul of a human.

Catherine was granted the stigmata, although because of her prayers, the marks did not show on her body until she died.

The early life of Teresa of Ávila was similar to that of many teens today. She attempted to run away from home, preferred romance novels, often caused trouble, and was known to care mostly for clothes, boys, and flirting. Upon turning sixteen, she was sent to a convent by her father and eventually grew to enjoy the religious life because of her growing love for God. Teresa had great difficulty with prayer. For eighteen years she felt that her prayers went unanswered and that the results she so desired would never come to pass. After falling ill at forty-one with malaria, she stopped praying but was convinced by a priest to return to prayer. Her prayerful reflections then grew daily. She poured out her spiritual life onto paper in the books *Life Written by Herself*, *Relations*, and *Interior Castle*. These books spoke of her life in prayer and her relationship with God. Her belief in prayer led her to reform the Carmelite order and found the (Discalced) Carmelites with the aid of Saint John of the Cross.

John of the Cross grew up in poverty and surrounded by suffering. John joined the Carmelites and was soon asked by Teresa of Ávila to aid in reforming the order and returning the Carmelites to a life of prayer. John was kidnapped by some members of the order who feared the reforms; he was placed in a small cell with a very small window at the top. In this location John focused on his love and his faith. He eventually escaped, and when he finally arrived at a safe location, he shared his poetry and stories with anyone who would listen. He wrote books that are mostly concerned with practicality and the ability we all have to grow spiritually. Among his books are *Ascent on Mount Carmel* and *Dark Night of the Soul*.

Prayer

Begin by praying the Sign of the Cross.

Leader: Ever living and ever loving Lord, you call us to be good to our neighbors and to care for all people. We learn from the Apostles in Acts that we should mission to those in need, and to show forth your grace in all we do. We ask your Son, Jesus, to empower our hearts to spread his word and aid all those in need. The response is "Lord Jesus, empower our hearts."

All: Lord Jesus, empower our hearts.

Leader: When we are in doubt of our abilities, and fearful of the road ahead . . .

All: Lord Jesus, empower our hearts.

Leader: When we have been arrested in our tracks, our path blocked by natural or unnatural causes . . .

All: Lord Jesus, empower our hearts.

Leader: When the storms of life cloud our vision, rock our boat, and send us in directions we never thought we would be sent in . . .

All: Lord Jesus, empower our hearts.

Leader: When we finally land where we belong, after being lost for so long . . .

All: Lord Jesus, empower our hearts.

Leader: Now we will join hands and pray the Lord's Prayer . . .

All: (when finished) Amen.

End by praying the Sign of the Cross.

Review

1. What factors have led many scholars to believe that the same person wrote the Gospel of Luke and Acts?

2. Explain why Peter proposed voting for Judas' replacement.

3. Describe some of the interactions the Apostles had with the Sanhedrin after the death of Jesus.

4. What happened to Saul after the stoning of Stephen? In what direction did his life turn?

5. How was Saul's background different from the other Apostles? Where was he raised? Was he wealthy or poor?

6. What differentiated the Church in Antioch from other early Churches?

7. Describe the first missionary journey of Paul and some of the controversies after Paul and Barnabas returned to Antioch. How were the controversies resolved?

8. Describe the differences in hospitality that Paul and Silas received during the second missionary journey of Paul.

9. Describe the differences and similarities between CRS and the CCHD.

10. Why is Acts sometimes called the Gospel of the Holy Spirit?

11. What is the communion of saints? How does it relate to canonization?

12. What are the unspoken themes in Acts that have become a monitor for the growth and faithfulness of the Church?

Key Words

canonization (p. 200)—An official Church statement by which a person is declared to have lived a holy life of heroic virtue. In the last stage of canonization, the person is named a saint.

civil disobedience (p. 185)—The act of breaking a law non-violently, usually with the intent to call into question the morality of the law.

communion of saints (p. 200)—All faithful Church members on earth, in heaven, and in purgatory; communion in holy things (*sancta*) and among holy persons (*sancti*).

martyr (p. 185)—The Greek word for "witness." They died for their beliefs.

persecution (p. 180)—The act of causing suffering because of a person's belief.

Teen to Teen

Jean Donovan and her fellow women martyrs were lay missionaries, administering care and starting a mission in El Salvador. The risks of personal harm and possibly death are present in almost every mission. Most missionaries, while aware of the dangers, volunteer their time to help make the world a better place. If you were a missionary, where would you want to help change the world?

"I want to go wherever the worst problems are. I hear about these places all the time on the news. After the hurricanes in the Caribbean, Haiti was in the midst of a hunger crisis. The civil war in the Sudan has created too many problems. In Chechnya, war still goes on. I want to go to these areas and let them know that I care, America cares, and God still cares. It's the least I can do for people who need me."

Britta E.

"I want to stay here in this country. There are parts of this country that have problems just as bad as any other in the world, and no one else is doing anything about it. When I look around at all I have, and the support of my family and my church, I just wonder what it's like for people who have less."

Marquell S.

"I want to administer help through a larger group in the U.S. I think I would work best on the administration side of things—to help identify where the next bad spot is going to be and get people there as soon as, or even before it gets worse. I think that even though it's rough going through bad times, having to wait for help for months while it's still bad is even worse."

Amberly K.

Personal Challenge

After high school you may be headed for college or a university. Using the Internet, research mission groups that offer scholarships for the colleges you are interested in attending. Many of these groups offer scholarships in return for volunteer work after graduation. This is an excellent way to both receive your education from a university and gain experience with mission work. Both of these traits will help you in your future job search and give you greater understanding of the world around you.

BReak Open *the* **Word**

Missionaries of the Church Read the quote from Acts 1:8 on the opening pages of the chapter, and then read Acts 1 in its entirety in your Bible. Jesus spoke these final words, recorded in Acts 1:8, before he ascended into heaven. These words promised the coming of the Holy Spirit who would empower Jesus' followers to be his witnesses throughout the world. The Holy Spirit enabled the followers of Jesus to begin the missionary actions of the Church. Make a chart on a piece of paper that shows the first disciples, where they traveled, and to what group their missions were directed.

A.D. 33
Crucifixion, death, and
Resurrection of Jesus

A.D. 41–43
Peter's ministry
to Gentiles

A.D. 50
Paul's arrival in Corinth

A.D. 14–37

A.D. 47

A.D. 33
Conversion of Paul of Tarsus

A.D. 41–43
Paul's house arrest in Rome
(Philippians likely written)

C. A.D. 50
First Pauline Letters written

Called to Be Church

"Bear with one another and, if anyone has a complaint against another, forgive each other...."

Colossians 3:12

Chapter Goals

In this chapter, you will:

- study the author and key themes of the Epistles.

- explore the Pauline Letters and how they encouraged early faith communities to commitment and worship.

- understand the common issues faced by these communities and how they are addressed in the Letters.

- learn about the Revelation to John and explore its imagery and symbolism.

- learn about modern letters written by the pope.

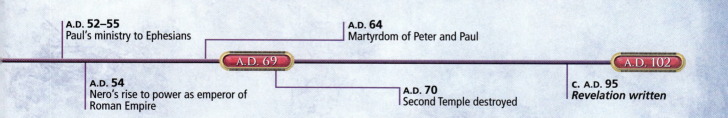

A.D. 52–55
Paul's ministry to Ephesians

A.D. 64
Martyrdom of Peter and Paul

A.D. 69

A.D. 102

A.D. 54
Nero's rise to power as emperor of Roman Empire

A.D. 70
Second Temple destroyed

C. A.D. 95
Revelation written

Overview of the Letters

Faith Activity

How Many Can You Name? In a small group and without looking in your Bible, name as many of the letters of the New Testament as you can. Why do you think so many letters were included in the canon? What benefit do you see from including letters to so many different groups of people or individuals?

▼ A professional scribe writes a Torah scroll using traditional writing tools.

These words, reflecting Paul's confidence in God, set the tone for the letters he wrote to the churches and for other New Testament writings. In this chapter, we consider Paul's letters, those of other disciples, and the Book of Revelation. Along with the four Gospels and the Acts of the Apostles, these form the New Testament writings. In treating them, we follow the general sequence of the letters and Revelation in the canon of the New Testament. Ambiguity surrounds the authorship of some of these works.

Most people are less familiar with the letters than they are with the Gospels. Many letters were written before the Gospels. They give us the earliest picture of the life of the first Christian churches. They were written to guide and encourage early Christians in their faith. They contain the challenges to the communities or individuals who needed reproof, and they describe the organization and structure of the first churches. They stress love, forgiveness, and faithfulness to the mission of Christ. Moreover these writings document the ministry of the early disciples and the community. They provide a useful guide for today's Christians.

The New Testament contains twenty-one letters, plus Revelation. All are faith-filled glimpses into the sacred Traditions from which our Church has grown. As the Apostles and the early missionaries shared the message of Jesus, they came across people of different economic, ethnic, and religious backgrounds. Ministering to such a diverse group was challenging, as was supporting the faith of the early Christian communities.

Each convert brought a different web of relationships from his or her life experiences. The common thread binding all converts together was their faith in God and their desire to follow Jesus in the faith life of the Christian communities.

The letters were instructions to communities of Christian converts. At first, they were read at church gatherings. Eventually, Church leaders collected them, scribes copied them, and couriers circulated them among other Christian communities. Paul or his followers wrote thirteen letters. Three are attributed to John, two to Peter, one to James, and one to Jude. Hebrews, although once thought to be one of Paul's letters, is unique.

Someone other than the named author wrote some of these letters. Why did this happen? This practice, called **pseudonymity**, was common during this time. It was a way of thanking or crediting one's mentor or teacher for the knowledge one had received. Besides, using a known person's name gave the writing more credibility.

This chapter arranges the letters according to the way they appear in the canon of the New Testament, which placed together letters written to the same community. Although the Third Council of Carthage in 397 approved this arrangement of the Scriptures, it was not accepted officially until the Council of Trent in 1546.

Faith Activity

Authorship What historical evidence indicates that Paul is the true author of all the letters credited to him? In your Bible, read the introductions to the letters in question, and then research in your library or on the Internet to find out about conflicting theories. Who do you think wrote the Pauline Letters in question?

Author, Date, Structure, and Themes of the Epistles The New Testament letters can be divided into two sections: the Pauline Letters and the Catholic Letters. The author to whom letters are attributed actually wrote some of them. In cases where the author is unknown, a disciple or member of an early Christian community probably wrote them.

Letters of the New Testament		
Pauline		
Missionary Journey Letters	**Captivity Letters**	**Pastoral Letters**
Romans	Colossians*	1 Timothy*
1 Corinthians	Ephesians*	2 Timothy*
2 Corinthians	Philippians	Titus*
1 Thessalonians	Philemon	
2 Thessalonians*		
Galatians		
Catholic		
Hebrews	2 Peter	3 John
James	1 John	Jude
1 Peter	2 John	

Note: * indicates that scripture scholars have doubts about authorship.

Work with the Chart

The Letters The letters vary between very short and very long.
Which letter in the chart is the longest? Which is the shortest? Which letter was likely written by one of the Gospel writers?

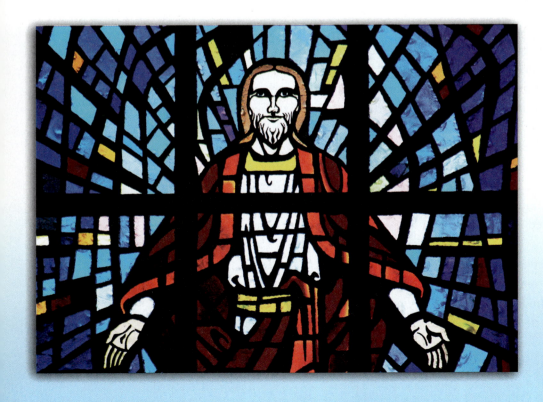

Paul's Letters

Paul wrote many of his letters during his missionary journeys. He wrote 1 and 2 Thessalonians on his second journey—though there are some doubts whether he actually wrote 2 Thessalonians. He wrote Galatians, 1 and 2 Corinthians, and Romans on his third journey.

Paul wrote other letters while in prison, probably in Ephesus, Caesarea, or Rome. These letters include Philippians, Philemon, Colossians, and Ephesians. Paul also wrote 2 Timothy while he was in prison. Scripture scholars have questioned the authorship of Colossians, Ephesians, and 2 Timothy as well; a skilled writer might simply have written in the style of Paul in these letters.

It is not clear from what part of Paul's life 1 Timothy and Titus were written, and again whether Paul actually wrote these letters is uncertain.

Sometimes called the *pastoral letters*, 1 and 2 Timothy and Titus describe the ministry of pastoral care for the entire Christian community. The authorship of all three pastoral letters has been questioned over the years. Most scholars believe that they were written not by Paul but by one of his followers after his death. The letters highlight the challenges faced by the Christian communities, as they shared Jesus' message in different cultures. These letters help us understand how the early Church was organized. Toward the end of the first century, Church leadership was in the hands of one bishop.

Paul's letters contain messages to the early Christian communities. His beliefs and convictions flowed from his conversion experience on the road to Damascus. This experience changed him and the world around him, as he made known Jesus' love and saving actions. Paul's teachings and theological insights came from God's grace and Paul's own faith and theological insight. At the heart of all he did and wrote was his conviction that Jesus was the Christ.

▲ Tradition holds that Christ was held in this prison chamber in the house of the High Priest Caiaphas when he was arrested.

Paul often stressed the importance and the participation of women in the early Church. Some of the women mentioned in the Letters and Acts include the following:

Women in Letters and Acts
Phoebe: a benefactor involved in different ministries in the Church at Cenchreae (See *Romans 16:2.*)
Priscilla: (Prisca) a preacher and missionary from Corinth (See *Acts 18:2, 18, 26*; *Romans 16:3*; *1 Corinthians 16:19*; and *2 Timothy 4:19.*)
Chloe: (See *1 Corinthians 1:11.*)
Lois: the grandmother, and Eunice, the mother of Timothy (See *2 Timothy 1:5.*)
Claudia: (See *2 Timothy 4:21.*)
Euodia and Syntyche: women of the Philippian church (See *Philippians 4:2–3.*)
Nympha: house church in her home (See *Colossians 4:15.*)
Lydia of Philippi: Paul's first European convert who established her home as possibly the first house church in Europe (See *Acts 16:14–15, 40.*)
Damaris: a woman from Athens who believed Paul's message when most Athenians did not (See *Acts 17:34.*)

Themes in Paul's Letters

The Trinity In Paul's letters and in all New Testament writings, we witness the centrality of the mystery of the Trinity—Father, Son, and Holy Spirit. The many references to the three Persons of the Trinity form the biblical background of the Church's classical doctrine of the Trinity. In Paul's letters to the Christian communities, we see the Church's living tradition in action.

The Paradox of the Cross The cross of Christ is a paradox—it's both a sign of defeat and death and a sign of victory and life. It is paradoxical that the God who made all things and keeps them in existence came to earth, lived, suffered, and died for our sins. The paradox of the cross shows what infinite love God has for us.

◄ Spire on Church of the Sagrada Familia by Antonio Gaudi y Cornet.

By his death Jesus became the Way through whom our sins are forgiven. The cross reconciled the world and humans to God, and offered us the gift of salvation. It is up to us to accept it.

The paradox of the cross shows us that strength can come from weakness and new life from apparent death. Christ's cross contradicted the expectations of the Jews and Gentiles. When we reflect on Jesus' life and death, we are invited to see beyond the world's expectations and trust in the power of the cross. In so doing, we illuminate our lives by the grace of Christ's death and Resurrection.

In 1 Corinthians, Paul says,

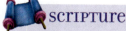 **scripture**

"For the message about the cross is foolishness to those who are perishing, but to us who are being saved it is the power of God . . . For since, in the wisdom of God, the world did not know God through wisdom, God decided, through the foolishness of our proclamation, to save those who believe. For Jews demand signs and Greeks desire wisdom, but we proclaim Christ crucified, a stumbling block to Jews and foolishness to Gentiles, but to those who are the called, both Jews and Greeks, Christ the power of God and the wisdom of God. For God's foolishness is wiser than human wisdom, and God's weakness is stronger than human strength."

1 Corinthians 1:18, 21–25

The Church: The Body of Christ Paul was the only New Testament writer who used the image of the Body of Christ. The phrase expresses the relationship of Christ with his Church and all its members. We are members, or parts, of Christ's body, the Church. As members of one body, Christ—the head of the Church—unites us, even though we have different gifts and different ways to serve. Jesus unites us into one body and calls us to use our gifts to serve one another. When we do so, we serve Jesus the head and the members of his body. Paul said,

 **scripture**

"For as in one body we have many members, and not all the members have the same function, so we, who are many, are one body in Christ, and individually we are members one of another. We have gifts that differ according to the grace given to us: prophecy, in proportion to faith; ministry, in ministering; the teacher, in teaching; the exhorter, in exhortation; the giver, in generosity; the leader, in diligence; the compassionate, in cheerfulness."

Romans 12:4–8

Faith Sharing

Unity In your faith-sharing group, read Colossians 3:12–14. How does this scripture passage relate to your family life or home situation? How do you celebrate joy, bear sufferings, and forgive one another in your family? What changes in your family life can make your family life stronger? What aspect of God is revealed in each of your family members? How does your family help you know God better?

The Sacraments Paul often related the unity of the body to celebration of the sacred mysteries, or sacraments. The early Church used Greek as its common language. The word sacrament comes from the Latin word *sacramentum*, meaning "a consecrating." The root of this word, *sacrare*, is the Church's Latin translation of the Greek word *mysterion*, meaning "mystery." Therefore, the Church used the expression *sacred mystery* to include what we refer to as sacraments. In Paul we see the significance of Baptism and the Eucharist. In the Church's sacraments, Paul recognized the special presence of the Lord in the community of believers and the need for unity and worship in the Body of Christ. In the ritualistic actions of Baptism and Eucharist, we find the highest expression of Christian prayer, which is central to the Church's life.

Grace For Paul, God's grace is the transforming power that changes and sustains us. To prove God's grace in changing a person, Paul told about his previous life in the flesh. No longer bound by the flesh, he had been transformed by God to live a new life in the Spirit. Although he still battled "a thorn" in his flesh, (See *2 Corinthians 12:7*.) Paul was strengthened in his weakness, when God's grace let him see that his real strength came from God. As with Paul, if we follow Jesus, God's grace strengthens us to overcome temptation and sin, and live an upright life. In striving to live this way, we participate in God's own life, for grace is a sharing in the life of God. God's friendship with us through grace is divine friendship. Grace, as a gift of God, invites us to respond by living our Christian lives in communion with the Church.

Justification Justification, which comes through Jesus' death, is bestowed on us by God's grace. It frees us from the enslavement of sin, reconciles us with God, and sanctifies and renews us. Our sharing in God's righteousness through grace does not result from human efforts, but comes as unmerited grace from the redemptive action of Christ on the cross. He gave himself as an offering for us to atone for our sins. The Sacrament of Baptism brings us justification and new life.

Catholic Letters

Hebrews; James; the First and Second Letters of Peter; the First, Second, and Third Letters of John; and the Letter of Jude are often called the catholic, or universal, letters. Unlike the epistles of Paul, which are addressed to specific churches, these letters are *catholic* or "universal" because they were written for the entire Church.

It is unlikely that James, Peter, John, or Jude wrote these letters. Those who wrote them probably knew these early Church leaders and the relationship they had with Jesus. The authors are unknown.

Letter Format Writing letters was common in the Greek world. Paul used this means of communication to convey Jesus' message in the Christian world. The format, described below, is followed in the seven undisputed letters of Paul (except in Galatians, which skips the thanksgiving):

Structure of Letters
Address: The author states the writer's name, the co-senders, and those receiving the letter.
Greeting: This includes a short greeting such as: "Grace to you and peace from God our Father and the Lord Jesus Christ" (*Romans 1:7*).
Thanksgiving: The writer expresses his thanks, gives the reason why he wrote, and indicates his attitude toward those addressed in the letter.
Message: In the body of the letter, the writer addresses issues, gives instructions, and encourages the readers.
Final Greetings: The writer often gives some personal comments about himself and those who were with him.
Blessing: The writer offers a prayer that the hearers will continue to follow Jesus and grow in their relationship with him and one another.

Break Open the Word

Greetings and Blessings Consider the greeting at the beginning and the blessing or farewell at the end of the following Pauline Letters:

Galatians
Colossians
Titus
Romans
Ephesians
Philippians
2 Corinthians

Compare the greetings with one another, and in your own opinion, explain Paul's choice of words to describe his dedication to the Lord Jesus Christ. Then, compare the farewells with one another. What is common among all the farewells? What is different? Do you recognize any of the farewells from the Mass?

The Pauline Letters

This chapter, which offers a small amount of information about each letter, cannot do justice to any of them in the limited space of this text. Each letter is discussed not in the order that it was written but in the order it is found in the Bible. An exception was made for the Letter to Philemon and the Letter to the Hebrews. Because these letters are, or once were, thought to be the writings of Saint Paul, they have been grouped with the Pauline Letters. Saint Paul's advice and that of other letter writers is still valuable and can direct our lives today.

The Importance of the Sacraments

The Letter to the Romans Paul wrote this letter before he met the community of Rome. He probably wrote it near the end of his third missionary journey. It served as an introduction to his visit. In this letter, Paul traced God's gift of salvation from Adam to Jesus. In tracing this lineage, Paul demonstrated that salvation is available for all humanity. Salvation and justification are God's free gift.

Romans 6:1–14 describes the significance of Baptism in the Christian life. Paul connected Baptism with liberation from sin and resurrection in Christ. He said:

scripture

"Do you not know that all of us who have been baptized into Christ Jesus were baptized into his death? Therefore we have been buried with him by baptism into death, so that, just as Christ was raised from the dead by the glory of the Father, so we too might walk in newness of life."

Romans 6:3–4

This entire section in Romans 6 indicates the importance of Baptism in the Christian life, the need to cooperate with God's grace to achieve salvation, and the significance of the sacramental life in the early Christian Church.

Break Open the Word

Getting Involved Read Romans 12:9–21. While you read, consider the general trend in society to not get involved with bad situations. After reading the verses, think about a time when you chose not to get involved and evil prevailed. Why did you make the choice you did? The next time you are confronted with a situation in which you can intervene, consider verse 21, and pray that you make a wise and loving choice.

The First Letter to the Corinthians Both letters to the Corinthians responded to the concerns of the Corinthian Church. Corinth, the largest city in Greece, was a port city. Many people from various backgrounds and nationalities passed through it. A diversity of economic, ethnic, and religious backgrounds existed there. Corinth's citizens worshiped many gods, including Roman, Greek, and Egyptian gods. A small community of Jews lived there. Each religious tradition also had temples or places of worship.

Paul stressed the importance of the Christian community and its unity. He was concerned that it would divide into factions over theological disagreements and divisions between those who were rich and the those who were poor. Within the context of upbraiding the Corinthian Church over their differences, Paul focused on the Lord's Supper. Here we have the earliest reference to the celebration of the Eucharist. We read,

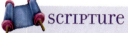
scripture

"For I received from the Lord what I also handed on to you, that the Lord Jesus on the night when he was betrayed took a loaf of bread, and when he had given thanks, he broke it and said, 'This is my body that is for you. Do this in remembrance of me.' In the same way he took the cup also, after supper, saying, 'This cup is the new covenant in my blood. Do this, as often as you drink it, in remembrance of me.'"

1 Corinthians 11:23–25

To emphasize the importance of unity in the body of believers, Paul described Church members as parts of Christ's body. As such, they needed to work together for the good of all. Paul also reminded them that charity could heal their divisions. He told them that as Christians, they were to follow different values and behave differently than did their neighbors of other faiths. This tested the faith of the early Christians.

break open the Word

Paul and the Corinthians Some scholars believe that there was communication between Paul and the Corinthians before the two letters contained in the canon. One of the main arguments for this belief is in 2 Corinthians 6:14—7:1, where the language and tone shift considerably from the sections preceding and following it. What does this section address? Read 2 Corinthians 6 and 7, excluding the above section. You can see that the message of Paul flows more logically without the "different" section included. What else does the different section indicate about authorship or history of these chapters of 2 Corinthians?

▼ We are reminded of the importance of the Eucharist when we pray the Lord's Prayer—as these teens are during World Youth Day.

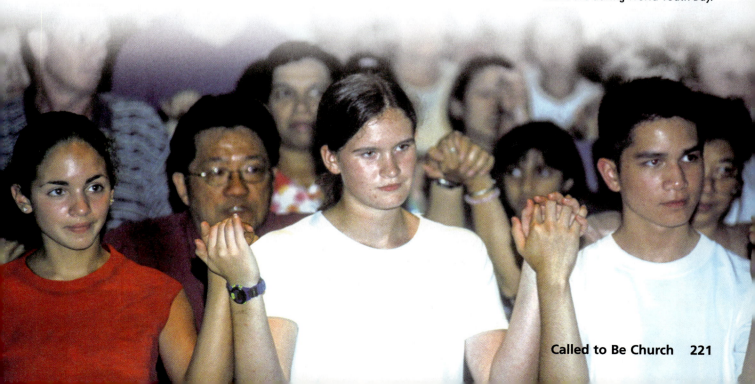

Reconciliation

The Second Letter to the Corinthians Paul's efforts in 1 Corinthians to unite the Corinthian Christians were not entirely successful. Paul made a brief, spontaneous visit to Corinth to try again to unite them, but was unsuccessful—a painful visit. Paul then tried to unite them and reconcile them to himself by writing another letter, a letter of tears. (See *2 Corinthians 2:3–4*.) At last he was successful. He wrote 2 Corinthians after he had received word that the Corinthians had answered his call for unity. (See *2 Corinthians 7:5–8*.) He wrote the letter to reinforce their unity and to warn them against further separation.

The Letter to the Galatians Paul's letter to the Galatians is addressed to Christians in several communities located in the Roman province of Galatia. These communities were probably in the northern part of that province, near the city of Ankyra. Paul had established these communities during his second missionary journey. After Paul's departure, other missionaries began to persuade the Galatians that they needed to keep the Jewish law. When Paul heard about this, he wrote the letter to argue that the Galatians should not keep the Jewish law. He was so concerned about making this point that he omitted the thanksgiving prayer, a customary part of his letters.

The Letter to the Ephesians Ephesians begins with a blessing that praises God: "With all wisdom and insight he has made known to us the mystery of his will, according to his good pleasure that he set forth in Christ, as a plan for the fullness of time, to gather up all things in him, things in heaven and things on earth" (*Ephesians 1:8–10*). The focus of this message is God's plan to bring unity to the world through Christ. Ephesians describes the Church as one, holy, catholic, and apostolic. This letter stresses the importance of the apostolic tradition.

Paul, or a disciple writing in his name, explained that forces were at work whose goal was to alienate people from each other. He warned his audience not to do the things that separate people but to adopt the attitudes of Jesus: humility, meekness, and patience.

The Marks of the Church

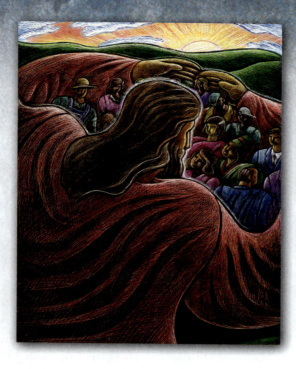

When we profess, "We believe in one holy catholic and apostolic Church" in the Nicene Creed, we state our belief in the Catholic Church. We proclaim the truth that Jesus, through the Holy Spirit, makes the Catholic Church one, holy, catholic, and apostolic. We call these the four essential, distinguishing marks of the Church.

One The Church is one because of her one founder, Jesus Christ; the one Holy Spirit who forms and unites the Church with all its many gifts of diversity; the one faith proclaimed and celebrated through the sacraments; and the leadership of the bishops united with the bishop of Rome, the pope.

Holy The Church is holy, or sacred and pure like God, because her founder, Jesus, is holy, and the Church is where the special presence of Christ can be found. The Church is also the way to holiness, for through her prayer and liturgy, her members are made holy.

Catholic The Church is catholic because through Christ's presence in the Church, the Church has the means of salvation for all people. The Church is catholic, which means universal, because Christ gave her the mission to share the Good News with all people. The Church welcomes members of all races, ages, cultures, and social and economic backgrounds.

Apostolic The Church is apostolic because she is built on the foundation of the Apostles, whom Christ chose to witness to his message and to lead his followers; guided by the Holy Spirit, as she continues to pass on the faith and teaching of the Apostles; and led by bishops, the successors of the Apostles.

We believe that the Catholic Church is the Church founded by Jesus and handed on to the Apostles. We believe that the Catholic Church, governed by the pope, who is the successor of Peter, and by the bishops in communion with him, has the fullness of grace and truth entrusted to it by Christ.

Call to Faithfulness

The Letter to the Philippians A group of women, including Lydia, were the first people to whom Paul preached at Philippi. His tone conveyed friendship and emotional warmth, a joy derived from his relationship with them. Within this community of friends, it was unthinkable that envy, rivalry, or competition should arise over the preaching of the Gospel. So Paul rebuked those who grumbled and complained, for they sought their own interests.

The Letter to the Colossians Colossae was in Phrygia, a region well known in the ancient world for its fascination with the magical and mysterious. Many cults promised perfection and maturity to their worshipers. Some recent converts to Christianity who desired these qualities and felt that Christianity was not offering them were turning to cults. Paul, or a disciple writing in his name, explained to these new Christians that they were still growing in the faith and had not yet borne fruit. He told them not to think of themselves as already perfect, because this would lead them to judge those who are not perfect. True wisdom and knowledge came only from their relationship with Christ. Their further growth and perfection would come through an ever-deepening recognition of what they had been given through Christ and of who they were in Christ. With obedience to God's Spirit, they were to extend love and support to each other, so that others could grow toward perfection in Christ.

The First Letter to the Thessalonians This letter to the community of Thessalonica in Macedonia, which Paul established, was the first Christian writing after the death of Jesus. It expresses thanks and appreciation and was addressed primarily to Gentile Christians. Paul indicated his gratitude for their faithfulness to the Lord. He attempted to strengthen their Christian identity by reminding them of their beginnings. His efforts included his preaching about Jesus and their response. Because they were God's assembly, they were to lead a holy life, turning away from their former ways of living. Their lives were not to stifle the work of the Spirit.

The Second Letter to the Thessalonians The early Christians were focused on the second coming of Christ at the end of the world, which they believed would happen soon. In this letter, Paul, or someone writing in his name, encouraged the Thessalonians not to assume that the second coming of Jesus was at hand, because the Second Coming would be preceded by signs to let them know it was near. The author told them to repent, remain focused on living a moral life, and keep the faith.

The First Letter of Paul to Timothy Paul sent Timothy to the churches in Macedonia, Thessalonica, Philippi, and Corinth to remind the people of Paul's teachings. These teachings included instructions on prayer, the attire and role of women in the liturgical assembly, the proper characteristics of bishops and deacons, the care of widows, the payment of elders for duties performed, and the attitudes of slaves toward their masters and of the rich toward their money.

This letter, along with 2 Timothy and Titus, stressed fide to the orthodox teaching of Jesus, in contrast to the false opinions and heresies that were emerging, especially Gnosticism. The author urged Church leaders to be faithful models of authentic Christianity. In these letters, we find out about the pastoral structure of Christian communities—a structure that has lasted through the ages. This structure focused around the *Episcopos*, or bishop, as the representative of Christ.

The Second Letter of Paul to Timothy In this letter, Paul reminded Timothy of what Paul had previously taught him. Paul wrote to Timothy about the struggles yet to come, encouraged him to persevere in his ministry, and reminded him of the resources that had been made available to him for sharing faith. These resources included the lessons from the Scriptures taught to him by his grandmother, his mother, and Paul. In it we read, "All scripture is inspired by God and is useful for teaching, for reproof, for correction, and for training in righteousness, so that everyone who belongs to God may be proficient, equipped for every good work" (*2 Timothy 3:16–17*).

Responsibilities of Christians

The Letter of Paul to Titus In this letter, Paul reminded Titus that he had left Titus in Crete to complete the work that Paul left unfinished and to see that each town had an appointed elder. Paul clearly described the qualities needed for leaders in the Church. He also gave a listing of appropriate attitudes that should be held by the community in Crete. These new attitudes and ways of treating others were possible because of the grace of God, redemption by Jesus, and the power and the strength of the Holy Spirit. Paul emphasized the importance of good works rooted in one's faith in God. Through the witness of Christian virtues and action, the social world could be transformed.

The Letter to Philemon The shortest of Paul's letters, this letter names several people in the greeting, but is basically a personal note to Philemon. Paul challenged Philemon to act as a responsible Christian and forgive his runaway slave, Onesimus. Onesimus should no longer be considered as property, but as his brother. As a fellow Christian, he was a brother in faith.

Faith
Activity

Wealth and Faith There are people who base their lives and the choices they make on the desire for financial wealth. As Christians we are called to make choices in life that increase our spiritual wealth. List and illustrate five things in your life that are more important than money. In a small group, explain your responses.

Messages for Everyone

The Catholic Letters serve a function similar to that of the letters attributed to Paul. The Christians first receiving and reading them needed the encouragement, direction, and instruction to grow in faith and understanding. As we look at the fundamental themes presented in each of the Catholic Letters, we need to remember the original audience: recent new believers who sought to follow Jesus' teachings in a world that did not necessarily accept him.

The experiences of these men and women nearly two thousand years ago were not that different from our experiences today. Some would say that today's society creates challenges similar to those faced by the early Church communities. The values perpetuated by modern mainstream society often contrast with the Gospel values Jesus taught. However, Jesus did not dismiss the culture and lifestyle of those to whom he preached, even if he called his followers to abandon both. He continually made reference to everyday occurrences and used images from the natural world to make his message sensible to his listeners. He understood that people's surroundings greatly influenced who they were and how they acted. The letter writers addressed the needs of their readers in a similar fashion, pointing out aspects of their previous lifestyle or practices that might keep them from accepting and living the Gospel message.

Foundation of Church Practices

The Letter to the Hebrews Unlike many of the other epistles, this writing does not have the form of a letter and seems more like a homily. Those the letter addressed probably consisted of Christians who were knowledgeable concerning Scripture. The author spoke of practices which have become a part of the Church's practices and beliefs, such as Baptism, the laying on of hands, the resurrection of the dead, and eternal judgment. The writer places emphasis on the Incarnation, Jesus as the Word of God, Jesus' death and Resurrection, and how Jesus' sacrifice and priesthood mediate our relationship with God.

Break open the Word

Titles of Jesus Using the list below, record some of the titles used by the writer of Hebrews to refer to Jesus. Illustrate one that you find interesting, and share your work with your classmates.

1:2	1:6
2:3	2:9
2:11	3:1
4:14	5:5
5:9	6:20
7:3	8:2
9:15	12:2
13:8	13:30

The Letter of James The authorship of this letter remains uncertain. The author wove references to Judaism and Jewish practices throughout the text. Other references in the letter lead us to believe the author knew Jesus personally or he was one generation removed from those who first followed Jesus. Either way, the author was aware of Jesus' sayings. He repeated them in this letter nearly word for word in at least a dozen different verses. The author stressed the need to witness to faith in both words and actions. The writer indicated that controlling our speech is the hardest of all human skills.

In James we find the importance of both faith and good works for salvation. (See *James 2:14*.) This letter teaches that to merit our justification, we must respond to God's grace through faith and good works.

The Letter of James contains the passage that gives witness to the earliest celebration of the sacrament of the Anointing of the Sick. We read,

scripture

"Are any among you suffering? They should pray. Are any cheerful? They should sing songs of praise. Are any among you sick? They should call for the elders of the church, and have them pray over them, anointing them with oil in the name of the Lord. The prayer of faith will save the sick, and the Lord will raise them up; and anyone who has committed sins will be forgiven."

James 5:13–15

Faith Activity

Bringing People Together In a small group, compile a list of words that can help bring people together—for example, "I love you" or "Let me help you." Choose some of these phrases, and compose a small skit that emphasizes the unity the Church can have when we work, live, and love together.

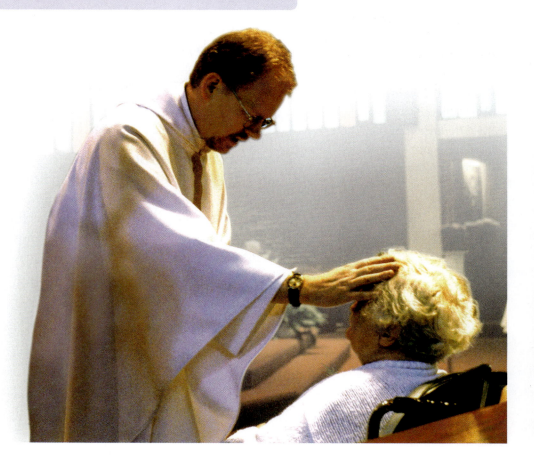

Faith Activity

Trials What "various trials" does the author of 1 Peter and 2 Peter address? What trials do you think the author would address in today's world?

Faith Activity

False Prophets Bring to class some magazines you won't mind cutting up. Select pictures from the magazines that illustrate some of the destructive opinions of false prophets. Next, write words or find pictures that illustrate what you think the new heavens and new earth will look like if we obey the word of God. Make a collage using the pictures and the words you have gathered to parallel the differences between the false prophets and the new heavens and new earth.

Perseverance and Endurance

The First Letter of Peter Bible scholars continue to dispute the authorship of 1 Peter. The writer was possibly Peter's secretary or a disciple carrying the message of Peter. The greeting of 1 Peter indicates that this letter was a correspondence from the author to groups of people living in Pontus, Galatia, Cappadocia, Asia, and Bithynia. These groups were experiencing "various trials."

This letter emphasizes Baptism. Some scripture scholars suggest that a major portion of this letter, 1 Peter 1:3—4:11, is a baptismal homily. It tells the baptized that their identity as Christians may cause them to suffer. The writer encouraged people to endure their suffering, not lose faith, and keep their hearts rooted in Christ the Lord. In this letter we find these words, indicative of our baptismal dignity, "But you are a chosen race, a royal priesthood, a holy nation, God's own people, in order that you may proclaim the mighty acts of him who called you out of darkness into his marvelous light" (*1 Peter 2:9*).

The Second Letter of Peter In spite of the opening greeting, which refers to Peter the Apostle and the later reference to this being the second letter written, (See *2 Peter 3:1*.) most scripture scholars believe the author of this letter is not the same as the author of 1 Peter. The differences in language and format from 1 Peter are so significant that it seems improbable that one author wrote both letters.

The Second Letter of Peter is one of the last books of the New Testament to be written. The author warned his audience about self-deception and advised them to grow in **virtue**—a moral or spiritual habit and desire to do good. He encouraged Christians to have faith in God's promises, which would give them the hope to persevere.

Conflict from Within

The First Letter of John This writing does not have the form of a letter, so the author of 1 John is not indicated explicitly. Most scholars agree that 1, 2, and 3 John were written for the same community for which the Gospel of John was written. Each letter carries the theme of a conflict that has arisen in the Christian community. The imagery of light and darkness reflects the tension between the truth and the heresies that surfaced at the time. Unlike the groups addressed in previous letters, it was not outside forces but forces from within the community that caused division and disruption.

The Second Letter of John In this letter and in the Third Letter of John, the author spoke of himself as the presbyter. Presbyter is another name for priest. The presbyter addressed the letter "to the elect lady and her children, whom I love in truth." In 2 John, verse 7, we hear of the **antichrist**. The antichrist is in the world and reflects the values of the world, especially displaying hatred for those who follow Christ. A person who is the opposite of the antichrist is one who believes in Jesus and professes this belief in the way one relates to and loves others. The author encourages the community to live in truth and love.

The Third Letter of John This letter is very short, and it is the only letter of John's addressed to a particular individual. It had two main purposes. First, it commended Demetrius who "walk[s] in truth." Second, it set the agenda for a future meeting about Diotrephes, a rival church leader.

The Letter of Jude The person who wrote the Second Letter of Peter probably used the Letter of Jude as a source, or perhaps the authors used a common source. Both letters contain a significant amount of the same material. The writer was honest and forceful, encouraging his listeners to stand firm in their beliefs and to develop attitudes opposite from their opponents. The writer assured his readers that God would reveal the truth in the Final Judgment.

Encouragement for Today

The letters written by Paul and others urge us, as they did the early Christians, to give ourselves to God instead of to the false illusions and temptations of the world. The good news shared in the letters is that we don't have to do this on our own. God's grace and presence are always with us. We can do all things in Christ.

When early Church communities began, many cultural divisions and barriers existed in secular society. Often people accepted these barriers without question—barriers between Greek and Jew, slaves and free persons, circumcised and uncircumcised, male and female. Jesus turned the accepted norms and expectations upside down. He treated everyone as equals, as children of the same God.

◄ Pope John Paul II talks with Greek Orthodox Ecumenical Patriarch Bartholomew I at the Vatican.

Faith Activity

Reflection The Letter to the Romans and your relationship with God,

"For I am convinced that neither death, nor life, nor angels, nor rulers, nor things present, nor things to come, nor powers, nor height, nor depth, nor anything else in all creation, will be able to separate us from the love of God in Christ Jesus our Lord" (*Romans 8:38*).

In the letter of the Romans Paul wrote that nothing can separate us from God's love. Through our decisions, however, we decide whether we accept that love. Write about choices that can help you have a stronger relationship with God.

Faith Activity

Group Discussion The First Letter to the Corinthians and trials in life,

"No testing has overtaken you that is not common to everyone. God is faithful, and he will not let you be tested beyond your strength, but with the testing he will also provide the way out so that you may be able to endure it" (*1 Corinthians 10:13*).

Saying "yes" to living for God is also saying "yes" to whatever trials and struggles that will come your way during our lives. Think about a time an unexpected trial came into your life. How did you respond? Did your relationship with God help you during this period of your life?

Faith Activity

Reflection The Letter to the Galatians and sexuality,

"For what the flesh desires is opposed to the Spirit, and what the Spirit desires is opposed to the flesh; for these are opposed to each other, to prevent you from doing what you want" (*Galatians 5:17*).

On a sheet of paper, write your long-range hopes and dreams for the future. Next, write what would happen to your hopes and dreams if you contracted AIDS or another sexually transmitted disease, became pregnant or fathered a child outside of a marriage relationship, or developed an addiction to alcohol or drugs. How would all these situations affect you physically, emotionally, spiritually, intellectually and socially?

Faith Activity

Group Activity The Letter to the Ephesians and anger/violence,

"Put away from you all bitterness and wrath and anger and wrangling and slander, together with all malice" (*Ephesians 4:31*).

Role play a situation of anger that leads to violence. Abuse can be verbal, physical or psychological. Role play the scene a second time, showing an appropriate response to the same situation. Discuss how abusive language is a form of violence.

Faith Activity

At-Home Activity The Letter to the Colossians and family relationships,

"Bear with one another and, if anyone has a complaint against another, forgive each other; just as the Lord has forgiven you, so you also must forgive" (*Colossians 3:13*).

At home today, be completely helpful and understanding. Offer to help with anything that needs to be done.

Faith Activity

Reflection and Discussion The First Letter to the Thessalonians and harmful addictions,

"So then let us not fall asleep as others do, but let us keep awake and be sober" (*1 Thessalonians 5:6*).

Write about someone you have read about who has or has had an addiction to alcohol or other drugs (including nicotine). Research the drug or drugs and write four facts about each drug. Share your information with your class.

Faith Activity

Reflection The Second Letter to the Thessalonians and faith,

"But the Lord is faithful; he will strengthen you and guard you from the evil one" (*2 Thessalonians 3:3*).

Copy 2 Thessalonians 3:3 into your notebook and place your name in it. Consider in writing what God is saying to you in this passage.

Faith Activity

Activity The First Letter of Paul to Timothy and the love of money,

"For the love of money is a root of all kinds of evil, and in their eagerness to be rich some have wandered away from the faith and pierced themselves with many pains" (*1 Timothy 6:10*).

As Christians our top priority is not the amount of money we will make. List or draw pictures of five things in your life that are more important than money.

Faith Activity

Group Activity The Letter of James and gossip,

"How great a forest is set ablaze by a small fire! And the tongue is a fire" (*James 3:5–6*).

Play the telephone game by whispering a message from person to person around the room. How did the message change? What problems are caused by gossip?

Faith Activity

Reflection The First Letter of Peter and giving your worries to God,

"Cast all your anxiety on him, because he cares for you" (*1 Peter 5:7–8*).

Write how prayer and God's love can keep you from worrying.

Faith Activity

Group Discussion The First Letter of John and school violence,

"Whoever says, 'I am in the light,' while hating a brother or sister, is still in the darkness" (*1 John 2:9*).

How can this scripture verse relate to violence that happens in school?

Messages of Hope in the World

Throughout our study of the Gospels and the New Testament letters, we have considered the many images and symbols Jesus used to describe himself, his Father and the Holy Spirit, the kingdom, and discipleship. Some of the writers of the letters reiterated Jesus' imagery, and others introduced symbols and images that form the way we understand who we are as the Church, such as Saint Paul's Body of Christ image in the First Letter to the Corinthians.

We speak of God and the mystery of his Church using images and symbols because God's reality is beyond our comprehension. We use images and make parallels with human nature and the physical aspects of the world because God's creation—most especially humans whom he made in his image and likeness—offer a glimpse into his infinite goodness, truth, and beauty. We use images and symbols to describe God, but he transcends all creatures and all language. We use language that evokes meaning on many levels, so that we can begin to express the relationship that is God. This is how Jesus taught, and his first followers continued to use metaphor, similes, and symbols to express their faith and to prompt faith among their listeners.

The Book of Revelation

The canon of the New Testament concludes with the Revelation to John, also called the Book of Revelation. The Book of Revelation has a distinct literary style, called **apocalyptic writing**, which uses highly symbolic language. The author of Revelation borrowed symbols from other apocalyptic writers, such as Daniel, Ezekiel, and Zechariah, and adapted them to meet his intentions.

All apocalyptic writings reveal the timeless struggle between good and evil in the world. In the Book of Revelation, prophetic visions convey the message that while the world is filled with evil and trials, God is always present and does not abandon those who are trusting and faithful. Like other writers after Jesus' Resurrection and Ascension, the author encouraged the readers to be faithful to Jesus' message. In this way, they will achieve their eternal salvation.

Themes and Perspectives Because of the symbolic imagery and codes used in this book, even scripture scholars are not certain of the meanings for all the symbols, numbers, and colors used. However, the audience for whom it was written would have understood this symbolic literature.

Break Open the Word

Prophecies The Book of Revelation leans heavily upon references to the Old Testament—no less than 170 references are made. Most notable, however, is the relationship that the author of Revelation shared with the authors of the Books of Daniel, Ezekiel, and Zechariah in the Old Testament. Read Isaiah 6 and Ezekiel 1, and compare the introductions and descriptions of the prophetic nature of the readings. What is similar? What is different? Describe some of the imagery in these sections and what you think it means.

Although the truths of the Bible are timeless, the text of the Book of Revelation is rooted in the history and cultural values of the seven communities of faith to which the author wrote: Ephesus, Smyrna, Pergamum, Thyatira, Sardis, Philadelphia, and Laodicea. Revelation is not only about the end of the world but also about the world of first-century Christians. The author encouraged them to be faithful in the midst of persecution, which came from their unwillingness to worship the emperor or to succumb to the dictates of false teachers within the Christian community itself.

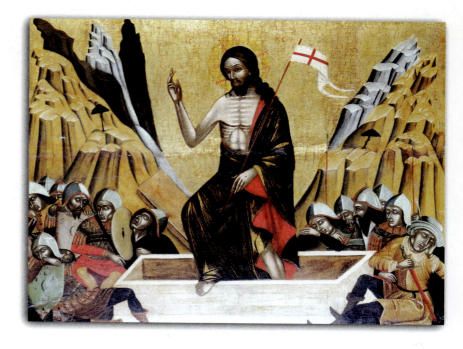

▲ The Resurrection by Italo-Cretan School, c. 1500.

This book is not primarily about God's anger and wrath with the world but about God's mercy and steadfast love, visible in the world. It is not primarily about the God's triumph over evil and death in the future but about God's triumph over evil and death which has already taken place through Jesus' death and Resurrection.

Authorship The author identified himself as John. (See *Revelation 1:1, 4, 9; 22:8*.) Scholars do not believe that this was John, the author of the fourth Gospel. Rather, many scholars believe that the writer was a Christian prophet familiar with John's community and tradition. It was probably written during the reign of Emperor Domitian (A.D. 81–96), who gave himself the title of Lord and God. In so doing, the Christians were challenged to respond to his imperial claim to divinity. Refusal to worship Domitian meant death.

The Book of Revelation offers hope that God's presence is the sustaining force amidst Christian suffering. The Book of Revelation may have been written while the author was exiled to the island of Patmos. In Revelation he encouraged Christians to stand fast in their convictions and witness to the truth of Jesus during their persecutions.

Since Nero's reign (A.D. 54–68), Christians had been subjected to occasional persecution in various places. The Christian communities had to devise ways to stand up to the political, social, and religious pressures of these persecutions. Many Christians suffered and died for their beliefs.

Faith Activity

Our Responses We see in Revelation that the aspects of God's anger and wrath can be incurred, but that the true message of the book is actually love and mercy. Responding with anger is easy when you have been wronged. How can you take a page from Revelation and show love and mercy instead?

SYMBOLISM IN REVELATION

Cosmic Symbolism

Alpha	Christ as the beginning
Angel	Messenger
First beast	Evil power of the Roman Empire
Beasts	Roman emperors
Book of Life	Names of faithful listed here
Bride	The faithful Church
Dragon	Devil
Eyes	Wisdom; all knowing
Horns; horse	Power
Key	Authority
Gog and Magog	Pagan nations against the Church
Lamb	Jesus Christ
Omega	Christ as the end
Saints	Persecuted and martyred Christians
Sea	Place of evil and death
Seals of scroll	Hardship and suffering
Seal of God	Faithfulness to God
Two-edged sword	Word of God that judges and punishes
Woman	Believers; faithful Church; Mary

Symbolism of Numbers

One	God
Three	Trinity
Four	Universal (north, south, east, and west)
Six	Imperfection
666	Absolute imperfection; refusing to be part of God's plan. Each letter in the Hebrew alphabet had a numerical equivalent. When the Greek words for "Caesar Nero" were written in Hebrew, the total was 666.
Seven	Perfection; completeness
Ten	Absolute completeness
Twelve	Completeness; twelve tribes of Israel; the Christian Church, twelve Apostles
1,260 days	Nonspecific time of struggle and persecution, which the faithful must endure
144,000	$12 \times 12 \times 1,000 = 144,000$, which represents perfection; those saved by the Lamb

Faith Sharing

Symbolism and You In your faith sharing group, choose a cosmic symbol and a number, and illustrate or write about what each means to you. As a group, discuss your ideas and how your interpretation compares to the biblical interpretation.

Symbols and Images of the Church

The Book of Revelation uses the image of a faithful bride to describe the Church, an image used in other New Testament works to describe the personal relationship between Jesus, the bridegroom, and his Church, the bride. The Scriptures contain many symbols for the Church, all hinging on the Old Testament image of People of God.

> "In the New Testament, all these images find a new center because Christ has become the head of this people, which henceforth is his Body.[13] Around this center are grouped images taken 'from the life of the shepherd or from cultivation of the land, from the art of building or from family life and marriage.'[14]"
>
> *Catechism of the Catholic Church, 753*

The Scriptures describe the Church as

- sheepfold or flock with her Good Shepherd, Jesus
- cultivated field
- branches, with Jesus the vine and the Father the vine grower
- building of God with Jesus her cornerstone
- house of God and holy temple
- our mother
- Jerusalem, which is above
- spotless spouse of the spotless lamb

From all these symbols, the Church has come to be known by four main images: People of God, Body of Christ, Bride of Christ, and Temple of the Holy Spirit. These images provide insight into the meaning, the characteristics, and the purpose of the Church.

People of God This image of the Church is solidly rooted in the call of Abraham and later of Moses, and the subsequent establishment of the people of Israel. In the Old Testament, we learn that God carefully made a covenant with the Israelites, desiring to create a people who would honor and serve him by their faithfulness and holiness.

By sending his only begotten Son into the world, God established a new and eternal covenant. Jesus called together a race made up of all races. He acquired a people who previously were not united as a people. Through the power of the Holy Spirit, he established the Catholic Church as the People of God, "a chosen race, a royal priesthood, a holy nation, God's own people" (*1 Peter 2:9*).

The People of God is a priestly, prophetic, and royal people. Through faith and Baptism, we become members of God's people. We share in Jesus' role as priest, prophet, and king. While ordained ministers have a distinct function in the People of God, all baptized members take part in Christ's priestly, prophetic, and royal office.

The Body of Christ We read in Saint Paul's first letter to the Corinthians that like the body with many parts, the Church has members with many functions. The analogy between the body and the Church rests on the fact that Jesus is the head of his Body, the Church. By sending his Holy Spirit, Jesus spiritually assembles as his Body all those brothers and sisters who are called from around the globe. Through the Holy Spirit and the grace of the sacraments, especially the Eucharist, Jesus constitutes the Church as his Body. With Jesus as the head of the Body, "The Church is this Body of which Christ is the head: she lives from him, in him, and for him; he lives with her and in her" (*Catechism of the Catholic Church, 807*).

We become members of Christ's Body and are incorporated into the Church through faith and Baptism. Jesus said, "I tell you, no one can enter the kingdom of God without being born of water and Spirit" (*John 3:5*). Thus, Baptism is necessary for salvation. Likewise, the Church is necessary for salvation. All salvation comes from Christ the Head through his Body, the Church.

Bride of Christ The personal relationship between Christ and his Church cannot be overstated. Think of the love between a husband and a wife, as well as the excitement and energy that typically surrounds newly married couples. The love and energy of Christ far surpasses any that we can understand. Christ loves his followers so much that he gave his life for his Church so his followers might know the divine love and life that is the Trinity.

The Temple of the Holy Spirit In many ways, the Holy Spirit is the Church's soul, "the source of its life, of its unity in diversity, and of the riches of its gifts and charisms" (*Catechism of the Catholic Church, 809*). The Spirit dwells with Christ as the Head of the Church and works throughout the Body of Christ. And as the ways of the Holy Spirit are a mystery, so too is the Church.

A Priestly, Prophetic, Royal People	
Priestly	We offer everything in our lives as a sacrifice to God through Jesus Christ. We participate in the sacraments and the worship of the Church. We also have the opportunity to serve the Church in its liturgy through a variety of liturgical ministries, such as altar servers, readers, extraordinary ministers of Holy Communion, and musicians.
Prophetic	We are called to speak God's word and to witness to Christ in our homes, schools, work place, and larger community. We yearn and pray for the coming of the kingdom, and we teach others about the kingdom in many ways. We stand up for those who can't stand up for themselves. We point out when the values of society do not correspond to Jesus' values.
Royal	Jesus taught his followers the importance of service, and he came as a servant king. He inaugurated God's kingdom on earth, and calls all of his followers to work for the kingdom. We work for justice and educate others about the responsibilities to help all people access basic human rights. We take an active role in our parish life, helping those in need among our parish, in our neighborhood, and around the world.

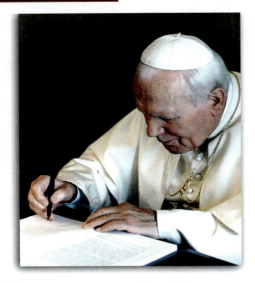

Writing Letters in the Modern World

Paul wrote his many letters of the New Testament to clarify the early Church's views and to reaffirm the faith of the early Christians. The letters written by other authors of the New Testament continued this intention.

Pope John Paul II continued the long tradition of papal letters to fellow priests, near or distant churches, or groups of people in need of reaffirmed faith. In 2004 the pope wrote two letters concerning the Social Weeks in both Italy and France. He reminded the people of France and Italy—as well as the religious leaders to whom he addressed the letters—why the Social Weeks are so important. The pope urged people to live the Church's social teachings, pursue freedom, and witness to the true love of Christ in the world.

Pope John Paul II wrote the following to the special envoy to the Social Weeks of France in September 2004:

". . . I thank God for the contribution Christians make to the reflection on the complex current economic, political and social problems in order to promote the renewal of our society. Drawing inspiration from the Church's social teaching, they contribute to the formation of the conscience of citizens who, each in his or her own capacity, are called to take part in civil life.

The centenary of the Social Weeks is an opportunity to rediscover the long tradition of the Church's social Magisterium and the many saints who have left their mark on the European Continent since the early centuries . . . they all showed that the Gospel and Christian values are fertile soil, both for the lives of persons and peoples, and for building society."

The pope continued his message in writing to the president of the Italian Bishop's Conference in October 2004 on the subject of Social Weeks:

"Catholics are therefore invited not only to work to make civil society more alive and dynamic through promotion of the family, associations, volunteer work and so forth, opposing undue restrictions and conditions put in the way by the political or economic authority; they must also reconsider the importance of commitment to public and institutional roles in those circles in which important collective decisions are taken and in the political context, understood in the most noble sense of the word, as today is hoped for by many.

Indeed, it cannot be forgotten that part of the vocation of the lay faithful is knowing and practicing the social teaching of the Church, hence, also of participating in the political life of the country in accordance with the methods and means of the democratic system."

Prayer

Begin by praying the Sign of the Cross.

Leader: Jesus led his followers and all humankind out of darkness and into the light of love, forgiveness, and new life. But after his Ascension, his followers were plunged once more into the darkness of confusion and fear. The Lord sent the Holy Spirit to his followers to help them preach the Good News to all and to help them record, in writing, his word. Jesus converted even the hardest of hearts—Saul—and made him one of the greatest vessels for the mission the world has known. Lord, grant us the wisdom to follow in the footsteps of your humble servants who have come before us.

All: Amen.

Reader 1: (Read aloud Ephesians 4:17–24.)

Leader: Paul called for all followers of Christ to live in the way that Christ lived, to cease living in their previous lives, to be converted as he had been.

All: Amen.

Reader 2: (Read aloud 2 Corinthians 2:5–11.)

Leader: Paul urges us to follow Jesus' law of love: to love our neighbors as ourselves and to forgive all those who wrong us.

All: Amen.

Leader: In closing, we will remember the marks of the Church, which so strongly guide us in our lives, reminding us of who we are, and how to live. We remember the guiding force of the Holy Spirit, compelling the first disciples to preach the Word of God. We pray . . .

All: We believe in the Holy Spirit, the Lord, the giver of life,
who proceeds from the Father and the Son.
With the Father and the Son he is worshiped and glorified.
He has spoken through the Prophets.
We believe in one holy catholic and apostolic Church.
We acknowledge one baptism for the forgiveness of sins.
We look for the resurrection of the dead,
and the life of the world to come. Amen.

End by praying the Sign of the Cross.

Review

1. How many letters appear in the New Testament? Why were they originally written?

2. How does pseudonymity affect who scripture scholars believe wrote particular letters?

3. Describe the format of the letters of Paul.

4. In your own words, describe the marks of the Church.

5. How did Paul connect Baptism with the Resurrection of Christ? What was Paul's main concern in writing the first letter to the Corinthians?

6. What was the purpose of Paul's letters to Titus and Philemon? What challenges did he propose to the two men?

7. How does Hebrews differ from other letters? What specific practices did the author address in his writing?

8. How do John's letters and Jude's letter address early conflict in the Church? What term for those who display hatred of those who follow Jesus do we first hear in 2 John?

9. List the stations of the cross. When did they become popular?

10. Which Old Testament writers did the author of Revelation borrow symbols from? What did apocalyptic writers reveal in their prophetic writings?

11. What four images represent the Church? What do they mean?

12. In Revelation, what does the number three represent? The number 666?

Key Words

antichrist (p. 229)—The antichrist is present in the world and displays hatred for those who follow Christ. The antichrist is the opposite of Jesus and his beliefs.

apocalyptic writing (p. 232)—A literary style that uses very symbolic language to convey its message.

pseudonymity (p. 213)—The act of another author writing in a named author's place. This occurs in some Pauline Letters.

virtue (p. 228)—A moral or spiritual habit and desire to do good.

Teen to Teen

Looking back on your journey and experiences learning about the New Testament, how do you think you have changed? What have you learned about yourself and your faith that has helped you become a better Christian?

"I think that I have changed by learning more answers to all of my why questions. I wondered why we did things a certain way during the Mass, or why the church I attend is built the way it is. Learning more about the traditions and rituals helped explain my questions. I've become a better Christian because I am really starting to understand the history of our faith. I understand the troubles that the early Christians had and the sacrifices they made to believe."

Andie F.

"I think that actually sitting down and reading some of the Gospels and letters has really helped reaffirm my faith. I found the stories and the lives the Apostles led very interesting, and I think that they are good models for how to live my life. I learned that I really enjoy reading the Bible—it is not as hard as I thought it would be. The more I read, and the more questions I asked and answered in my group, the more I really understood."

Verron A.

Personal Challenge

The tradition of writing letters to fellow Christian communities began with the first Apostles and evangelists and continued throughout the centuries with popes, bishops, conferences, and priests writing letters as well. This week, pair off with another student and choose one student to write a letter and the other to write a response. The topics of the letters should be taking your place as a part of the body of the Church and facing challenges to your faith.

BREAK OPEN the Word

Fitting In Read the quote from 1 Corinthians that opens the chapter. Then read 1 Corinthians 12 in your Bible. We can learn from these verses that all people, great and small, just as all parts of the body, are necessary to the Lord and necessary to the body. What other object could you use to describe the Church that is many pieces of one whole? What part of the body and of the Church do you fit into?

Catholic Source Book

Scripture & Liturgy

Catholics gather to praise and worship God in liturgy, the official public prayer of the Church. The original meaning of the word *liturgy* was a public work, or a service in the name of or on behalf of the people. In Christian terms, the word *liturgy* describes the participation of the whole People of God in the work of God. The liturgy consists of the celebration of the sacraments, first and foremost the Eucharist, and the Liturgy of the Hours.

Scripture is integral to how we pray and worship. The celebration of each sacrament includes a Liturgy of the Word. This proclamation of Scripture expresses the meaning of the sacrament and calls those who receive the sacrament to respond in faith.

Liturgy of the Hours The Liturgy of the Hours is a prayer that includes psalms and readings and is prayed several times a day as a way to mark time as holy and recall God's saving work in creation. The psalms are an integral part to the Liturgy of the Hours.

The Seven Sacraments

In the sacraments Jesus continues his saving work. During his life Jesus welcomed, fed, healed, and forgave people. Through the sacraments he continues to share God's life and love with his followers. Because the sacraments were founded by Jesus and witnessed to in the early Church, we can find Biblical roots for the sacraments.

Sacraments of Initiation Three sacraments together complete initiation into the Church: Baptism, which begins new life in Christ; Confirmation, which strengthens that life; and, Eucharist, which nourishes that life and transforms the recipient to become more Christ-like.

- Baptism—John 3:5; Matthew 28:19–20; Romans 6:3–11
- Confirmation—Acts 8:14–17, 9:17–19, 19:5; Titus 3:4–8
- Eucharist—John 6:1–15, 25–71; Matthew 26:26–28; Mark 14:22–25; Luke 22:7–20

Sacraments of Healing In the Sacraments of Healing God's forgiveness of sins and healing are given to those suffering physical and spiritual sickness.

- Reconciliation (also called the Sacrament of Penance, the Sacrament of Conversion, and the Sacrament of Confession)—John 20:19, 22–23; Mark 1:15, 2:5, 10; Luke 7:48, 15:18

- Anointing of the Sick—Mark 6:12–13, 16:17–18; Matthew 10:8; James 5:14–15

Sacraments at the Service of Communion In these sacraments Catholics receive the grace to commit to and serve God and the community.

- Holy Orders—John 10:36; Acts 1:8, 2:4; 1 Timothy 4:14; 2 Timothy 1:6–7

- Matrimony—Matthew 19:6; John 2:1–11; 1 Corinthians 7:39; Ephesians 5:31–32

The Mass

Several ritual books are used in the celebration of the Eucharist. The lectionary is the collection of readings assigned by the Church for liturgical proclamation. The Church promulgated the current lectionary for use in 1970, and it was revised in 1998. The lectionary is comprised of:

1. A three-year cycle of Sunday readings (first and second readings)

2. A two-year weekday cycle

3. A one-year sanctoral cycle

4. A variety of other readings for various occasions

5. Responsorial psalms and alleluia verses

The Book of Gospels is used for the proclamation of the Gospels during Mass. The Church released the most recent revision in 1999. The bishop presents a Book of Gospels to new deacons upon their ordination; the book is also raised over the heads of new bishops during their ordination ceremonies.

The Liturgical Year

The liturgical year is the Church's annual cycle of seasons and feasts that celebrates the Paschal mystery. It begins on the First Sunday of Advent and ends on the feast of Christ the King. Throughout all the season, the Church celebrates some aspect of Christ's Paschal Mystery.

Holy Days of Obligation in the United States The Vatican has listed ten holy days of obligation, but each conference of bishops determines which holy days will be locally observed. In the United States we celebrate six. Catholics are required to participate in Mass on all Sundays and on these holy days.

Mary the Mother of God (January 1)

The Ascension of the Lord (40 days after Easter or the Sunday nearest the end of the 40-day period)

The Assumption of Mary (August 15)

All Saints' Day (November 1)

The Immaculate Conception of Mary (December 8)

Christmas (December 25)

Fast, Abstinence, and Days of Penance All Christians are obliged to live in a spirit of penance whereby their exterior act of prayer, self-denial, and charity bear witness to the inner values of their faith.

Fasting is the limitation to one full meal and two lighter meals a day, with no food between meals. In the United States the obligation to fast binds those from eighteen years of age to the beginning of the sixtieth year.

The Eucharistic fast requires that a person fast from food and drink for one hour before receiving Communion. This does not include water and medicine. The fast for those who are elderly or sick is fifteen minutes.

- Grave circumstances—sickness, dietary needs, social obligations—excuse a person from the obligations to fast and abstain, but not from seeking out other forms of penance.

- Abstinence generally refers to refraining from eating meat on certain days. The obligation to abstain from meat binds Catholics from the age of fourteen throughout life.

Ash Wednesday and Good Friday are days of fast and abstinence, as are all Fridays during Lent. All Fridays during the year and the entire Season of Lent are days of penance. Works of penance include voluntary abstinence, fasting, prayer, works of charity, and other acts of self-denial.

Vocations

The Resurrection of Jesus is one of the defining mysteries of the Catholic faith. All of us are called to live in light of the risen Jesus and be a sign of life and hope for the world. God created each of us to be in his friendship and to share in his life. He continually calls all people to believe in him and to grow in his friendship.

Through Baptism, Christ calls each of us to holiness— to become more like him. We are called to take part in the Church's mission of spreading the good news through our words and actions. This call is our baptismal or common vocation. The word *vocation* refers to one's calling or purpose. In religious terms a vocation is one's call to love and serve God and others. God calls us to live out this shared vocation in different ways.

Single life: Through the single life, people profess to the mystery of the Incarnation and bring the message of the Good News to others through their work, civic involvement, and family life.

Married life: In married life husband and wife affirm the image of God in one another and welcome children to share in their lives. Like those in the single life, married people are called to be a witness to their faith in the world.

Ordained life: Men receive the Sacrament of Holy Orders to become deacons, priests, or bishops and minister to the Church through teaching, leading, and worship.

Consecrated life: Religious sisters, brothers, and priests live, pray, and work in community to stand together in opposition to the culture and the values in the world that are not Gospel values.

As Christians, we are called to make the world holy. Which vocation will you choose to bring holiness and wholeness, or resurrection, to the world?

Scripture & Morality

The Ten Commandments

1. I am the Lord your God: you shall not have strange gods before me.
   - Place one's faith in God alone.
   - Believe in, trust, and love God.

2. You shall not take the name of the Lord your God in vain.
   - Speak God's name, and that of Jesus and the saints, with reverence.
   - Don't curse or call on God to witness to a lie.

3. Remember to keep holy the Lord's day.
   - Gather to worship at the Eucharist.
   - Rest and avoid unnecessary work on Sunday.

4. Honor your father and your mother.
   - Respect and obey parents, guardians, and others who have proper authority.

5. You shall not kill.
   - Respect and protect your life and the lives of others.

6. You shall not commit adultery.
   - Be faithful and loyal to spouses, friends, and family.
   - Respect God's gift of sexuality, and practice the virtue of chastity.
   - Learn to appreciate the gift of sexuality by practicing self-mastery.

7. You shall not steal.
   - Respect the things that belong to others.
   - Share what you have with those in need.

8. You shall not bear false witness against your neighbor.
   - Be honest, truthful, and avoid bragging.
   - Don't say untruthful or negative things about others.

9. You shall not covet your neighbor's wife.
   - Practice modesty in thoughts, words, dress, and actions.

10. You shall not covet your neighbor's goods.

- ■ Rejoice in others' good fortune.
- ■ Don't be jealous of others' possessions and don't be greedy.

The Great Commandment

"You shall love the Lord your God with all your heart, and with all your soul, and with all your strength, and with all your mind; and your neighbor as yourself."

Luke 10:27

The New Commandment

"I give you a new commandment, that you love one another. Just as I have loved you, you also should love one another."

John 13:34

The Beatitudes

Blessed are the poor in spirit,
   for theirs is the kingdom of heaven.
Blessed are they who mourn,
   for they will be comforted.
Blessed are the meek,
   for they will inherit the earth.
Blessed are they who hunger and thirst for righteousness,
   for they will be filled.
Blessed are the merciful,
   for they will receive mercy.
Blessed are the pure in heart,
   for they will see God.
Blessed are the peacemakers,
   for they will be called children of God.
Blessed are they who are persecuted for the righteousness sake,
   for theirs is the kingdom of heaven.

Matthew 5:3–10

Works of Mercy

Matthew 25:31–46 lays the foundation for the Works of Mercy, particularly the Corporal Works of Mercy.

Spiritual Works of Mercy

Teach the ignorant.

Counsel the doubtful.

Comfort the sorrowful.

Bear wrongs patiently.

Forgive injuries.

Warn the sinner.

Pray for the living and the dead.

Corporal Works of Mercy

Feed the hungry.

Give drink to the thirsty.

Shelter the homeless.

Clothe the naked.

Visit the sick.

Visit the imprisoned.

Bury the dead.

Virtues

Theological Virtues The theological virtues are gifts from God. They are called the theological virtues because they are rooted in God, directed toward him, and reflect his presence in our lives. (In Greek *theos* means "god.")

- Faith means believing in him and all that he has revealed to us and that the Church proposes for our belief.

- Hope is the desire, bolstered by trust, to do God's will and achieve eternal life.

- Through charity, we love God above all else, and our neighbors as ourselves.

Cardinal Virtues The cardinal virtues are the principal moral virtues that help us lead a moral life by governing our actions, controlling our passions and emotions, and keeping our conduct on the right tract.

- prudence (careful judgment)

- fortitude (courage)

- justice (giving God and people their due)

- temperance (moderation, balance)

Precepts of the Church

The precepts of the Church are laws that name specific actions that all Catholics are obligated to carry out. According to the *National Catechetical Directory,* the following precepts apply to Catholics in the United States.

1. To keep holy the day of the Lord's Resurrection: to worship God by participating in Mass every Sunday and holy day of obligation; to avoid those activities that would hinder renewal of soul and body on the Sabbath (e.g., needless work and business activities, unnecessary shopping, etc.).

2. To lead a sacramental life; to receive Holy Communion frequently and the Sacrament of Reconciliation regularly—minimally, to receive the Sacrament of Reconciliation at least once a year (annual confession is obligatory only if serious sin is involved); minimally also, to receive Holy Communion at least once a year, between the First Sunday of Lent and Trinity Sunday.

3. To study Catholic teaching in preparation for the Sacrament of Confirmation, to be confirmed, and then to continue to study and advance the cause of Christ.

4. To observe the marriage laws of the Church; to give religious training, by example and word, to one's children; to use parish schools and catechetical programs.

5. To strengthen and support the Church—one's own parish community and parish priests, the worldwide Church and the pope.

6. To do penance, including abstaining from meat and fasting from food on the appointed days.

7. To join in the missionary spirit and apostolate of the Church.

Catholic Social Teaching

Strengthened by the grace of God the Father and the power of the Holy Spirit, the Church reaches out to the entire world with the saving message of Christ's Passion, death, and Resurrection. The Church defends those who are poor and impoverished—those whom the world has cast aside. The Church protects life in all its forms and in all its stages. The Church struggles for justice where there is hatred and prejudice.

In these ways the Church lives out Jesus' message of just action and living. Over the past century, popes and bishops have appealed to the Church to honor the dignity of all people and to work to ensure that the rights of all are protected and upheld. This is the core of Catholic Social Teaching. The U.S. Bishops have identified the following seven themes or principles of Catholic Social Teaching:

- The Life and Dignity of the Human Person
- Call to Family, Community, and Participation
- Rights and Responsibilities of the Human Person
- Option for the Poor and Vulnerable
- The Dignity of Work and the Rights of Workers
- The Solidarity of the Human Family
- Care for God's Creation

The mission of the Church to bring the saving love and forgiveness of Jesus "to all the world" begins with loving God and loving our neighbors. We are called to be "good Samaritans," to be people of forgiveness, to heal and invite, to convert and reconcile, to be the loving, healing, forgiving presence of Christ in the world.

Catholic Prayers and Practices

The Lord's Prayer
Matthew 6:9–13, Luke 11:2–4

Our Father, who art in heaven,
hallowed be thy name.
Thy kingdom come;
they will be done on earth as it is in heaven.
Give us this day our daily bread
and forgive us our trespasses
as we forgive those who trespass against us.
And lead us not into temptation,
but deliver us from evil. Amen.

Hail Mary
Luke 1:28 and Luke 1:42

Hail, Mary, full of grace!
The Lord is with you.
Blessed are you among women
and blessed is the fruit of your womb, Jesus.
Holy Mary, Mother of God,
pray for us sinners,
now and at the hour of our death. Amen.

Magnificat
Luke 1:46–55

My soul proclaims the greatness of the Lord,
my spirit rejoices in God my Savior
for he has looked with favor on his lowly servant.
From this day all generations will call me blessed:
the Almighty has done great things for me,
and holy is his Name.
He has mercy on those who fear him
in every generation.
He has shown the strength of his arm,
he has scattered the proud in their conceit.
He has cast down the mighty from their thrones,
and has lifted up the lowly.
He has filled the hungry with good things,
and the rich he has sent away empty.
He has come to the help of his servant Israel
for he has remembered his promise of mercy,
the promise he made to our fathers,
to Abraham and his children for ever.

The title of this prayer—*Magnificat*—is the Latin word for "proclaim."
It is derived from Mary's response to Elizabeth's greeting during the
Visitation. The Church sings Mary's song during Evening Prayer, also
known as Vespers.

The Rosary

Early Christians used beads or knotted strings to keep count of prayers. As devotion to Mary increased, it became popular to create psalters or books dedicated to Jesus or Mary, using biblical scenes. The Rosary we know today developed from both of these practices. As you pray each decade of beads, you think of one mystery in the life of Jesus or Mary.

Praying the Rosary   The rosary begins at the cross with the Sign of the Cross and then the Apostles' Creed. Then at the first bead, the Lord's Prayer followed by three Hail Mary's—one for each bead. After moving past the third Hail Mary bead, pray a Glory to the Father. At the last bead, announce the first mystery of the Rosary, and then pray the Lord's Prayer again.

After passing the medallion, move to the right on the rosary and pray ten Hail Mary's while contemplating the first mystery of the Rosary. After the tenth Hail Mary, pray a Glory to the Father, announce the next mystery of the rosary, and pray the Lord's prayer. Pray ten Hail Mary's until you have announced and contemplated the remaining mysteries of the Rosary.

Mysteries of the Rosary

Joyful Mysteries
- Annunciation
- Visitation
- Nativity
- Presentation of Jesus
- Finding Jesus in the Temple

Sorrowful Mysteries
- Agony in the Garden
- Scourging at the Pillar
- Crowning with Thorns
- Jesus Carries his Cross
- Crucifixion

Glorious Mysteries
- Resurrection of Jesus
- Ascension
- Descent of the Holy Spirit
- Assumption of Mary
- Coronation of Mary

Luminous Mysteries
- The Baptism of Christ in the Jordan
- Jesus' Self-manifestation at the Wedding Feast of Cana
- The Announcement of the Kingdom Along with the Call to Conversion
- The Transfiguration
- The Institution of the Eucharist as the Sacramental Expression of the Paschal Mystery

The Stations of the Cross

The Stations of the Cross commemorate the journey of Christ from the praetorium—where Pilate held court—to Calvary and the tomb. Many crusaders retraced this path, and the prayerful reflection many people experienced while retracing these steps was brought back to Churches throughout Europe.

1. **Jesus is condemned to death.**
   - Scripture reference: Matthew 27:11–31; Mark 15:2–15; Luke 23:2–25; John 19:1–16
   - Scripture reflection: "For God so loved the world that he gave his only Son, so that everyone who believes in him may not perish but may have eternal life" (*John 3:16*).

2. **Jesus carries his cross.**
   - Scripture reference: Matthew 27:31; John 19:17
   - Scripture reflection: "If any want to become my followers, let them deny themselves and take up their cross daily and follow me" (*Luke 9:23*).

3. **Jesus falls the first time.**
   - Scripture reference: none directly
   - Scripture reflection: "All we like sheep have gone astray; we have all turned to our own way, and the Lord has laid on him the iniquity of us all" (*Isaiah 53:6*).

4. **Jesus meets his mother.**
   - Scripture reference: John 19:25–27
   - Scripture reflection: "Is it nothing to you, all you who pass by? Look and see if there is any sorrow like my sorrow . . ." (*Lamentations 1:12*).

5. **Simon helps Jesus carry his cross.**
   - Scripture reference: Matthew 27:32; Mark 15:21; Luke 23:26
   - Scripture reflection: "Truly I tell you, just as you did it to one of the least of these who are members of my family, you did it to me" (*Matthew 25:40*).

6. Veronica wipes the face of Jesus.
   - ■ Scripture reference: none directly
   - ■ Scripture reflection: "Whoever has seen me has seen the Father" (*John 14:9*).

7. Jesus falls the second time.
   - ■ Scripture reference: none directly
   - ■ Scripture reflection: "Come to me, all you that are weary and carrying heavy burdens, and I will give you rest" (*Matthew 11:28*).

8. Jesus speaks to the women of Jerusalem.
   - ■ Scripture reference: Luke 23:27; Matthew 27:55; Mark 15:40
   - ■ Scripture reflection: "Daughters of Jerusalem, do not weep for me, but weep for yourselves and for your children" (*Luke 23:28*).

9. Jesus falls the third time.
   - ■ Scripture reference: none directly
   - ■ Scripture reflection: "For all who exalt themselves will be humbled, and these who humble themselves will be exalted" (*Luke 14:11*).

10. Jesus is stripped of his garments.
    - ■ Scripture reference: John 19:23–25
    - ■ Scripture reflection: "None of you can become my disciple if you do not give up all your possessions" (*Luke 14:33*).

11. Jesus is nailed to the cross.
    - ■ Scripture reference: Matthew 27:35; Mark 15:24; Luke 23:33
    - ■ Scripture reflection: "For I have come down from heaven, not to do my own will, but the will of him who sent me" (*John 6:38*).

12. Jesus dies on the cross.
    - ■ Scripture reference: Matthew 27:50; Mark 15:37; John 19:30
    - ■ Scripture reflection: "And being found in human form, he humbled himself and became obedient to the point of death—even death on a cross" (*Philippians 2:7–8*).

13. Jesus is taken down from the cross.

- ■ Scripture reference: Matthew 27:59; Mark 15:46; Luke 23:53; John 19:31–38

- ■ Scripture reflection: "Was it not necessary that the Messiah should suffer these things and then enter into his glory?" (*Luke 24:26*).

14. Jesus is laid in the tomb.

- ■ Scripture reference: Matthew 27:59–60; Mark 15:47

- ■ Scripture reflection: "Unless a grain of wheat falls into the earth and dies, it remains just a single grain; but if it dies, it bears much fruit" (*John 12:24*).

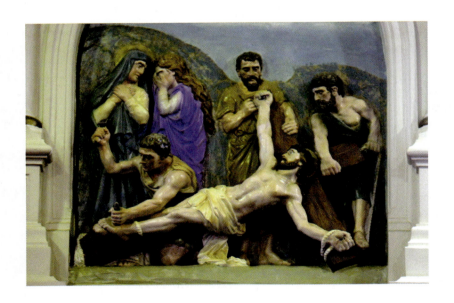

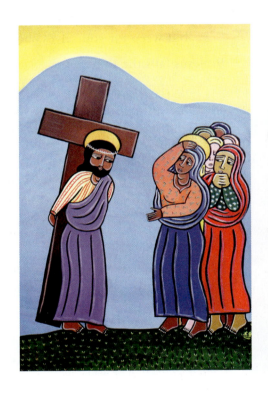

Glossary

A

allegories (p. 156)—Expressions of truths or generalizations of human experiences through the use of symbolic fictional figures or actions.

anawim (p. 137)—A Hebrew word referring to those who are materially or spiritually poor and are seeking God.

antichrist (p. 229)—The antichrist is present in the world and displays hatred for those who follow Christ. The antichrist is the opposite of Jesus and his beliefs.

apocalyptic writing (p. 232)—A literary style that uses very symbolic language to convey its message.

apostolic succession (p. 45)—The uninterrupted succession of bishops, from the Apostle Peter to each of his legitimate successors. The continuity of shepherding responsibility given by Christ to the Church leadership is realized in this line of authority.

B

Baptism (p. 37)—Baptism is the first of the Sacraments of Initiation. In Baptism the infant has holy water poured on his or her head and is anointed with chrism. He or she is then forgiven of Original Sin and united with Jesus.

Beatitudes (p. 77)—Jesus' teachings about the meaning and path to true happiness; descriptions of the way to attain eternal blessedness, or holiness, to which God calls all of us.

biblical exegesis (p. 25)—The explanation or critical interpretation of a passage of sacred Scripture.

biblical inerrancy (p. 25)—Freedom from error: The books of Scripture faithfully and without error teach the truth that God, for the sake of our salvation, wishes to have communicated through the sacred Scriptures.

biblical inspiration (p. 24)—This is the process by which God the Holy Spirit assisted a human author in writing a book of the Bible. Because of this, God is the author of the Bible, and the truth that he willed us to know was conveyed without error.

blasphemy (p. 115)—To proclaim oneself as God, to claim to have the attributes of God, or to insult God or his name.

C

canonization (p. 200)—An official Church statement by which a person is declared to have lived a holy life of heroic virtue. In the last stage of canonization, the person is named a saint.

Christ (p. 66)—The Greek word for "anointed" and "Messiah." Jesus, as Messiah, restored all people to communion and friendship with God through his life, death, and Resurrection.

civil disobedience (p. 185)—The act of breaking a law nonviolently, usually with the intent to call into question the morality of the law.

communion of saints (p. 200)—All faithful Church members on earth, in heaven, and in purgatory; communion in holy things (*sancta*) and among holy persons (*sancti*).

Confirmation (p. 135)—Through the Sacrament of Confirmation we are sealed with the gifts of the Holy Spirit. Confirmation strengthens the spiritual life received in Baptism.

conversion experience (p. 111)—An experience that turns us toward God and away from sin, and encourages us to search to understand and do what God desires of us.

covenant (p. 5)—A solemn promise, or agreement, made between two parties; the word means testament.

D

discipleship (p. 101)—A life rooted in Jesus and expressed in union with his Church.

divine revelation (p. 24)—God's communicating of himself and his plan of goodness throughout history.

E

ecumenism (p. 168)—The effort to strive toward unity among all Christians.

Essenes (p. 15)—People who withdrew completely from the world and political activity to prepare for the imminent coming of God. They typically avoided all contact with foreign cultures and followed the Law of Moses to the last detail.

Eucharist (p. 113)—The sacrament of Jesus' Body and Blood, truly and really present under the appearances of the bread and wine.

Evangelists (p. 54)—The Gospel writers: Matthew, Mark, Luke, and John. They told the stories of Jesus to uncover what was at the center of the religious encounter of the community with God.

Gifts of the Holy Spirit (p. 135)—Conveyed through Confirmation, the seven gifts of the Holy Spirit strengthen us to spread and defend the faith.

Gospels (p. 54)—All the Gospels tell the Good News, which is the meaning of the word *Gospel*. They present the story of Easter faith rooted in the life, death, and Resurrection of Jesus Christ, the incarnate Son of God. There are four Gospels: Matthew, Mark, Luke, and John.

Hellenistic (p. 17)—Another word for Greek influence.

Holy Trinity (p. 36)—The three Persons in one God. The Holy Trinity comprises the Father, the Son, and the Holy Spirit.

Incarnation (p. 73)—The second Person of the Holy Trinity, who, while remaining God, assumed a human nature and became man.

Infancy Narratives (p. 69)—Recorded stories in the Gospels of Jesus' conception, birth, and early years.

kingdom of heaven (p. 75)—Also known as the kingdom of God or the reign of God; the gift of salvation and eternal life; God's rule of justice, love, and peace.

martyr (p. 185)—The Greek word for "witness." People who died for their beliefs.

Messiah (p. 66)—The Hebrew word for "anointed"; a savior sent by God to redeem his people from the power of sin and everlasting death and to restore them to his friendship.

miracles (p. 51)—Signs of wonder that can be attributed to God only.

monotheism (p. 5)—The belief in one God.

parables (p. 48)—Metaphors or similes drawn from common life experiences or nature to illustrate moral or spiritual truths.

Parousia (p. 127)—The second coming of Christ at the end of time, when God's plan for salvation is accomplished and humanity is glorified.

Paschal mystery (p. 112)—Christ's work of redemption through his Passion, death, Resurrection, and Ascension.

Pentecost (p. 34)—The fiftieth day following Easter when the Holy Spirit is made present, given, and communicated as a divine Person of the Trinity.

persecution (p. 180)—The act of causing suffering because of a person's belief.

Pharisees (p. 13)—They were the most influential religious sect during the lifetime of Jesus. As well-educated religious leaders, they focused on keeping the Jews faithful to the law. They also acknowledged the oral traditions of the elders.

polytheistic (p. 20)—This means that many gods were worshiped.

pseudonymity (p. 213)—The act of another author writing in a named author's place. This occurs in some Pauline Letters.

sacrament (p. 37)—An effective sign that conveys grace and which was established by Jesus and given to the Church.

Sadducees (p. 14)—They did not believe in anything that wasn't mentioned in the Torah. As part of the wealthy, conservative, aristocratic ruling class, many Sadducees actively worked with the Romans.

salvation history (p. 4)—The saving action of God through human history.

scribes (p. 14)—They were the interpreters and the teachers of the law most closely affiliated with the Pharisees, but also associated with the Sadducees. Scribes were not a religious party; rather, they were the Jewish scholars who assisted in writing and telling Jews about their religious traditions.

Shema (p. 124)—A Hebrew word meaning "hear," the first word of Deuteronomy 6:4–9, "Hear, O Israel . . ."

sin (p. 130)—An offense against God—any word, action, or thought contrary to God's law. Sin weakens, and at times can even break, our relationship with God.

synoptic Gospels (p. 53)—The Gospels of Matthew, Mark, and Luke; so labeled because of their similar vision.

Ten Commandments (p. 8)—These ten laws—often called the Decalogue and given by God to Moses—prescribed the moral obligations for the Israelites. The commandments later evolved into the 613 laws which comprise the Torah, the written law of the Hebrew people.

threefold pattern (p. 99)—A writing technique, notably used by Mark, to emphasize particular subjects, such as the declarations of Jesus as the Son of God.

Tradition (p. 23)—The living and authentic transmission of the teachings of Jesus in the Church.

Transfiguration (p. 108)—The culminating moment in the public life of Jesus. Jesus' appearance changed in the presence of his disciples, and Elijah and Moses appeared beside him to reveal him as the true Messiah. This event points toward the Resurrection of Jesus.

treason (p. 115)—An attempt or desire to overthrow and replace the head of the government to which one owes allegiance.

virtue (p. 228)—A moral or spiritual habit and desire to do good.

Works of Mercy (p. 86)—Charitable acts by which we care for the physical and spiritual needs of others.

YHWH (p. 75)—Hebrew name for God, sometimes translated "I AM," or "the One Who Is," or "The One Who Causes to Be What Is."

Z

Zealots (p. 15)—A group that formed a rebellious movement of militant Jews who yearned and battled for the recovery of Jewish independence. They considered the acceptance of foreign government and the subsequent payment of taxes to Rome as blasphemy against God.

Index

A

Abraham (Abram), 2, 5, 6, 7, 65
Acts of the Apostles, 52, 63
Alexander the Great, 3
allegories, 156, 176, 257
anawim, 135, 148, 257
antichrist, 230, 240, 257
Antioch, 64
apocalyptic literature (writing), 26, 53, 231, 240, 257
Apostles, 45, 48–49
apostolic succession, 45, 60, 257
artisan, 19

B

Baptism, 35–37, 46, 60, 237, 257
Barnabas, 192, 193–194
Bartimaeus, 110–111
Beatitudes, 77–79, 90, 247, 257
biblical exegesis, 25, 30, 257
biblical inerrancy, 25, 30, 257
biblical inspiration, 24, 30, 257
blasphemy, 115, 120, 257
bride of Christ, 237

C

Canaan, 5
canon, 27
canonization, 200, 208, 257
canticles, 26
Catholic Campaign for Human Development (CCHD), 197
Catholic Relief Services (CRS), 197
Catholic Social Teaching, 250
Christ, 66, 90, 257
Christian service, 165
Christianity, 22
civil disobedience, 185, 208, 257
communion of saints, 200, 208, 257
Confirmation, 60, 135, 257
Constantine, 47
conversion experience(s), 111, 257
covenant, 5, 7, 9, 30, 257
    new and everlasting, 114
crèche, 72
Cult
    of Demeter, 21
    of Dionysus, 21
    of the Emperor, 21
    of Isis, 20, 22
    of Mithras, 21
Cynics, 21

D

David, 3, 65
Dead Sea, 3, 16
Dead Sea Scrolls, 16, 33
didache, 50
discipleship, 94, 101, 120, 257
Discourses, 67
divine inspiration, 24
divine revelation, 24, 30, 257
Doctors of the Church
    Catherine of Siena, Saint, 206
    John of the Cross, Saint, 206
    Teresa of Avila, Saint, 206
Dom Helder Camara, 174
Dorothy Day, 28
Dorothy Stang, 88

E

ecumenism, 168, 176, 257
Elijah, 108
Epicureans, 21
Epistles, 53
Essenes, 15, 30, 257
Eucharist, 46, 113, 120, 144–145, 258
Evangelist(s), 54, 60, 127, 152, 258
Exodus, 7, 8

F

folktales, 26
Francis of Assisi, 72

G

Genesis, Book of, 67
Gentiles, 65, 127, 193–195
Gifts of the Holy Spirit, 60, 135, 258
Good News, 40, 44, 49, 54, 133, 135, 182, 186
Gospels, 51, 54, 55, 60, 258
governor, 19
grace, 218
great commandment, 247
Greece, 125

H

Hail Mary, 131, 251
Hellenistic (Hellenist), 17, 30, 187, 258
Herod 3, 17–18, 71, 97
Herodians, 97
historical accounts, 26
Holy Spirit, 42, 100, 111, 127, 132–134, 165, 166, 186, 198, 237
Holy Trinity, 36, 39–40, 42, 48, 60, 216
house churches, 47

I

Incarnation, 73, 90, 258
Infancy Narrative(s), 67, 69–71, 90, 127, 258
Islam, 22

J

Jerusalem, 112, 128
Jesus
    Ascension of, 49
    baptism of, 32, 34, 100
    birth of, 3
    blood and water from, 170
    Body of, 217, 237
    crucifixion, 32, 116
    as fulfillment of the covenant, 9
    genealogy, 70
    and the Law, 14
    life and teaching, 48, 50
    the Messiah, 70, 96, 106, 117
    passion, 96, 169
    public ministry, 32, 75, 96
    Resurrection, 9, 32, 48, 49, 96, 117, 145, 172–173
    seamless tunic of, 170
    Son of God, 73
    Son of Man, 100
    Suffering Servant, 107
    Temptation of, 73–75
Jewish life, 12–13
John the Baptist, 3, 32, 100, 101
John Paul II, 238
Josephus, 56
Judaism, 4, 11, 13, 46
Judas, 183
Judea, 32
Judgment of Nations, 86
Julius Caesar, 3, 19
justification, 218

K

Kateri Tekakwitha, Blessed, 146
kergyma, 49
kingdom of heaven (God), 75–76, 90, 258

L

Last Supper, 50, 113, 164
lepers, 19
letters, 26, 212–213
    catholic, 219, 226–227, 229–230
    pastoral letters, 215
    Pauline, 53, 220–222, 224–225
liturgia, 50
liturgical year, 244
liturgy, 242
logos, 154
Lord's Prayer, 50, 80, 131, 251

M

Magnificat, 130, 252
marks of the Church, 223
Martha, 140
martyr, 185, 208, 258
Mary, 130, 131, 140
merchant, 19
Messiah, 49, 66, 90, 258
Messianic Secret (mystery), 106
miracle(s), 50–51, 144, 148, 258
monotheism, monotheistic, 5, 30, 258
Moses, 2, 8, 108
Mount Sinai, 8
mystery cults, 20–21

N

Narratives, 67, 101
Nero, 62, 63
new commandment, 165, 247
New Testament Letters, 52, 214
Nicene Creed, 40
Nicodemus, 160–161

O

oral proclamation, 49

P

Palestine, 3, 11
parables, 26, 49–50, 66, 90, 258
paradox of the cross, 216

Parousia, 127, 148, 258
Paschal mystery, 112, 120, 258
Passover, 8, 9, 113
Paul, 49, 65, 182, 189, 191, 193–194, 196, 198
peasant, 19
Pentecost, 35, 42, 49, 60, 183–184, 258
persecution, 180, 208, 258
Peter, 65, 85, 116, 182, 191, 195
Pharisees, 13, 30, 67, 97, 129
Philip, 187
Pio of Pietrelcina, Saint, 118
Pliny the Younger, 57
polytheistic, 20, 30, 258
Pontius Pilate, 32, 115, 169
prayer, 134
psalms, 26
pseudonymity, 213, 240, 258

Q

Q document, 51
Qumran, 3, 16, 33

R

rabbi, 66, 68
Revelation, 53, 63, 232–233
Rome, Roman Empire, 3, 18, 32–33, 47, 49, 95
rosary, 131, 253
ruler, 19

S

sacrament(s), 35, 60, 204–205, 218, 242–243, 258
Sadducees, 14, 30, 97, 258
salvation history, 4, 30, 259
Samaria, 11, 12, 32
Samaritan(s), 138–139, 162
Sanhedrin, 97, 115
Saul, 186, 188–189
scribes, 14, 30, 67, 129, 259
Septuagint, 27
Sermon on the Mount, 77
Shema, 124, 126, 148, 259
short stories, 26
sign(s), 158–159
Simon Peter, 19
sin, 130, 148, 259
social classes, 19
Solomon, 3
Stations of the Cross, 254–256

Stoics, 21
Suetonius, 56
symbols, symbolism, 233, 234
synoptic Gospels, 51, 60, 259

T

table fellowship, 143
Tacitus, 56–57
Temple, 3, 10, 33
Ten Commandments, 8, 78, 246–247, 259
Testament
    New, 4, 27, 40, 212
    Old, 4, 27, 42
Thea Bowman, Sister, 58
Theodosius I, 22
threefold pattern, 99, 120, 259
Tiberius, 32
Torah, 12, 67
Tradition, 23, 48, 152, 259
Transfiguration, 108, 120, 259
treason, 115, 120, 259

U

unclean, 19
unity, 168

V

virtue(s), 228, 240, 248, 259
vocations, 245

W

woman caught in adultery, 163
Works of Mercy, 86–87, 90, 248, 259
written proclamation, 50

Y

YHWH (YAHWEH), 75, 90, 259

Z

Zacchaeus, 19
Zealots, 15, 30, 259
Zechariah, 125
Zoroastrianism, 21, 22

Credits

AFP/Getty Images: 204; © AINACO/CORBIS: 72 (top); © Alinari Archives/CORBIS: 23; Dominick D Andrea: 96; © LICHTENSTEIN ANDREW/CORBIS SYGMA: 92; AP/Wide World Photos: 88, 225, 229, 237, 238; © Archivo Iconografico, S.A./CORBIS: 5, 13, 34, 40, 198; Arquivo Nacional da Torre do Tombo, Lisbon, Portugal/Giraudon/Bridgeman Art Library: 234; © Arte & Immagini srl/CORBIS: 7 (top), 117, 161; © 2004 Artists Rights Society (ARS), New York/ADAGP, Paris. Image courtesy of Erich Lessing/Art Resource, NY: 172; Ashmolean Museum, University of Oxford/Bridgeman Art Library: 139; © Marc Asnin/CORBIS SABA: 79; © Dave Bartruff/CORBIS: 74; © Annie Griffiths Belt/CORBIS: 10; © Bettmann/CORBIS: 44, 57, 224; © Tibor Bognár/CORBIS: 186; © Bohemian Nomad Picturemakers/CORBIS: 27; Brooklyn Museum of Art, New York/Bridgeman Art Library: 108, 173; © David Butow/CORBIS SABA: 136; © Fabian Cevallos/CORBIS SYGMA: 118; Chiesa di Santa Maria Maddalena, Gressan, Italy/Bridgeman Art Library/Seat Alinari: 194; © Christie's Images/CORBIS: 191, 233; Christie's Images, London/Bridgeman Art Library: 158; © Elio Ciol/CORBIS: 43 (inset and background), 66; © Corbis: viii–ix, 51, 76 (left), 175, 214, 245 (right), 246–247, 248–249, 250–251 (border); Stephanie Dalton Cowan/Getty Images: 156; © Andrew Cowin; Travel Ink/CORBIS: 20; © Keith Dannemiller/CORBIS: 107; © Dennis Degnan/CORBIS: 12; © Rick D'Elia/Corbis: 197; © M. ou Me. Desjeux, Bernard/CORBIS: x–xi, 105 (top), 193, 252–253, 254–255, 256–257; Digital Stock: 81; © Ric Ergenbright/CORBIS: 4; Stephen Ferry/Getty Images: 9; © ORIGLIA FRANCO/CORBIS SYGMA: 168; © LUIS GALDAMEZ/Reuters/Corbis: 201; © Getty Images: 174, 182 (bottom); © Getty Images/118087: 178; © Getty Images/1254: 46 (far left); © Getty Images/1313: 47 (upper left); © Getty Images/32328: 75; © Getty Images/32292: 121; © Getty Images/32297: 130; © Getty Images/5076: 47 (center right); © Getty Image/56281: 72 (middle); © Getty Images/80178: 207; © Getty Images/OS38019: 76 (right); © Getty Images/PhotoDisc/41009: 250; © Antoine Gyori/CORBIS SYGMA: 17; Harcourt Religion Publishers: 127; Harcourt School Publishers: 46 (center left, center right, and far right), 47 (far left, far right, and upper right), 70, 145 (left); © John Henley/CORBIS: 150; © Ralf-Finn Hestoft/CORBIS: 134; HIP/Art Resource, NY: 105 (bottom); © George H. H. Huey/CORBIS: 131 (bottom); © Hanan Isachar/CORBIS: 32, 113 (top); © Images.com/CORBIS: 223; © LANGEVIN JACQUES/CORBIS SYGMA: 205; © *Mississippi Today*, photo courtesy of FSPA archives: 58; © Reed

Kaestner/CORBIS: 14; © Ronnie Kaufman/CORBIS: 26; © France Keyser/In Visu/Corbis: 141; Erica Lansner/Getty Images: 2; © David Lees/CORBIS: 114, 202–203; Erich Lessing/Art Resource, NY: 45, 190, 190 (background); © Massimo Listri/CORBIS: 78; Louvre, Paris, France/Peter Willi/Bridgeman Art Library: 21; Richard Nebesky/Robert Harding World Imagery/Getty Images: 112–113; © Richard T. Nowitz/CORBIS: 16, 215; © D. C. Lowe/SuperStock: 29; Marquette University Archives: 28; © Francis G. Mayer/CORBIS: 185 (bottom); Musee Conde, Chantilly, France, Giraudon/Bridgeman Art library: 199; Musee de Picardie, Amiens, France/Giraudon/Bridgeman Art Library: 188; Musee de la Ville de Paris, Musee du Petit-Palais, France/Giraudon/Bridgeman Art Library: 111; Museo di San Marco dell'Angelico, Florence, Italy/Bridgeman Art Library: 171; © Pablo Corral V/CORBIS: 128; © Tim Page/CORBIS: 22 (top); St. Peter's, Vatican, Rome, Italy/Joseph Martin/Bridgeman Art Library: 83 (bottom); PhotoDisc: 61, 73, 101 (bottom); Photodisc Green/Getty Images: 235; Photospin: vi–vii, 242–243, 244–245 (border); Gene Plaisted, The Crosiers: 36, 54–55, 132, 166; Private Collection/Bridgeman Art Library: 69, 144; Z. Radovan, Jerusalem: 212; © Eldad Rafaeli/CORBIS: 126; © Reuters/CORBIS: 48, 83 (top), 122, 164; © Ariel Skelley/CORBIS: 143; Norbert Rosing/National Geographic/Getty Images: 98–99; © Bob Rowan; Progressive Image/CORBIS: 192; © Royalty-Free/CORBIS: 84, 154, 210; Roger Spooner/Getty Images: 104; © Tom Stewart/CORBIS: 62; © Strauss/Curtis/CORBIS: 7 (bottom), 109; © Streetstock Images/CORBIS: 222; SW Productions/Getty Images: 22 (bottom); SW Productions/Brand X Pictures: 31; GREAT CATCH, © 1993 by John August Swanson, Serigraph 22" by 32", www.JohnAugustSwanson.com: 102; Scala/Art Resource, NY: 145 (right), 162; Time & Life Pictures/Getty Images: 37; © Peter Turnley/CORBIS: 137; Vatican Museums and Galleries, Vatican City, Italy/Bridgeman Art Library: 53; Victoria & Albert Museum, London/Art Resource, NY: 129; © Sandro Vannini/CORBIS: 182 (top), 184, 195, 216; *The Coming of the Holy Spirit*, by Soichi Watanabe (Japan). Permission for reprinting this image is granted by Asian Christian Art Association: 183; © Nik Wheeler/CORBIS: 39 (top); W. P. Wittman Limited: x, 24, 39 (bottom), 47 (center left), 68, 87, 101 (top), 103, 135, 142, 149, 155, 160, 165, 167, 169, 180, 185 (top), 218, 219, 220, 221, 227, 241, 245 (left); © Adam Woolfitt/CORBIS: 72 (bottom); Lois Woolley: 43, 146, 206

Endnotes

1. see Jn 20:31; 2 Tim 3:16; 2 Pet 1:19–21; 3:15–16

2. See Vatican Council I, Dogmatic Constitution on the Catholic Faith, *Dei Filius*, ch. 2: Denz. 1787 (3006). Pontficial biblical commission, Decree 18 June 1915: Denz. 2180 (3629); EB 420. Holy Office, *Letter*, 22 Dec. 1923: EB 499.

3. See St Augustine, *De Gen.ad Litt.*, 2, 9, 20: PL 34, 270–271; *Epistola* 82, 3: PL 33, 277; CSEL 34, 2, p. 354. St Thomas Aquinas, *De Veritate*, q. 12, a 2, C. Council of Trent, Session IV, On the canonical scriptures: Denz. 783 (1501) Leo XIII, Encyclical *Providentissimus Deus*: EB 121, 124, 126–127. Pius XII, Encyclical *Divino Afflante*: EB 539.

4. 2 Tim 3:16–17, Greek text

5. St Augustine, *De Civitate Dei*, XVII, 6, 2: PL 41, 537: CSEL 40, 2, 228.

6. Pius XII, loc. cit.: Denz. 2294 (3829–3830); EB 557–562.

7. *Col* 1:15

8. cf. *Eph* 1:3–6; *Rom* 8:29

9. *2 Pet* 1:4

10. St. Thomas Aquinas, *Sth* III, 45, 4, *ad* 2.

11. *Heb* 9:26

12. *Heb* 9:26

13. Cf. *Eph* 1:22; *Col* 1:18; *LG* 9.

14. *LG* 6